BLAISE PASCAL

Pensées

EDITED AND TRANSLATED BY

Roger Ariew

Hackett Publishing Company
Indianapolis/Cambridge

Copyright © 2004 by Hackett Publishing Company, Inc.

14 13 12 11 10   2 3 4 5 6 7

For further information, please address:
  Hackett Publishing Company, Inc.
  P.O. Box 44937
  Indianapolis, IN 46244-0937
  www.hackettpublishing.com

Auguste Rodin, *La Pensée* (Thought), Musée D'Orsay, Paris. Reprinted by
permission of the photographer, Dr. Jeffrey Howe, Department of Fine Arts,
Boston College.

Cover design by Abigail Coyle
Text design by Jennifer Plumley
Composition by Professional Book Compositors, Inc.
Printed at Versa Press, Inc.

Library of Congress Cataloging-in-Publication Data
Pascal, Blaise, 1623–1662.
    [Pensées. English]
    Pensées / Blaise Pascal ; edited and translated by Roger Ariew.
            p.   cm.
    Includes bibliographical references and index.
    ISBN 0-87220-718-8 (cloth) — ISBN 0-87220-717-X (pbk.)
            1. Philosophy—Early works to 1800. 2. Apologetics—Early works to
1800.   I. Ariew, Roger.   II. Title.
B1901.P42E5   2004b
230'.2—dc22   2004021245

ISBN-13: 978-0-87220-718-9 (cloth)
ISBN-13: 978-0-87220-717-2 (pbk.)

BLAISE PASCAL

Pensées

For Roby

CONTENTS

Pensées

INTRODUCTION

The *Pensées*: A Brief History of the Text

Several good biographies of Blaise Pascal have been published, starting with the one written by Gilberte Périer, his sister. They all describe the brilliant universal genius, details of whose life and times are sketched in the chronology on page xv. During Pascal's very brief life, he made significant advances in mathematics and physics and contributed several technological innovations. But he is best known for his religious and political polemics, the *Provincial Letters*, and the *Pensées*. Pascal above all was a subtle thinker and a master of the French language.

When Pascal died in 1662, he left behind the notes to the project (or projects) he had been working on, including the *Apology for the Christian Religion*, which he had outlined at a meeting at Port-Royal. These notes became known as the *Pensées*, though neither *Pensées* nor *Apologie* were Pascal's titles. Pascal's usual procedure while composing was to write down thoughts on large sheets of paper, separating them from one another with a short horizontal line, and then cutting the papers along that line and organizing the fragments into various bundles (*liasses*) sewn together. In 1658 (according to Philippe Sellier, or in 1660, according to Jean Mesnard), Pascal decided on a core twenty-seven bundles and put seven others aside. These two sets constitute Parts I and II of the present translation; fragments written afterward or of diverse origins make up Parts III through V. At Pascal's death, the whole collection was handed down to his sister Gilberte and her family.

The problem of what to do with Pascal's bundles of fragments, handwritten by Pascal or recopied by young assistants, then came to the forefront—a problem of significantly greater magnitude than if, at a given time, your relative decided to publish all of your computer files or everything on your desk. Here is how Pascal's nephew, Etienne Périer, expresses the difficulty in his preface to what was eventually published in 1670, known as the Port-Royal edition: *Pensées de M. Pascal sur la religion et sur quelques autres sujets, qui ont esté trouvées après sa mort parmy ses papiers*:

> Since we knew Pascal's intent to work on religion, we took great care after his death to gather together all his writings on the subject. We found them all sewn together into different bundles, but without any order or sequence, because, as I have already noted, they were only the first ex-

pressions of his thoughts that he wrote down on small pieces of paper as
they came to his mind. And all these were so imperfect and so badly written that we had all the pains of the world to decipher them.

The first thing we did was to have them copied such as they were and
in the same confusion in which we had found them. But when we saw
them in this state, with greater facility to read them and to examine them
than when they were in their original state, they seemed at first so infirm,
so badly thought out, and most of them so ill-explained that for a long
time we did not think at all to publish them.

Périer conveys the embarrassment caused by the condition of Pascal's work for a 17th-century editor. To publish some mere jottings was
just not something that was done then. Pascal's relatives took a while to
consider their options. But a key to that process was their decision to
make copies of all the fragments at hand. In fact, they had two copies
made: one for themselves and another they sent to Port-Royal, to Antoine Arnauld and Pierre Nicole, for their editorial assistance. Pascal's
relatives ultimately decided to publish something. But what?

[W]e took some time to determine the path we ought to take.

The first that came to mind, and the one that was no doubt the easiest,
was to have the fragments published immediately in the state in which
we found them. But soon we judged that to do it that way would be to
lose almost the whole fruit for which we could hope. The most perfect
thoughts, those most ordered, clear, and developed, were mixed in and,
as it were, lost among so many other imperfect, obscured, and half-di-
gested ones—some almost unintelligible to anyone other than the person
who wrote them. Hence, there was reason to believe that the ones could
put off the others and that people would think this volume uselessly en-
larged with so many imperfect thoughts, like a confused mass without
order, without sequence, and of no use to anyone.

There was another way to give these writings to the public, which was
to work on them beforehand: to illuminate the obscure thoughts, to complete the incomplete ones, and, taking into account Pascal's aim in all
these fragments, to supplement in some way the work he intended to accomplish. This way was assuredly the most perfect, but also the most difficult to execute well. We decided on that path and began, in fact, to
work on it. But in the end we rejected it as we did the first path, because
we thought that it was almost impossible to enter very well into the
thought and aim of an author, especially that of a dead author; and that
we would not be giving the work of Pascal, but a completely different
work.

Thus, to avoid the disadvantages in these two ways of producing these
writings, we have chosen a middle path, which we have followed in this
collection. Among the great numbers of thoughts, we have taken only the
ones that seemed clearest and most complete, and have given them such

as we have found them without adding anything to them; except that, instead of their being without sequence, without linkage, and dispersed confusedly at various places, we have put them in some sort of an order and placed under the same titles those that were about the same subjects, and we have suppressed all the others that were either too obscure or too imperfect.

Accordingly, Périer's middle path was to publish a selection of fragments, reordered according to topics imposed externally, and, ultimately (though he denies it), to retouch and subtly alter Pascal's words. Périer's own judgment was that the fragments did not adequately represent the summary of the project Pascal had sketched at Port-Royal. As Périer stated:

We will see among the fragments we give to the public something of Pascal's design, though we will see rather little of it. The very things we will find there are so imperfect, so little developed, and so little digested, that they can only give an extremely crude idea of the way he wanted to treat them.

Moreover, we should not be surprised if, in the little we give of them, we have not kept the order and sequence of the distribution of subjects. Since we had almost nothing that followed, it would have been useless to keep them in that order; we have been satisfied to dispose them approximately in the manner we have deemed to be the most suitable to what we had.

And so began the practice, which continued for about 300 years, of publishing selections of *Pensées* and ordering them according to one's own conception, along externally determined themes. Perhaps the best such arrangement was that of Léon Brunschvicg at the end of the 19th century. But Brunschvicg also responded to the call by Victor Cousin for a more accurate new edition of the *Pensées*, producing as well a photographic reproduction of the fragments extant at the beginning of the 20th century. The "Recueil Original," as it is called, consists of the fragments as the Bibliothèque Nationale had received them: Pascal's heirs had cut up and pasted the fragments into sheets, but many of them (known from their copies) were missing, and the order in which they were pasted was not at all likely to have been Pascal's.

A generation of scholars followed whose intent was to recover all the notes that Pascal left, exactly as he had left them, and in the order he had left them. Most important in this process was Zacharie Tourneur, with his edition of the *Pensées* that showed all variants. In the 1960s, Louis Lafuma turned to one of the copies made for Pascal's sister—copy A, as it is called—and produced the first reliable edition of the fragments. (Another photographic reproduction of the Recueil Original was published for the tercentennial commemoration of Pascal's death in 1962, with the fragments rearranged according to Lafuma's ordering.) But in 1976, Sellier produced a different edition, based on copy B, arguing convincingly that the order of copy B more likely corresponded to the way in which Pascal left his notes: copy B is a continuous manuscript and the sections could not be reordered, while copy A appears as a collection of discontinuous sections and may well have been reordered. (These arguments are summarized in Anthony R. Pugh's *The Composition of Pascal's Pensées.*)

This is the state of the editions of the *Pensées* to date, until the publication of volume VI of Mesnard's critical edition of Pascal's works (begun in 1964), containing the *Pensées*. The latest French editions of the *Pensées* all follow Sellier's edition, which is also superior for a number of other reasons: it reproduces Pascal's horizontal line between thoughts within particular fragments; it reorders some fragments internally; and it reconsiders the issue of what is to be counted as a fragment, renumbering Lafuma's 993 fragments into 813 fragments. The present translation is a complete translation of all the fragments, following Sellier's edition of copy B. (Deletions by Pascal are placed between angle brackets < >. This translation uses the King James Version of the Bible to translate Pascal's biblical references, except in cases where Pascal's use clearly depends on the Vulgate or its 17th-century French version. In those cases, the translation reflects Pascal and his sources, rather than the King James text.)

Still, one should keep in mind the historical importance of a number of editions and manuscripts, especially those of Port-Royal, the Recueil original, Lafuma's edition following copy A, and Sellier's edition following copy B. Thus, the present translation indicates both Sellier's and Lafuma's numbering of the fragments on the margins and includes a concordance enabling one to locate a Sellier-numbered passage, if one has a citation using Lafuma's numbering. Other interesting later developments include Pol Ernst's attempt to reconstitute the order in which the fragments were actually written, based on evidence from watermarks, and Emmanuel Martineau's effort to reorder the fragments according to their internal logic (not according to topics, as was previously done). The multiplicity of editions and orders may well be appropriate for such a challenging and multilayered work as the *Pensées.**

---

*I would like to thank Marjorie Grene, Daniel Garber, and Deborah Wilkes for their assistance and encouragement with this project. I am also grateful to Prudence Steiner, who perused the whole translation assiduously and suggested numerous alternative translations and readings.

Selected Bibliography

Primary Sources

Pascal, Blaise. *Pensées de M. Pascal sur la religion et sur quelques autres sujets, qui ont esté trouvées après sa mort parmy ses papiers.* Paris, 1670. The Port-Royal edition with a Preface by Pascal's nephew, Etienne Périer.

———— *L'original des Pensées de Pascal.* Léon Brunschvicg, ed. Paris: Hachette, 1905. A facsimile of the original fragments that are extant.

———— *Pensées.* W.F. Trotter, trans. London: J.M. Dent, 1908.

———— *Pensées de Blaise Pascal.* Zacharie Tourneur, ed. Paris: Vrin, 1942. "Paleographic" edition of the *Pensées*, showing all variants.

———— *Le Manuscript des Pensées de Pascal.* Louis Lafuma, ed. Paris: Les Libraires associés, 1962. A facsimile of the extant original fragments ordered following copy A.

———— *Oeuvres complètes.* Louis Lafuma, ed. Paris: Editions du Seuil, 1963. The complete works in a single volume containing an edition based on copy A.

———— *Oeuvres complètes.* Jean Mesnard, ed. Paris: Desclée De Brouwer, 1964–?. Critical edition of the complete works; vol. 6, containing the *Pensées*, has yet to be published.

———— *Pensées et opuscules.* Léon Brunschvicg, ed. Paris: Hachette, 1967. First ed. 1897.

———— *Discours sur la religion et sur quelques autres sujets, qui ont été trouvés après sa mort parmi ses papiers.* Emmanuel Martineau, ed. Paris: Fayard/Armand Colin, 1992. An interesting attempt to reorder the fragments according to their internal logic.

———— *Pensées.* A.J. Krailsheimer, trans. Hammondsworth: Penguin, 1995. First ed. 1966; an excellent English translation of almost the whole of copy A.

———— *Pensées and Other Writings.* Honor Levi, trans. Oxford: Oxford University Press, 1995. A partial English translation following copy B, with some other selections.

———— *Oeuvres complètes,* 2 vols. Michel Le Guern, ed. Paris: Editions Gallimard, 1998–2000. The complete works, containing an edition based on copy A (revised L. Lafuma ordering), in v. 2.

———— *Pensées.* Philippe Sellier, ed. Paris: Classiques Garnier, 1999. First ed. Paris: Mercure de France, 1976; edition based on copy B.

———— *Pensées.* Gérard Feyerolles, ed. Paris: Livre de Poche, 2000. Edition based on copy B (following P. Sellier).

Secondary Sources

Alexandrescu, Vlad. *Le Paradoxe chez Blaise Pascal.* Berne: Peter Lang, 1997.

Armour, Leslie. *"Infini Rien" Pascal's Wager and the Human Paradox.* Carbondale, Ill.: Southern Illinois University Press, 1993.

Brunschvicg, Léon. *Descartes et Pascal lecteurs de Montaigne.* Neuchâtel: La Baconnière, 1945.

Carraud, Vincent. *Pascal et la Philosophie.* Paris: Presses Universitaires de France, 1992.

Cousin, Victor. *Des Pensées de Pascal, rapport à l'Académie française sur la nécessité d'une nouvelle édition de cet ouvrage.* Paris: Librairie philosophique de Ladrange, 1843.

Davidson, Hugh M.. *The Origins of Certainty: Means and Meaning in Pascal's Pensées.* Chicago: The University of Chicago Press, 1979.

Davidson, Hugh M., and Pierre H. Dubé. *A Concordance to Pascal's Pensées.* Ithaca: Cornell University Press, 1975.

Ernst, Pol. *Les Pensées de Pascal, Géologie et stratigraphie.* Oxford: Voltaire Foundation, 1996. An attempt to reconstitute the order in which the fragments were written, based on evidence from watermarks.

Hammond, Nicholas, ed. *The Cambridge Companion to Pascal.* Cambridge: Cambridge University Press, 2003.

Krailsheimer, A.J. *Pascal.* Oxford: Oxford University Press, 1980.

Mesnard, Jean. *Pascal, His Life and Works.* Harvill, London, 1952. Trans. of *Pascal, l'homme et l'oeuvre.* Paris: Boivin, 1951.

——— *Pascal et les Roannez.* Paris: Desclée De Brouwer, 1965.

——— *Pascal.* Paris: Hatier, 1967.

——— *Les Pensées de Pascal.* Paris: Société d'édition d'enseignement supérieur, 1976.

Périer, Gilberte. *La Vie de Monsieur Pascal.* Amsterdam, 1684. Pascal's biography, written by his sister.

Pugh, Anthony R. *The Composition of Pascal's Apologia.* Toronto: The University of Toronto Press, 1984.

Sellier, Philippe. *Pascal et Saint Augustin.* Paris: Armand Colin, 1970.

——— *Port-Royal et la Literature, I: Pascal.* Paris: Honoré Champion, 1999.

CHRONOLOGY OF PASCAL'S LIFE AND TIMES

1623   Birth of Blaise Pascal at Clermont on June 19 to Etienne (born 1588) and Antoinette Pascal (née Begon in 1596); an older sister, Gilberte, was born in January 1620

1625   Birth of Jacqueline Pascal, younger sister of Blaise

1626   Death of Antoinette Begon

1631   The family moves to Paris in November

1635   Having shown mathematical ability, Blaise begins to accompany his father to the meetings supervised by Marin Mersenne at the Minim convent in Paris, where mathematics and philosophy are regularly discussed

1638   Etienne Pascal takes part in a political demonstration and must hide to avoid being imprisoned

1639   Jacqueline is instrumental in obtaining a pardon from Cardinal Richelieu on behalf of her father

1640   The family moves to Rouen, where Richelieu names Etienne tax commissioner; Blaise publishes *Essai pour les coniques*; publication of Jansenius' *Augustinus*

1641   Marriage of Gilberte to her cousin, Florin Périer

1642   To assist his father with his work collecting taxes, Pascal invents one of the first digital calculators; the device allows the addition or subtraction of two numbers of up to six digits. Pascal develops it over the course of three years and puts it into production

1646   In January, Etienne falls on ice and breaks his thigh; the brothers Deschamps, belonging to a group dedicated to the sick and connected with the Abbey of Saint-Cyran, help him heal; as a result, the whole family is gradually converted to a more intense Christianity; in October, Blaise learns from Mersenne of Evangelista Torricelli's experiments with the mercury barometer and undertakes a series of experiments on atmospheric pressure and the possibility of a void

1647   Blaise Pascal, who has been ill since the spring, returns to Paris during the summer, together with his sister Jacqueline; René Descartes visits him in September and discusses the issue of the void; Pascal publishes *Expériences nouvelles touchant le vide*; Blaise and Jacqueline become affiliated with the monastery of Port-Royal, where they are reacquainted with the spirituality of Saint-Cyran

1648   Death of Mersenne on September 1; Pascal arranges for an experiment designed to show that the height of the mercury column is determined by atmospheric pressure; he has Florin Périer carry a barometer up the Puy-de-Dôme Mountain near Clermont; as predicted, the mercury column drops as the device is moved up the mountainside; Pascal then publishes *Récit de la grande expérience de l'équilibre des liqueurs*

1649   Fleeing the Fronde uprising in Paris, the Pascals leave for Clermont, staying there until November 1650

1650   Death of Descartes on February 11

1651   Pascal works on a *Traité du vide*; death of Etienne Pascal, September 24

1652   Jacqueline enters Port-Royal; Pascal begins his "worldly" period

1653   Pope Innocent XI condemns five propositions attributed to the *Augustinus* of Jansenius

1654   Pascal enters into correspondence with Pierre de Fermat on questions of probability; the exchange produces fundamental results now regarded as the foundation of the subject; he publishes *Traité du triangle arithmétique*; during the night of November 23, he has a vision; he subsequently practices a severe asceticism, abandoning the world of scientific and mathematical research for the theological matters discussed at Port-Royal

1656   Pascal undertakes the public defense of Jansenism against the Jesuits by publishing the first of a series of eighteen anonymous *Lettres provinciales* (from January 23 to March 24 of the following year); on March 24, Pascal's niece, Marguerite Périer, is miraculously healed at Port-Royal of a reputedly incurable ulcer to her lachrymal duct

1658   Pascal works on an *Apologie de la religion chrétienne*, what will become known as the *Pensées*, organizing his notes into various bundles of fragments, and gives an outline of it at Port-Royal

1661   Port-Royal is persecuted for its Jansenism; death of Jacqueline on October 4

1662   Initiation of the "carrosses à cinq sols," the first form of public transportation, began in Paris by Pascal and the duc de Roannez; Pascal, gravely ill, is taken to Gilberte's house on June 29; he dies August 19 and is buried two days later in the church of Saint-Etienne-du-Mont

[I. THE PROJECT OF JUNE 1658]

[1. Table, etc.]¹

Order	A. P. R.³	S1
	Beginning	
Vanity	Submission and use of reason	
	Excellence	
Wretchedness	Transition	
	Nature is corrupt⁴	
Boredom	Falsity of other religions	
	Religion attractive	
<Sound opinions of the people>	Foundation	
Causes of effects	Figurative law	
Greatness	Rabbinism	
	Perpetuity	
Oppositions²	Proofs of Moses	
	Proofs of Jesus Christ	
Diversion	Prophecies	
	Figures	
Philosophers	Christian morality	
The supreme good	Conclusion	

---

¹ This table, containing the titles to the various fragments of Part I, together with a deleted and an empty heading, is thought by some to contain the rationale and order of Pascal's apologetic project of June 1658, but by others as another descriptive fragment.

² Pascal's word is *contrariétés*, often translated as contradictions. In traditional logic, contrarieties or contrary propositions say the opposite about the same subject; contradictions are direct negations of one another. Thus "all roses are red" and "all roses are nonred" or "no roses are red" are contraries. They cannot both be true, but they both might be false. "All roses are red" and "some roses are not red" are contradictories. They cannot both be true and cannot both be false. Depending on the context, I will reserve opposition and contrary for all verbal forms of *contrariété* and contradiction for *contradiction*.

³ A. P. R. is generally taken to mean "A Port-Royal," though that would make it an odd title, compared to the other titles. See fragments S155, S182, and S274.

⁴ This category is empty. Pascal probably merged these fragments with those of the next category.

To be insensitive to the point of despising things of interest   S2/L383
and to become insensitive to what interests us most.

The Maccabees after they no longer had prophets.   S3/L384
The Masorah since Jesus Christ.[5]

But it was not enough that there were prophecies: they had   S4/L385
to be distributed to all places and maintained at all times.

And, so that the coming should not be taken as the result of chance,
it had to be foretold.

———

It is much more glorious for the Messiah that they should be the ob-
servers and even the instruments of his glory—other than that God had
chosen them.

The fascination for trivialities.[6]   S5/L386

So that passion can do no harm, let us act as if we had only
one week to live.

Order   S6/L387

I would be much more afraid of being wrong and finding
out that the Christian religion is true than of being wrong in believing it
to be true.

Jesus Christ, with whom the two *Testaments* are concerned: S7/L388
the *Old* as its hope, the *New* as its model, and both as their
center.

Why did Jesus Christ not come in a visible way instead of   S8/L389
drawing his proof from previous prophecies?

———

Why did he have himself foretold by figures?[7]

Perpetuity   S9/L390

Let us consider that, since the beginning of the world, the
Messiah has been expected or worshiped continuously. That there were
men who said that God had revealed to them that a Redeemer would be
born to save his people. That Abraham then came to say he had a reve-

———

[5] The Maccabees were Jewish high priests and dissidents who led a successful rebellion
during the second century. The Masorah is a series of Jewish commentaries attempting to
maintain the integrity of the original scriptures.

[6] *Fascinatio nugacitatis.* Wisdom of Solomon 4:12.

[7] Figures are symbols—that is, types (people, events, institutions) containing the seeds of
what they prefigure. For example, in fragment S11 below, Adam prefigures Christ. The
Scriptures thus contain figurative language.

lation that the Redeemer was to be born of him through a son he would have. That Jacob declared that, of his twelve children, the Redeemer would be born of Judah. That Moses and the prophets then came to proclaim the time and manner of his coming. That they said the law they had would last only while awaiting that of the Messiah—until then it would be permanent—but the latter would last forever. That thus their law or that of the Messiah of which it was the pledge would always be on the earth. That in fact it has always lasted. That finally Jesus Christ came with all the circumstances foretold. This is remarkable.

If this was so clearly foretold to the Jews, why did they not   S10/L391
believe it, or why were they not destroyed for resisting so clear
a thing?

I reply. First, it was foretold both that they would not believe so clear a thing and that they would not be destroyed. And nothing is more glorious for the Messiah, for it was not enough that there should be prophets; they had to be kept above suspicion, but, etc.

Figures   S11/L392

God, wishing to create a holy people whom he would sep-
arate from all the other nations, whom he would deliver from its enemies and bring to a place of peace, promised to do it and foretold through his prophets the time and manner of his coming. And yet, to strengthen the hope of his chosen in every age, he showed them an image of it, never leaving them without assurances of his power and his will for their salvation. For, in the creation of man, when men were still so close to the Creation that they could not have forgotten their creation and fall, Adam was the witness and guardian of the promise of a savior, who would be born of woman. When those who had seen Adam were no longer in the world, God sent Noah and saved him, and drowned the whole earth by a miracle that clearly showed his power to save the world and his will to do it, and to cause the one he had promised to be born from the seed of woman.

This miracle was sufficient to strengthen the hope of the [chosen].

The memory of the deluge being so fresh among men while Noah was still alive, God made promises to Abraham, and while Shem was still alive, he sent Moses, etc.

Man's true nature, his true good, true virtue, and true re-   S12/L393
ligion, are things that cannot be known separately.

Instead of complaining that God has hidden himself, you   S13/L394
will thank him for revealing so much of himself; and you will
also thank him for not revealing himself to arrogant sages unworthy of knowing so holy a God.

Two kinds of persons know him: those who have a humble heart and who embrace lowliness, whatever their degree of intellect, high or low; and those who have sufficient understanding to see the truth, whatever they may have against it.

When we want to think of God, is there nothing that turns   S14/L395
us away, tempts us to think of something else? All of this is bad
and is born with us.

It is wrong for anyone to become attached to me, even   S15/L396
though they do it gladly and freely. I will disappoint those in
whom I have aroused this desire, for I am nobody's end and do not have
the means of satisfying them. Am I not ready to die? And thus the object
of their attachment will die. Therefore, just as I would be guilty if I
caused a falsehood to be believed, even though I argued for it gently
and they believed it with pleasure and it gave me pleasure, in the same
way I am guilty if I make anyone love me and attract people to become
attached to me. I must warn those who are ready to consent to the lie
that they should not believe it, whatever advantage I might derive from
it; likewise they should not become attached to me because they should
spend their life and efforts in pleasing God or in seeking him.

True nature having been lost, everything becomes his   S16/L397
nature.

In the same way, the true good having been lost, everything becomes
his true good.

The philosophers did not prescribe feelings proportionate   S17/L398
to the two states.

They inspired impulses of pure greatness, and this is not man's state.

They inspired impulses of pure lowliness, and this is not man's state.

There must be impulses of lowliness, not from nature, but from penitence; not to retain them, but to go on to greatness. There must be impulses of greatness, not from merit but from grace, and after having passed through lowliness.

If man is not made for God, why is he happy only in God?   S18/L399
If man is made for God, why is he so opposed to God?

Man does not know what rank he should occupy. He has   S19/L400
obviously gone astray and fallen from his true place, lacking
the power to find it again. He looks for it everywhere anxiously and unsuccessfully, in impenetrable darkness.

We want truth and find only uncertainty in ourselves.   S20/L401
We seek happiness and find only wretchedness and death.
We are incapable of not wanting truth and happiness and are incapable of certainty or happiness.

We have been left with this desire as much to punish us as to make us
perceive from whence we have fallen.

Proofs of religion S21/L402
Morality./Doctrine./Miracles./Prophecies./Figures.
Wretchedness S22/L403

Solomon and Job understood best and spoke best about
the wretchedness of man, one the happiest and the other the unhappi-
est of men; one knowing the vanity of pleasures through experience, the
other the reality of pains.

All these oppositions that seemed to take me farthest from   S23/L404
the knowledge of religion are what led me most directly to the
true one.

I blame equally those who decide to praise man, those who   S24/L405
blame him, and those who amuse themselves; and I can approve only of those who search in anguish.

Instinct, reason S25/L406

We have an inability to prove that no dogmatism can overcome.

We have an idea of truth that no skepticism can overcome.

The Stoics say, "Withdraw into yourself, where you will   S26/L407
find peace." And this is not true.

Others say, "Go out, seek happiness in diversion." And this is not
true. Illnesses arise.

Happiness is neither outside of us nor within us. It is in God, both
outside and within us.

A *Letter* on the folly of human knowledge and philosophy.   S27/L408
This *Letter* before the section on *Diversion*.
Happy is the man who could [know the reason for things].[8]
Happy is he who is surprised at nothing.[9]
Two hundred eighty kinds of supreme good in Montaigne.[10]

The falsity of philosophers who did not discuss the immor-   S28/L409
tality of the soul.
The falsity of their dilemma in Montaigne.[11]

---

[8] *Felix qui potuit.* Virgil, *Georgics*, 2. 490.

[9] *Felix nihil admirari.* Horace, *Epistles*, 1.6.1.

[10] See Montaigne, *Essays* II, chap. 12: "There is no battle so violent among philosophers,
and so bitter, as that which turns on the question of the sovereign good for man, from
which, according to Varro, there sprang 288 sects." (Ariew and Grene trans., p. 138.)

[11] See Montaigne, *Essays* II, chap. 12: "The philosophers always have this dilemma to
console us for our mortal condition on their tongues: 'Either the soul is mortal or it is

This internal war between reason and the passions has   S29/L410
divided those who wanted peace into two sects. Some wanted
to renounce their passions and become gods; others wanted to renounce reason and become brute beasts. Des Barreaux.[12] But neither
can succeed: reason remains to condemn the lowliness and injustice of
the passions and to disturb the peace of those who surrender to them;
and the passions stay alive in those who want to renounce them.

Greatness of man   S30/L411
We have such a lofty idea of man's soul that we cannot
bear being despised and not esteemed by some soul. And all the happiness of men consists in this esteem.

Men are so necessarily mad that it would be another kind   S31/L412
of madness not to be mad.

Whoever wants to know man's vanity fully has only to con-   S32/L413
sider the causes and effects of love. The cause is a *something I
know not what*. Corneille.[13] And the effects are frightening. This *something I know not what*, so insignificant that we cannot recognize it, dis-
turbs the whole earth, princes, armies, the entire world.

Cleopatra's nose: had it been shorter, the whole face of the earth
would have been changed.

Wretchedness   S33/L414
The only thing that consoles us for our miseries is diver-
sion, and yet this is the greatest of our miseries. For it is mainly what prevents us from thinking about ourselves, leading us imperceptibly to our
ruin. Without it we would be bored, and this boredom would drive us to
seek a more solid means of escape. But diversion amuses us and guides
us imperceptibly to death.

Agitation   S34/L415
When a soldier, or a laborer, etc., complains of his toils,
give him nothing to do.

Nature is corrupt   S35/L416
Without Jesus Christ, man must be mired in vice and
wretchedness.
With Jesus Christ, man is free from vice and wretchedness.
In him are all our virtue and all our happiness.

---

immortal. If mortal, it will be without pain; if immortal, it will go on improving.' They
never touch the other horn of the dilemma: 'What if it goes on getting worse?' and they
leave to the poets the threats of future pains." (Ariew and Grene trans., pp. 112–13.)

[12] Jacques Vallée Des Barreaux (1599–1673), libertine poet.

[13] *je ne sais quoi*. Pierre Corneille, *Medea*, II, 6.

Apart from him, there is only vice, wretchedness, error, darkness, death, despair.

Not only do we not know God except through Jesus Christ,   S36/L417
but also we do not know ourselves except through Jesus
Christ. We know life and death only through Jesus Christ. Apart from
Jesus Christ, we do not know what is our life, or our death, or God, or
ourselves.

Thus without Scripture, whose only object is Jesus Christ, we know
nothing, and see only darkness and confusion in the nature of God and
in the very nature [of man].

[2] Order

The Psalms are sung throughout the earth.   S37/L1
Who bears witness to Mahomet? Himself.
Jesus Christ wants his witness to be nothing.[14]

The quality of witnesses requires that they always exist, both everywhere and wretched.[15] He is alone.

Order   S38/L2

by dialogues

"What should I do? I see only darkness everywhere. Shall I believe
that I am nothing? Shall I believe that I am God?"

——

"All things change and succeed one another."   S38/L3
"You are wrong; there is . . . "

——

"Why, do you not yourself say that the sky and the birds prove God?"
No. "And does not your religion say so?" No. For while this is true in a
sense for some souls to whom God gave this illumination, nevertheless
it is false for most of them.

——

Letter to induce the search for God.   S38/L4

And then have them seek him among the philosophers,
skeptics, and dogmatists, who will trouble those studying them.

---

[14] See John 5:31: "If I bear witness of myself, my witness is not true."

[15] Christ's witnesses are the Jews.

Order   S39/L5

A letter of exhortation to a friend to induce him to seek. And
he will reply, "But what good will seeking do for me? Nothing comes of
it." Then reply to him, "Do not despair." And he will answer that he
would be glad to find some illumination, but that, according to this very
religion, if he believed it in his way, it would not do him any good, and
hence he prefers not to seek. The answer to that is: "The machine."[16]

First part: Wretchedness of man without God.   S40/L6
Second part: Happiness of man with God.

———

otherwise

First part: That nature is corrupt, proved by nature itself.
Second part: That there is a Redeemer, proved by Scripture.

Letter indicating the usefulness of proofs. By the machine.   S41/L7
Faith is different from proof. One is human; the other is a
gift of God. *The righteous live through faith.*[17] It is this faith that God
himself puts into the heart, and proof is often its instrument. *Faith
comes by hearing.*[18] But this faith is in the heart and makes us say not *I
know*, but *I believe.*[19]

Order   S42/L8

See what is clear and indisputable in the whole state of the
Jews.

In the letter on injustice can come: S43/L9
The absurdity of first-born sons receiving everything. "My
friend, you were born on this side of the mountain; it is therefore right
that your older brother should have everything."
"Why are you killing me?"

The miseries of human life have unsettled all this.   S44/L10
As they have become aware of it, they have taken up
diversion.

Order. After the letter about the necessity of seeking God,   S45/L11
put in the letter about removing obstacles, which is
the discourse on the machine, on preparing the machine, on
searching through reason.

———

[16] See below, fragments S41, S45, and S59. What we call "The Wager" (fragment S680)
is found in the chapter called *Discourse on the Machine.*

[17] *Justus ex fide vivit.* Romans 1:17.

[18] *Fides ex auditu.* Romans 10:17.

[19] ". . . et fait dire non *Scio* mais *Credo.*"

Order S46/L12

Men despise religion; they hate it and fear that it is true. To
cure this, we must begin by showing that religion is not contrary to
reason, but worthy of veneration and respect. Next we must make it
attractive, to make the good wish it were true, and then we must show
that it is true.

Worthy of veneration because it has properly understood man.

Attractive because it promises the true good.

[3] Vanity

Two similar faces, though neither by itself is particularly S47/L13
funny, are funny together because of their similarity.

True Christians nevertheless obey these follies, not because S48/L14
they respect them, but rather God's command, which has sub-
jected them to follies for their punishment. *For all creatures are subject to
vanity.* [. . .] *They shall be freed.*[20] Thus Saint Thomas explains the passage in Saint James on giving preference to the rich, that, if they do not do
it in the sight of God, they are transgressing the order of religion.[21]

Perseus, King of Macedonia. Paulus Emilius.[22] S49/L15
Perseus was criticized for not killing himself.

Vanity S50/L16

That something so obvious as the vanity of the world is so
little known that it would be odd and surprising to say that it is foolish to
seek greatness, this is remarkable.

Inconstancy and oddity S51/L17

To live by one's work alone and to rule over the most powerful state in the world are very different things. They are combined in the
person of the great Sultan of the Turks.

751. A piece of cowl brings 25,000 monks to arms.[23] S52/L18

---

[20] *Omnis creatura subjecta est vanitati. Liberabitur.* Romans 8:20–21; cf. Ecclesiastes
3:19.

[21] Thomas Aquinas, *Summa Theologiae* II, 2, quest. 63, referring to James 2:1: "Whoever
honors the rich for their riches, sins."

[22] Montaigne, *Essays* I, chap. 20: "There is nothing evil in life for the person who thoroughly understands that the privation of life is not an evil. Paulus Emilius replied to the
messenger whom that miserable king of Macedonia, his prisoner, sent to beg him not to
lead him in his triumph: 'Let him make that request to himself.'" (Frame trans., p. 60;
Screech trans., p. 96.)

[23] "751" is a page reference to the 1652 edition of Montaigne's *Essays*, concerning the
emptiness of human affairs.

He has four lackeys.   S53/L19

He lives across the water.   S54/L20

Those too young do not judge well; so also those too old.   S55/L21
Not thinking enough or thinking too much about things
makes us stubborn and opinionated.

———

If we look at our work immediately after completing it, we are still altogether possessed with it; if we delay too long, we can no longer get in-
volved with it.

———

It is the same with pictures seen from too far or too near. And there is
only one indivisible point, which is the right place. The others are too
near, too far, too high, or too low. Perspective determines that point in
the art of painting. But in truth and in morality, who will determine it?

The power of flies: they win battles, hinder the activity of   S56/L22
our souls, eat our bodies.[24]

Vanity of the sciences   S57/L23

The knowledge of physical things will not console me for
the ignorance of morality in a time of affliction. But the knowledge of
ethics will always console me for ignorance of the physical sciences.

Man's condition   S58/L24

⌈Inconstancy, boredom, anxiety.⌉

The custom of seeing kings accompanied by guards, drums,   S59/L25
officers, and all the things that direct the machine to yield respect and fear, makes their faces, when they are sometimes seen alone
without these trappings, impress respect and fear in their subjects, because we cannot separate in thought their persons from what usually
accompanies them. And the world, which does not know that this effect is
the result of custom, believes that it derives from a natural force. From
this come these words: *the character of divinity is stamped on his face*, etc.

The power of kings is based on reason and on the folly of   S60/L26
the people; indeed, much more on folly. The greatest and
most important thing in the world has weakness as its foundation, and
this foundation is wonderfully secure, for there is nothing more secure

———

[24] See Montaigne, *Essays* II, chap. 12: "If you let loose even some of our flies, they will
have both the power and the courage to disperse the horde" (Ariew and Grene trans., p.
37). The flies Montaigne refers to are actually honeybees (*mouches à miel*). Montaigne
gives an example of bees having been used successfully against a Portuguese army that
was laying siege to a town.

than that the people will be weak. What is based on reason alone is truly ill founded, like esteem for wisdom.

Man's nature is not always improving; it has its gains and its losses.   S61/L27

Fever has its shivers and its hot flashes. And the cold indicates the magnitude of the fever's temperature as well as the hot.

It is the same with man's inventions from century to century. It is the same with the kindness and the malice of the world in general.

Changes are most always pleasing to princes.[25]

Weakness   S62/L28

All of man's pursuits aim at acquiring some good, but he cannot have a title to show that he owns the good rightly, for he has only human fancy; nor does he have the strength to own it securely.

It is the same with knowledge, for illness takes it away.

✦ We are equally incapable of truth and good. ✦

A warlike people for whom there is no life without arms.[26]   S63/L29
They prefer death to peace; others prefer death to war.

Every opinion can be preferable to life, the love of which seems so strong and natural.

We do not choose as captain of a ship the passenger who comes from the best home.   S64/L30

We do not worry about being esteemed in the towns we travel through. But when we have to stay there a little while, we do worry about it. How much time is needed? A time proportionate to our futile and puny duration.   S65/L31

Vanity   S66/L32

Respect means: inconvenience yourself[27]

What astonishes me most is to see that everyone is not astonished by his own weakness. We behave seriously and each follows his calling, not because it is in fact good to do so (as fashion will have it), but as if each knew with certainty where reason and justice lie. We are constantly disappointed, and with ridiculous humility think it is our fault and not that of the skill we always boast about. But it is good for the reputation of skepticism that there are so many people in the world who are not skeptics, showing that man is quite capable of the   S67/L33

---

[25] *Plerumque gratae principibus vices.* Horace, *Odes,* III. xxix. 13.

[26] *Ferox gens, nullam esse vitam sine armis rati.* Montaigne, *Essays* I, chap. 14 (Frame trans., p. 42; Screech trans., p. 65.), quoting Livy, 24. 17.

[27] See fragment S115 for Pascal's development of this thought.

most extravagant opinions, since he is capable of believing that he is not naturally and inevitably weak, and is, on the contrary, naturally wise.

Nothing strengthens skepticism more than the fact that there are some people who are not skeptics; if all of them were, they would be wrong.

This sect[28] is strengthened by its enemies more than by its   S68/L34
friends, for man's weakness is much more apparent in those
who do not recognize it than in those who do.

Heel of a shoe   S69/L35

Oh, how well shaped it is! Now, there's a skillful workman! What a brave soldier! This is the source of our inclinations and choice of conditions. This person drinks too much! That person drinks too little! This is what makes people sober or drunk, soldiers, cowards, etc.

Anyone who does not see the vanity of the world is himself   S70/L36
very vain.

Indeed, who does not see it, other than young people absorbed in noise, diversion, and thoughts of the future?

But take away their diversion, and you will see them shrivel out of boredom.

Then they feel their nothingness without recognizing it, for it is indeed wretched to be insufferably depressed, as soon as you are reduced to introspection without any means of diversion.

Occupations   S71/L37

The sweetness of fame is so great that we love every object to which it is attached, even death.

Too much and too little wine. Give him none, he cannot   S72/L38
find truth. Give him too much, the same thing.

Men spend their time chasing a ball or a hare. It is the   S73/L39
entertainment even of kings.

How vain is painting, which attracts admiration by its   S74/L40
similarity to originals we do not admire!

When we read too fast or too slowly, we understand   S75/L41
nothing.

How many kingdoms are unaware of us!   S76/L42

It takes little to console us because it takes little to distress   S77/L43
us.

Imagination   S78/L44

In man it is that dominant part, that master of error and falsity, and all the more deceptive because it is not always so; for it

---

[28] Skepticism.

would be an infallible rule of truth, if it were an infallible one of false-hood. But being more often false, it gives no indication of its quality, impressing the same mark on the true and the false. I am not speaking of fools; I am speaking of the wisest, and they are the ones whom imagination is most entitled to persuade. Reason may well protest; it cannot determine the price of things.

This arrogant power, which likes to control and dominate reason, its enemy, to show how all-powerful it is, has established a second nature in man. It has its happy, its sad, its healthy, its sick, its rich, and its poor. It makes them believe, doubt, and deny reason. It suspends the senses; it sharpens them. It has its fools and its wise men, and nothing upsets us more than to see it satisfy them more fully and completely than reason. Those with a capable imagination are far more pleased with themselves than prudent people could reasonably be. They look down on people with an air of authority. They argue boldly and confidently—the others timidly and carefully. And this cheerful look often gives them the advantage in the opinion of their listeners: such is the favor that those wise by imagination enjoy with their judges of the same nature.

Imagination cannot make fools wise, but it can make them happy, as opposed to reason, which can only make its friends miserable, the one covering them with glory, the other with shame.

What dispenses reputation? What gives respect and veneration to people, works, laws, and the great, other than this imagining faculty? How insufficient are all the riches of the earth without its consent.

Would you not say that this magistrate whose venerable age commands everyone's respect is ruled by pure, sublime reason, and that he judges things by their true nature without considering those trivial circumstances damaging only the imagination of the weak? See him go to a sermon, bringing a wholly devout zeal, reinforcing the soundness of his reason with the warmth of his charity. He is ready to listen with exemplary respect. When the preacher appears, if nature has given him a hoarse voice and an odd sort of face, or his barber has shaved him badly, if by chance he is dirtier than usual, however great the truths he announces, I wager that our old magistrate will lose his composure.

Put the world's greatest philosopher on a plank hanging over a precipice, but wider than it needs to be. Although his reason will convince him of his safety, his imagination will prevail. Many could not bear the thought of it without getting pale and sweating.[29]

---

[29] See Montaigne, *Essays* II, chap. 12: "Put a philosopher in a cage of small bars of thin iron suspended at the top of the towers of Notre Dame de Paris, he will see for obvious

I will not relate all the effects of imagination. Who does not know that the sight of cats or rats, the crunching of coal, etc., can unhinge reason completely? Tone of voice affects the wisest men and perforce changes a discourse or a poem. Love or hate alters the face of justice. How much more righteous does a lawyer, well paid in advance, find the case he is pleading! How much better does his bold manner make his case appear to the judges taken in by his appearance! Ludicrous reason, blowing with the wind in every direction! I would have to enumerate almost all the actions of men, which hardly waver except under the assaults of imagination. For reason has had to yield, and the wisest reason takes as its principles the ones human imagination has rashly introduced everywhere. <We must, since it has been ordained, work all day for benefits recognized as imaginary; and, after sleep has refreshed our tired reason, we must jump up at once to rush after phantoms and endure the impressions of this master of the world.>

Our magistrates have well understood this mystery. Their red robes, the ermine in which they wrap themselves like furry cats, the palaces in which they administer justice, the fleurs-de-lis, and all such stately apparatus were truly necessary. If physicians did not have gowns and slippers, if learned doctors did not have square caps and robes four times too large, they would never have duped the world, which cannot resist so original a display. If they possessed true justice, and if physicians possessed the true art of healing, they would have no need of square caps. The majesty of these sciences would command enough respect by itself. But having only imaginary knowledge, they must take up those vain tools that strike the imagination to which they must appeal; and in this way they do, in fact, inspire respect.

Soldiers alone are not disguised in this way, because their role is really more essential. They establish themselves by force—the others by affectation.

That is why our kings have not sought such disguises. They have not masked themselves in extraordinary costumes to appear as they do, but have accompanied themselves with guards and soldiers. Those armed troops, whose hands and power are for them alone, the trumpets and drums marching before them, and the legions surrounding them, make

reasons that it is impossible for him to fall, and yet (unless he is used to the roofer's trade) he will not be able to keep the vision of that height from frightening and astonishing him. [. . .] There are some who cannot even bear the thought of it. Set a plank between those two towers, of a size such as is needed for us to walk on it: there is no philosophical wisdom of such firmness as to give us the courage to walk on it as we would do if it was on the ground." (Ariew and Grene trans., p. 155.)

the steadiest men tremble. They do not just have the trappings; they
have the power. You would need a very refined reason to regard the
Grand Turk, surrounded in his superb seraglio by 40,000 janissaries, as
just another man.

We cannot even see a lawyer in cap and gown without forming a
favorable opinion of his ability.

The imagination disposes of everything. It creates beauty, justice,
and happiness, which are the whole of the world.

I would gladly see the Italian book, of which I know only the title,
Opinion, Queen of the World,[30] which alone is worth many books.
Without knowing the book, I approve of what it says, except for any evil
it may contain.

These are more or less the effects of that deceptive faculty, which
seems to have been given to us specifically to lead us into necessary
error. We have many other principles of error.

Old impressions are not the only things that can mislead us; the
charms of novelty have the same power. All disputes arise from this,
people blaming each other for following their false impressions from
childhood or rashly pursuing new ones. Who keeps the golden mean?
Let him come forward and prove it. There is no principle, however natural it has been ever since childhood, [that cannot] be made to pass for
a false impression whether of education or the senses.

Some people say, "Because you have believed since childhood that a
box was empty when you saw nothing in it, you believed the void possible. This is an illusion of your senses, strengthened by habit, which
science must correct." Others say, "Because you have been told at
school that there is no such thing as a void, your common sense, which
comprehended it clearly before this false impression, has been corrupted and must be corrected by returning to your original state."
Which then has deceived you, the senses or education?

We have another principle of error, illnesses. They impair our judgment and our senses. And if major illnesses disturb them noticeably, I
do not doubt that lesser ones make a proportionate impression.

Our own interest is another marvelous instrument for blinding ourselves agreeably. The fairest man in the world is not allowed to be judge
in his own case. I know some people who, in order to avoid this partiality
for themselves, have been most unjust as counterbalance. The sure way
of losing a perfectly just case is for people to have their close relatives
recommend it to them. Justice and truth are two points so fine that our

---

[30] *Dell'opinione regina del mondo.*

tools are too blunt to touch them exactly. If they get at it, they either crush the point or press in all around, more on the false than on the true.

<Man is therefore so happily constituted that he has no exact principle of the true and several excellent ones of the false. Let us now see how many.

But the most amusing cause of his errors is the war between the senses and reason.>

Man is but a subject full of natural error that cannot be   S78/L45
eradicated without grace. [Nothing] shows him the truth.
Everything deceives him. (The chapter on the deceptive powers must begin with this.) These two principles of truth, reason and the senses, besides both lacking authenticity, mutually deceive one another. The senses deceive reason with false appearances, and in turn receive from the soul the very tricks they play on it. Reason takes its revenge. The passions of the soul trouble the senses and give them false impressions. They rival each other in lying and deception.

But apart from this error that happens accidentally and through a lack of understanding between these heterogeneous faculties . . .

Vanity   S79/L46

The cause and effects of love.
     Cleopatra.

We never keep to the present time. We anticipate the future   S80/L47
as too slow in coming, almost to hurry it up, or we remember
the past, to stop it as having gone too fast. So imprudent are we that we wander about in times that are not ours and do not think of the one that belongs to us, and so vain are we that we dream of those that are nothing and let slip away without reflection the one that exists. It is that the present is usually painful. We hide it from our sight because it distresses us; and, if it is agreeable, we regret seeing it slip away. We try to support it with the future and think of arranging things we cannot control, for a time we have no certainty of reaching.

Examine your thoughts, and you will find them wholly occupied with the past or the future. We almost never think of the present, and if we do so, it is only to shed light on our plans for the future. The present is never our end. The past and the present are our means; only the future is our end. So, we never live, but hope to live, and, as we are always planning to be happy, it is inevitable we should never be so.

The mind of this supreme judge of the world is not so   S81/L48
independent that it is not liable to be disturbed by the first
noise in its vicinity. The din of a cannon is not necessary to hinder its thoughts; it needs only the creaking of a vane or pulley. Do not be sur-

prised if right now it does not reason well: a fly is buzzing in its ears. This is enough to render it incapable of good reflection. If you wish it to be able to reach the truth, chase away the animal holding its reason in check and disturbing that powerful intellect, ruler of towns and kingdoms.

Here is a comical god! *Most ridiculous hero!*[31]

Caesar was too old, it seems to me, to amuse himself by   S82/L49
going off to conquer the world. Such entertainment was good
for Augustus or Alexander. They were still young men and difficult to restrain. But Caesar should have been more mature.

The Swiss are offended by being called gentlemen, and   S83/L50
establish their working-class origins in order to be judged
worthy of high office.

"Why are you killing me?" "Well, do you not live on the   S84/L51
other side of the water? If you lived on this side, my friend, I
would be a murderer, and it would be wrong to kill you in this way. But since you live on the other side, I am a brave man and it is right."

Good sense.   S85/L52

They are compelled to say, "You are not acting in good
faith, we are not asleep," etc. How I love to see this proud reason humbled and suppliant! For this is not the language of someone whose rights are challenged and who defends them with the force of weapons in hand. He does not bother to say that they are not acting in good faith, but punishes this bad faith with force.

[4] Wretchedness

The vileness of man, going as far as submission to the   S86/L53
beasts, to the point of worshiping them.

Inconstancy   S87/L54

Things have diverse qualities and the soul diverse inclina-
tions; for nothing presented to the soul is simple, and the soul never presents itself simply to any object. That is why we cry and laugh at the same thing.

Inconstancy   S88/L55

We think we are playing on ordinary organs when playing
on men. They are organs, indeed, but odd, changeable, and variable <with pipes that do not follow a normal pattern. Those who only know how to play on ordinary organs> will not produce chords on these. We must know where [the keys are].

---

[31] *O ridicolosissimo heroe!*

We are so unhappy that we can only take pleasure in   S89/L56
something on condition of our being annoyed if it turns out
badly, as thousands of things can and do every hour. Anyone who found
the secret of rejoicing in the good without being annoyed by its contrary
evil would have found the point. It is perpetual motion.

It is not good to be too free.   S90/L57

_____

It is not good to have all the necessities.

Tyranny   S91/L58

Tyranny is wanting to have by one means what can only be
had by another. We have different duties to different sorts of merits: the
duty of love to charm, fear to strength, belief to knowledge.

We must fulfill these obligations; it is wrong to deny them and wrong
to ask for others.

Thus this discourse is false and tyrannical: "I am handsome, so I
must be feared. I am strong, so I must be loved. I am . . ." And it is even
false and tyrannical to say: "He is not strong, so I will not admire him;
he is not clever, so I will not fear him."

Tyranny consists in the universal desire   S92/L58
to dominate beyond one's order

There are various compartments of the strong, the handsome, the
sensible, the pious; each of them rules there but not elsewhere. Sometimes they intersect. And the strong and the handsome fight to see who
is master, but this is foolish, for their mastery is of different kinds. They
do not understand one another. Their mistake is to want to rule everywhere. Nothing can do this, not even strength, which is of no use in the
realm of knowledge and governs only external actions.

When it is a question of deciding whether we should make   S93/L59
war and kill so many men—condemn so many Spaniards to
death—it is one man alone who decides, and an interested party at that.
It should be a third, disinterested party.

On what will he base the organization (*économie*) of the   S94/L60
world he wants to govern? On the whim of each individual?
What confusion! On justice? He does not know what it is. Certainly, if
he did know, he would not have laid down this maxim, the most general
of all human maxims, that each should follow the customs of his own
country. True equity would have swayed all people by its brilliance and
legislators would not have taken as their model the fancies and whims

of Persians and Germans, instead of this steady justice.[32] We would have seen it planted in all the states of the world, at all times; whereas we see nothing, whether just or unjust, that does not change its quality with a change in climate. Three degrees of latitude reverse all jurisprudence; a meridian decides what is true. Fundamental laws change after being kept for a few years; rights have their terms. The entry of Saturn into Leo marks the origin of a given crime. Odd kind of justice that is bounded by a river! Truth on this side of the Pyrenees, error on the other.[33]

They admit that justice does not reside in these customs, but in natural laws common to every country. They would certainly maintain this stubbornly if reckless chance, which has distributed human laws, had found at least one that was universal; but the joke is that human whim has so many varieties that there is no such <general> law.

Theft, incest, infanticide, parricide, all have been considered virtuous actions. Can anything be more ridiculous than that a man should have the right to kill me because he lives on the other side of the water and his prince has a quarrel with mine, though I have none with him?

Doubtless there are natural laws, but this fine reason having been corrupted, it corrupted everything. *Nothing more is ours; what we call ours is by convention.*[34] *It is by virtue of senatorial decrees and plebiscites that crimes are committed.*[35] *As we once suffered from our vices, we now suffer from our laws.*[36]

---

[32] See Montaigne, *Essays* II, chap. 12: "If it is from ourselves that we draw the regulation of our customs, into what confusion we throw ourselves! For what our reason advises us as most likely is, generally, that each person obey the laws of his country, <like the view of Socrates, inspired, he says, by divine counsel.> And what can be meant by this, except that our duty has no rule but chance? Truth must have an identical and universal countenance. If man knew what gave body and true being to right and justice, he would not attach them to the condition of the customs of this or that country; it would not be through the fancy of the Persians or the Indians that virtue would take its form." (Ariew and Grene trans., p. 140.)

[33] See Montaigne, *Essays* II, chap. 12: "There is nothing subject to more continual agitation than the laws. [. . .] And even among us, I have seen what was a capital offense become legitimate; and in the same way as we ourselves think of others according to the uncertainty of the fortunes of war, we go from being one day guilty of *lese majesté* both human and divine, our justice falling to the mercy of injustice, to taking an opposite nature in the space of a few years' possession. [. . .] What virtue is it that I see approved today and not tomorrow, and that crossing a river makes a crime? What truth is it that is bounded by these mountains, and that is falsehood in the world beyond them?" (Ariew and Grene trans., p. 140.)

[34] *Nihil amplius nostrum est; quod nostrum dicimus, artis est.* Cicero, *De finibus*, V. 21.

[35] *Ex senatus-consultis et plebiscitis crimina exercentur.* Seneca, *Epistles*, xcv.

[36] *Ut olim vitiis, sic nunc legibus laboramus.* Tacitus, *Annals*, iii. 25.

The result of this confusion is that one says the essence of justice is the authority of the legislator, another the interest of the sovereign, another present custom.[37] And the last is the surest. Nothing, according to reason alone, is just in itself; everything shifts with time. Custom constitutes the whole of equity for the sole reason that it is accepted. This is the hidden (*mystique*) basis of its authority; whoever tries to reduce it to its first principles destroys it. Nothing is so faulty as the laws that correct faults. Whoever obeys them because they are just obeys an imaginary justice, and not the essence of the law. It is altogether self-contained; it is the law and nothing more. Whoever wants to examine the basis for this will find it so weak and trivial that, if he is not used to contemplating the wonders of human imagination, he will be amazed that it has gained such pomp and reverence in the course of a century. The art of subversion and revolution is to unsettle established customs by probing them to their core to show their lack of authority and justice. We must, it is said, get back to the primitive and fundamental laws of the state, which an unjust custom has abolished. It is a game certain to result in the loss of everything; on these scales nothing will be just. Yet people readily listen to such discourses. They throw off the yoke as soon as they recognize it; and the mighty profit by their ruin and by the ruin of those inquisitive investigators of accepted customs.[38] That is why the wisest of legislators used to say that it was necessary to deceive people for their own good; and another, a good politician, said: *When he searches for the truth that would bring him freedom, it is good that he should be misinformed.*[39] He must not become aware of the usurpation; it was originally introduced without reason and has become reasonable. It must be made to seem authentic and eternal, and its origin must be concealed, if we do not want it to end soon.

---

[37] See Montaigne, *Essays* II, chap. 12: "Protagoras and Ariston give the justice of laws no other essence but the authority and opinion of the legislator, and they claim that, apart from that, goodness and honesty would lose their qualities and remain empty names of indifferent things. Thrasymachus, in Plato, holds that there is no other right than the advantage of the superior." (Ariew and Grene trans., p. 141.)

[38] See Montaigne, *Essays* II, chap. 12: "For the common people, [. . .] once they have been given the temerity to despise and contradict the opinions they had held in extreme reverence, [. . .] soon cast into equal uncertainty all the other items of their belief, for these had no greater authority or foundation among them than those just questioned, and they shake off like a yoke all the impressions they had received from the authority of the law or reverence for long usage: *For once too much dreaded, now it is easily trampled.*" (Ariew and Grene trans., p. 2.)

[39] *Cum veritatem qua liberetur ignoret, expedit quod fallatur.* Saint Augustine, *City of God*, iv. 27.

Justice   S95/L61
As fashion determines charm, so also it determines justice.

\<Three hosts\>   S96/L62
Could anyone who had the friendship of the King of
England, the King of Poland, and the Queen of Sweden ever have be-
lieved he would be without refuge and shelter in the world?[40]

Glory   S97/L63
Admiration spoils everything as early as childhood. "Oh,
well said! Oh, well done! How well behaved!" and so forth. The children of Port-Royal, who are not spurred on by envy and glory, fall into
indifference.

Mine, yours   S98/L64
"This is my dog," said those poor children. "That is my
place in the sun." Here is the origin and image of the usurpation of the
whole earth.

Diversity   S99/L65
Theology is a science, but how many sciences is it all at
once? A man is an individual substance (*suppôt*), but if he is dissected,
will he be the head, heart, stomach, veins, each vein, each portion of a
vein, the blood, each humor of the blood?

From afar a town, a farmland, is a town and a farmland; but as you
approach, there are houses, trees, tiles, leaves, grass, ants, ant legs, to infinity. All this is contained under the word "farmland."

Injustice   S100/L66
It is dangerous to tell the people that the laws are not just,
for they obey them only because they believe them to be just. That is
why they must be told at the same time that laws are to be obeyed because they are laws, just as superiors are to be obeyed because they are
superiors, not because they are just. In this way sedition is prevented if
they can be made to understand this, and that it is the proper definition
of justice.

Injustice   S101/L67
Jurisdiction is not given for the sake of the governor, but
for the governed. It is dangerous to tell the people this. But the people
have too much faith in you; it will not harm them and may serve you. It

---

[40] King Charles I of England was beheaded in 1649, and Charles II was in exile in the
1650s; King Casimir of Poland was deposed for a few months in 1656; Queen Christina of
Sweden abdicated her throne in 1654.

should, therefore, be disseminated. *Feed my sheep, not yours.*[41] You owe me pasturage.

When I consider the brief duration of my life absorbed in   S102/L68
the eternity that lies before and after—*The memory of a guest who stays only a day*[42]—the small space I occupy and can even see, engulfed in the infinite immensity of spaces I do not know and that do not know me, I am frightened and astonished to see myself here rather than there; for there is no reason why I am here rather than there, why now rather than then. Who put me here? By whose order and direction have this place and time been allotted to me?

Wretchedness   S103/L69

Job and Solomon.[43]

If our condition were truly happy, we would not need to   S104/L70
divert ourselves from thinking about it.

Contradiction   S105/L71

Pride counterbalances all miseries. Either he hides his miseries or, if he displays them, he glories in knowing them.

You must know yourself. If this does not serve to find the   S106/L72
truth, at least it serves to order your life. And nothing is better.

The awareness that present pleasures are false, together   S107/L73
with the ignorance that absent pleasures are vain, causes inconstancy.

Injustice   S108/L74

They have not found another means of satisfying their concupiscence[44] without doing harm to others.

Job and Solomon.   S109/L74

Ecclesiastes shows that man without God is totally igno-   S110/L75
rant and inevitably wretched. For it is wretched to want but not to have power. Now, he wants to be happy and certain of some truth, and yet he can neither know nor desire not to know. He cannot even doubt.

---

[41] *Pasce oves meas, non tuas.* John 21:17

[42] *Memoria hospitis unius diei praetereuntis.* Wisdom of Solomon 5:15.

[43] See fragment S22.

[44] *Concupiscence* is sometimes translated as lust, but this does not do justice to Pascal's broader concept, which does not refer simply to sensuality and afflictions of the body, but also to those of the mind and will. For Pascal, concupiscence is similar to inordinate self-love, which, in its concrete expression, may involve lasciviousness, but may also consist in excess curiosity or pride.

13. <Is the soul therefore too noble a subject for its feeble   S111/L76
perceptions? Let us take it down, then, to the level of matter.
Let us see if it knows of what the very body it animates, and the others it
contemplates and moves at its will, are made.

What have these great dogmatists who are ignorant of nothing
known of this?

393.[45]

On these opinions.[46]

This would be sufficient, no doubt, if reason were reasonable. It is
reasonable enough to admit that it has been unable to find anything
firm so far, but it does not yet despair of discovering it. On the contrary,
it is as ardent as ever in this search and confident it has within itself the
necessary strength for this conquest.

We must therefore complete it, and, after having observed its powers
through their effects, examine them in themselves. Let us see if it has
strength enough and a grasp capable of getting hold of the truth.

13—But perhaps this subject goes beyond the reach of reason. Let us
therefore examine its solutions to things within its powers. If there is
something in its own interest to which it must have applied itself most
earnestly, it is the inquiry into its own supreme good. Let us see then
where these strong and clear-sighted souls have placed it and whether
they agree.

One says that the supreme good consists in virtue, another in pleasure, another in following nature, another in truth—*Happy is he who
could know the causes of things*[47]—another in peaceful ignorance, another in idleness, others in resisting appearances, another in wondering
at nothing—*To wonder at nothing is almost the only thing that can produce and maintain happiness*[48]—and the brave skeptics in their indifference (*ataraxia*), doubt, and perpetual suspension of judgment; and
others, still wiser, say that it cannot be found, not even by wishing. We
have been well rewarded.

---

[45] The page references are to Montaigne, *Essays* II.

[46] *Harum sententiarum*. Cicero, *Disputationes Tusculanae*, i, ii.

[47] *Felix qui potuit rerum cognoscere causas*. Virgil, *Georgics*, ii.

[48] *Nihil mirari prope res una quae possit facere et servare beatum*. Horace, *Epistles*, I. vi. 1.

{

Whether we ought to see if this fine philosophy has
not acquired something certain from so long and so
intent a study. Perhaps at least the soul will know
itself. Let us listen to the leaders of the world on this
subject.

Transpose
after the
laws the
following
article

What have they thought about its substance?

395

Have they been luckier in locating it?

395

What have they discovered about its origin, its
duration, and its departure?

399>

[5] Boredom and the Qualities Essential to Man

Pride S112/L77

Curiosity is most often only vanity. We want to know
something simply to talk about it. In other words, we would not travel
the sea in order to say nothing about it, just for the pleasure of seeing
without the hope of ever communicating anything of it.

Description of man S113/L78
Dependence, desire for independence, needs

Our boredom in leaving pursuits to which we are   S114/L79
attached. A man lives happily at home. Let him see an attractive woman or gamble happily for five or six days; you will find him miserable if he returns to what he was doing before. Nothing is more
common than that.

[6] Cause of the Effects

Respect means: inconvenience yourself.   S115/L80

This is seemingly empty but quite right, for it says: "I
would truly inconvenience myself if you needed it, since I do it even
when it is of no use to you." Further, respect serves to distinguish the
great. Now, if respect was shown by sitting in an armchair, we would be
showing respect to everybody, and so no distinction would be made; but
by inconveniencing ourselves, a distinction is very well made.

The only universal rules are the laws of the country in   S116/L81
ordinary things and of the majority in others. Where does this
come from? From the power that resides in them.

That is why kings, who have power from elsewhere, do not follow the majority of their ministers.

Equality of goods is no doubt just; but, since we are unable to make might obey justice, we have made it just to obey might. Unable to strengthen justice, we have justified might, so that justice and might should unite and there be peace, which is the supreme good.

Wisdom leads us back to childhood. *Unless you become*   S116/L82
like little children.[49]

The world judges things well, because it is in a state of   S117/L83
natural ignorance, which is man's true state. Knowledge has
two extremes that meet. The first is the pure, natural ignorance of every-one at birth. The other extreme is reached by great souls who run through everything that can be known, only to find that they know nothing and to find themselves in the same ignorance from which they set out; but this is an erudite ignorance that knows itself. Between the two are those who have put natural ignorance behind them but have not been able to reach the other. They possess a tincture of adequate knowledge and pretend to be learned. They trouble the world and judge everything badly. Ordinary and clever people are the run of the world; they despise it and are despised. They judge all things badly, and the world judges them rightly.

<Descartes   S118/L84

We must say in general: "This happens through shape and motion," because it is true. But to say which shapes and motions and to constitute the machine is ridiculous, for it is useless, uncertain, and laborious. And if it were true, we do not believe all of philosophy to be worth an hour of labor.>

The strictest law, the greatest injustice.[50]   S119/L85

———

Majority opinion is the best way, because it is visible and has the strength to make itself obeyed. <u>Yet it is the opinion of the least clever people.</u>

If it could have been done, we would have put might in the hands of justice. But since we cannot handle might as we like, because it is a palpable quality, whereas justice is a spiritual quality we manipulate at will, we put justice in the hands of might. And so we call just what we are forced to obey.

---

[49] *Nisi efficiamini sicut parvuli.* Matthew 18. 3.

[50] *Summum jus, summa injuria.* Terrence, *Heauton Timorumenus*, iv. 5. 47; Cicero, *De officiis*, i. 10.

[From this] arises the right of the sword, for the sword gives a true right.

Otherwise we would see violence on one side and justice on the other. End of the twelfth *Provincial Letter*.

Hence the injustice of the Fronde,[51] which raises its alleged justice against might.

It is not the same in the Church, for there is true justice without violence.

Of true law.[52] We no longer have it. If we did have it, we   S120/L86
would not accept following the customs of the country as a
rule of justice.

Thus, not finding justice, we have found might, etc.

The chancellor is solemn and dressed in fine clothes,   S121/L87
because his position is a false one. Not so the king: he has
power. He has no use for imagination. Judges, physicians, etc., have
only imagination.

It is the effect of might, not of custom, because those   S122/L88
capable of originality are rare. The greatest in number want
only to follow and refuse recognition to the ones seeking it by their originality. And if they persist in wanting recognition and despising those
who are not original, they will be called ridiculous names and physi-
cally abused. Let no one, then, boast of his subtlety, or let him keep it to
himself.

Cause of the effects   S123/L89

This is remarkable: they do not want me to honor a man
clothed in brocade and followed by seven or eight lackeys. Why, he will
have me thrashed, if I do not salute him. His costume is power. It is the
same with a horse in fine harness, as compared with another. Montaigne is amusing when he does not see the difference, wonders at our
finding any, and asks the reason for it.[53] "**Indeed,**" he says, "**how does it
happen,**" etc.

---

[51] A reference to the French civil wars, 1648–1653.

[52] *Veri juris*. Cicero, *De officiis*, iii. 17.

[53] Montaigne, *Essays* I, chap. 42: "We praise a horse because it is vigorous and skilled . . .
not for its harness. . . . Why do we not likewise esteem a man by what is his own? He has

Cause of the effects   S124/L90

Gradations. Ordinary people honor persons of high birth.
Semi-clever ones despise them, saying that birth is not a privilege of the
person, but of chance. Clever ones honor them, not for the same reason
as ordinary people, but for a deeper reason in back. Devout ones, who
have more zeal than knowledge, despise them, in spite of the reason
that makes the clever honor them, because they judge them by a new
light that piety gives them. But perfect Christians honor them by another, higher light.

Thus opinions succeed one another for and against, according to
one's own lights.

Cause of the effects   S125/L91

We must have a deeper reason in back and judge everything by it, while talking like ordinary people.

Cause of the effects   S126/L92

It is, therefore, true to say that everyone is under an illusion; for, although the opinions of ordinary people are sound, they are
not so as conceived by them, since they think the truth to be where it is
not. Truth is indeed in their opinions, but not where they imagine it to
be. It is true that we must honor gentlemen, but not because birth is an
effective privilege, etc.

Cause of the effects   S127/L93

Continual reversal of pro and con.

We have, therefore, shown that man is vain because of the value he
places on things that are not essential. And all these opinions are refuted.

Then we have shown that all these opinions are perfectly sound and
that thus, since all these vanities are very well founded, ordinary people
are not as foolish as they are said to be. And so we have refuted the opinion that refuted the opinion of the people.

But we must now refute this last proposition and show that it remains
always true that the people are vain, although their opinions are sound,
because they do not see the truth where it is and, placing it where it is
not, their opinions are always false and completely unsound.

Sound opinions of the people   S128/L94

Civil wars are the greatest of all evils.

---

a great retinue, a beautiful palace, so much credit, so much income; all that is around
him, not in him." (Frame trans., p. 189; Screech trans., pp. 288–89.)

Civil wars are certain, if we want to reward merit, because everyone will claim to be meritorious. The evil to be feared from a fool who succeeds by right of birth is neither so great nor so certain.

Sound opinions of the people S129/L95

To be elegant (*brave*) is not mere vanity, for it shows that a great number of people work for you. Your hair shows that you have a valet, a perfumer, etc. As does your band, thread, lace, etc. Now it is not for simple appearance or superficial show that you have many hands at your service.

The more hands you have, the more powerful you are. To be elegant is to show your power.

Cause of the effects S130/L96

Human weakness is the reason for many standards of beauty, like being able to play the lute well. [Not playing the lute] is a bad thing only because of our weakness.

Cause of the effects S131/L97

Concupiscence and force are the sources of all our actions. Concupiscence causes voluntary actions, force involuntary ones.

Why does a lame person not annoy us, but a lame mind   S132/L98
does? Because a lame person recognizes that we are walking straight, whereas a lame mind says that it is we who are limping. Were this not so, we should feel pity and not anger.

Epictetus asks even more strongly: Why do we not get angry if we are told we have a headache, and we do get angry when we are told we reason badly, or choose wrongly?[54]

The reason is that we are quite certain that we do not have   S132/L99
a headache and that we are not lame, but we are not so sure
that we are choosing the right thing. So, being certain only to the extent that we see with all our vision, it puts us into suspense and surprises us when another sees the opposite with all his vision, and still more so when a thousand others deride our choice. For we must prefer our own lights to those of so many others. And this is daring and difficult. This contradiction of feelings does not happen about a lame person.

Man is so made that, by virtue of telling him he is a fool, he believes it. And by virtue of telling it to ourselves, we make ourselves believe it. For man alone holds an internal conversation with himself, which it is important to keep well in check: *Evil communications corrupt good*

------

[54] Epictetus, *Discourses*, 4.6, 2.14.

manners.[55] We must maintain silence as much as possible and talk with ourselves only of God, whom we know to be the truth, and in this way convince ourselves of it.

Cause of the effects   S133/L100

Epictetus, those who say: "You have a headache."

It is not the same thing. We are certain about health, but not about being right. And in fact his own thought was nonsense.

And yet he believed he was proving it by saying: "It is either in our power or not."

But he did not see that it is not in our power to regulate the heart, and he was wrong to conclude that it is, since there were Christians then.

The people have very sound opinions. For example: S134/L101

1. In choosing diversion, and the hunt rather than the kill. The semi-learned scoff at this and glory in showing that this proves the foolishness of the world. But, for a reason not grasped by these men, the people are right.

2. In distinguishing men by external marks, as by birth or wealth. Again the world glories in showing how unreasonable this is. But it is very reasonable. Cannibals laugh at an infant king.[56]

3. In taking offense at a slap or in desiring glory so much.

    But it is very desirable because of the other essential goods joined to it. And a man who receives a slap without resentment is overwhelmed with insults and deficiencies.

———

4. Working for an uncertain goal; sailing on the sea; walking over a plank.

Justice, might   S135/L103

It is just to follow the just. It is necessary to follow the strongest.

Justice without might is powerless. Might without justice is tyrannical.

Justice without might is challenged, because there are always evil people. Might without justice is indicted. We must therefore combine justice and might and, to that end, make what is just strong, or what is strong just.

---

[55] *Corrumpunt bonos mores colloquia prava.* I Corinthians 15. 33.

[56] In *Essays* I, chap. 31, Montaigne relates the surprise of some native Brazilians who, seeing Charles IX at Rouen, "said that they thought it very strange that so many grown men, bearded, strong and armed, who were around the king . . . should submit to obey a child, and that one of them was not chosen to command instead" (Frame trans., p. 159).

Justice is subject to dispute. Might is easily recognized and beyond dispute. So, we have not been able to give might to justice, because might has challenged justice, calling it unjust, and calling itself just.

And thus, being unable to make what is just strong, we have made what is strong just.

What a great advantage is noble birth, giving an eighteen- S136/L104
year-old the standing, recognition, and respect that someone
else might earn in fifty years. It is thirty years gained without effort.

[7] Greatness

If an animal did with a mind what it does by instinct, and S137/L105
if it spoke with a mind what it speaks by instinct when hunting and warning its mates that the prey is found or lost, it would certainly also speak about things that affect it more, as for example, "Gnaw
on this cord that is hurting me and I cannot reach."

Greatness S138/L106

The cause of the effects marks man's greatness, in having
derived so fine an order from concupiscence.

The parrot's beak, which it wipes although it is clean. S139/L107

What feels pleasure in us? Is it the hand, the arm, flesh, S140/L108
blood? We will see that it must be something immaterial.

Against skepticism S141/L109

<It is therefore strange that we cannot define these
things[57] without obscuring them.> We assume that everybody conceives
of them in the same way. But this assumption is quite gratuitous, since
we have no proof of it. I do see that we use these words on the same occasions and that every time two men see a body change place, they use
the same words to express their view of this same object, both saying that
it moved. And from this conformity of application, we derive a strong
conviction of conformity of ideas. But, even though it is enough to support a wager for the affirmative, it is not ultimately fully convincing, because we know that the same conclusions are often derived from
different premises.

It is enough, at least, to muddle the issue. Not that it completely ex-
tinguishes the natural clarity that makes us certain about such things.
The Academics would have wagered positively, but this tarnishes the
issue and troubles the dogmatists to the glory of the skeptical crowd,

---

[57] Pascal is referring to things such as space, time, motion, number, equality, and so forth, which, in "On the Geometrical Mind," he says are words that cannot be defined without being made more obscure (Lafuma ed., p. 350).

which revels in this ambiguous ambiguity and in a certain doubtful obscurity, from which our doubts cannot remove all clarity any more than our own natural light can chase away all darkness.

We know the truth, not only through reason, but also   S142/L110
through the heart. It is through the latter that we know first
principles, and reason, which has no part in it, tries in vain to challenge them. The skeptics, who have only this for their object, labor uselessly. We know we are not dreaming, however powerless we are to prove it by reason. This inability demonstrates only the weakness of our reason, and not, as they claim, the uncertainty of all our knowledge.

For knowledge of first principles, such as space, time, motion, number, [is] as firm as any we derive from reasoning. Reason must use this knowledge from the heart and instinct, and base all its arguments on it. The heart feels that there are three dimensions in space and numbers are infinite, and reason then shows that there are no two square numbers of which one is double the other. Principles are felt, propositions are proved; all with certainty, though in different ways. And it is as useless and absurd for reason to demand from the heart proofs of its first principles before accepting them, as it would be for the heart to demand from reason an intuition of all demonstrated propositions before receiving them.

This inability must serve, then, only to humble reason, which would want to be judge of everything, but not to attack our certainty. As if reason alone were capable of teaching us! Would to God, on the contrary, that we never had need of it, and that we knew everything by instinct and intuition. But nature has refused us this good, giving us instead very little knowledge of this kind. And all other knowledge can be acquired only by reasoning.

That is why those to whom God has given religion by intuition of the heart are very fortunate and, in fact, properly convinced. But [to] those who do not have it, we can give it only through reasoning, until God gives it to them by intuition of the heart. Without this, faith is only human and useless for salvation.

I can certainly conceive of a man without hands, feet,   S143/L111
head, for it is only experience that teaches us the head is
more necessary than the feet. But I cannot conceive of man without thought. He would be a stone or a beast.

Instinct and reason, marks of two natures.   S144/L112

Thinking reed   S145/L113

It is not in space that I must seek my dignity, but in the
ordering of my thought. I will gain no advantage in possessing worlds. Through space the universe encompasses and swallows me up like a mere point; through thought I encompass it.

Man's greatness lies in his knowing himself to be   S146/L114
wretched.

A tree does not know itself to be wretched.

So it is to be wretched to know oneself wretched, but it is to be great to know that one is wretched.

Immateriality of the soul. Philosophers who have sub-   S147/L115
dued their passions.

What material thing could have done that?

All these forms of wretchedness prove his greatness.   S148/L116

They are the wretchedness of a great lord, the wretchedness of a deposed king.

Man's greatness   S149/L117

Man's greatness is so obvious that it can be derived even
from his wretchedness. For what in animals is nature, we call wretchedness in man. In this way we recognize that, his nature being now like
that of animals, he has fallen from a better nature that once was his own.

For who is unhappy not being a king, except a deposed king? Did
anyone think Paulus Emilius was unhappy no longer being consul? On
the contrary, everybody thought he was happy having been consul, because the office could not be held indefinitely. But people thought
Perseus was so unhappy no longer being king, because the position was
permanent, that they found it strange he could bear life. Who would be
unhappy having only one mouth? And who would not be unhappy
having only one eye? Probably no person has ever thought of being distressed not having three eyes, but we are inconsolable having none.

Man's greatness, even in his concupiscence, from having   S150/L118
known how to derive an admirable system of rules from it
and to make it into an image (*tableau*) of charity.

[8] Oppositions

After having shown the lowliness and greatness of man.   S151/L119

Let man judge his worth now. Let him love himself, for
there is in him a nature capable of good; but let him not, on that account, love the lowliness in him. Let him despise himself, because this
capacity is empty; but let him not, on that account, despise this natural
capacity. Let him hate himself; let him love himself. He has in himself
the capacity for knowing truth and being happy, but he possesses no
truth, either constant or satisfactory.

I would then arouse in man the desire to find the truth; to be ready,
free from passions, to follow it where he may find it, knowing how much

his knowledge is obscured by the passions. I would want him to hate his concupiscence, which is self-determined, so that it may not blind him in making his choice, nor stop him when he has chosen.

We are so presumptuous that we would like to be known   S152/L120
throughout the world, even by people who will come when
we are no more. And we are so vain that the esteem of five or six people close to us pleases and satisfies us.

It is dangerous to show man too clearly how much alike   S153/L121
he is to the beasts without showing him his greatness. It is
also dangerous to show him too clearly his greatness without his lowliness. It is still more dangerous to leave him in ignorance of both, but it is very advantageous to show both to him.

Man must not believe that he is equal either to the beasts   S154/L121
or to angels, nor must he be ignorant of either, but he must
know both.

A. P. R. Greatness and wretchedness   S155/L122

Wretchedness being inferred from greatness and greatness from wretchedness, some have concluded for wretchedness all the more because they have used greatness to prove it, and others have concluded for greatness with even more force because they concluded it from wretchedness. Everything that the former have been able to say as proof of greatness has served only for the others as an argument for wretchedness, because the greater our fall, the more wretched we are. And the others conclude the opposite. They come back on one another in an endless circle, since it is certain that, to the extent that men possess enlightenment, they discover both greatness and wretchedness in man. In short, man knows he is wretched. He is therefore wretched because he is so. But he is truly great because he knows it.

Contradiction, contempt for our existence, dying for   S156/L123
nothing, hatred of our existence.

Oppositions   S157/L124

Man is naturally credulous, incredulous, fearful, bold.

What are our natural principles other than our accus-   S158/L125
tomed principles? And in children, [are they not] those they
received from the customs of their fathers, like hunting in animals?

A different custom will produce different natural principles. This is perceived in experience. And if there are some principles custom cannot erase, there are also customs against nature that nature or a second custom cannot erase. It depends on one's disposition.

Fathers fear that their children's natural love may be   S159/L126
erased. What, then, is this nature that can be erased?

Custom is a second nature that destroys the first.

But what is nature? Why is custom not natural?

I greatly fear that nature is itself only a first custom, as custom is a second nature.

Man's nature may be considered in two ways. One   S160/L127
according to his end, and then he is great and incomparable.
The other according to the masses, as the nature of the horse and the dog are judged by the masses, seeing their speed and their **dislike of strangers**;[58] and then man is abject and vile. These two ways make us judge him differently and provoke such disputes among philosophers.

For each denies the assumption of the other. One says, "He is not born for this end, because all his actions are repugnant to it." The other says, "He falls short of his end when his actions are so base."

Two things teach man about his whole nature: instinct   S161/L128
and experience.

Occupations   S162/L129

Thoughts

All is one, all is diverse. How many natures exist in man! How many vocations, and through what chance! Each person normally takes up what he has heard praised. A well-turned heel.

If he exalts himself, I humble him.   S163/L130

If he humbles himself, I exalt him.

And I continue to contradict him

Until he comprehends

That he is an incomprehensible monster.

The most powerful argument of the skeptics—setting   S164/L131
aside the lesser ones—is that we have no certainty of the
truth of these principles (apart from faith and revelation), except insofar as we naturally perceive them in ourselves. Now, this natural sensation is not a convincing proof of their truth. There is no certainty, apart from faith, as to whether man was created by a good God, by an evil demon, or by chance, so depending on our origin, it is doubtful whether these principles given to us are true, or false, or uncertain.[59]

Moreover, no person has any certainty, apart from faith, whether he is awake or asleep, seeing that during sleep we believe we are awake as firmly as we are now. We believe we see spaces, shapes, and motions. We feel the passing of time, we measure it, and in fact we behave as we

---

[58] *et animum arcendi.*

[59] Compare these and the following arguments with Descartes, *Meditations* I.

do when we are awake. Given that half of our life is spent in sleep, we have by our own admission no idea of truth, whatever we may imagine. All our sensations, then, are simply illusions. Who knows whether this other half of our life, in which we think we are awake, is not another sleep slightly different from the first half, from which we awake when we think we are asleep?[60] <Since we often dream that we are dreaming, piling up dream upon dream, it could well be that this half of our life, in which we think we are awake, is itself only a dream on which the others are grafted and from which we awaken at death. During this state we have as few principles of truth and good as we have during natural sleep; this flowing of time and life, these various bodies we feel, these different thoughts disturbing us are perhaps only illusions similar to the passage of time and the vain phantoms of our dreams.>

These are the strongest arguments of the two sides.[61] I set aside the lesser ones, such as the discourses of the skeptics against the impressions of custom, education, local manners, and the like. The least puff of skepticism upsets these, though they influence the majority of common people, who have only these empty foundations for their dogmas. If we are not sufficiently convinced, we have only to read their books and very soon we will be, perhaps too much so.

I pause at the dogmatists' only strong point, which is that, speaking in good faith and sincerely, we cannot doubt natural principles.

The skeptics oppose against this: in a word, the uncertainty of our origin, which includes that of our nature. The dogmatists have been trying to answer this objection ever since the world began.

So, there is open warfare in which each person must take part and side either with dogmatism or skepticism, for whoever thinks he can remain neutral will unquestionably be a skeptic. This neutrality is the essence of the conspiracy. Whoever is not against them is powerfully for

---

[60] Pascal then wrote and crossed out the following sentence not reproduced in Copy B: <And who doubts that, if we dreamed in company of others and the dreams happened to agree—something common enough—and if we were always alone when awake, we would not think that things were reversed?> See also Montaigne, *Essays* II, chap 12: "Those who have likened our life to a dream were right, perhaps more so than they thought. When we are dreaming, our soul lives, acts, exercises all its faculties, no more nor less than when it is awake [. . .]. We are awake while asleep and sleeping while awake. [. . .] Since our reason and our soul receive the fancies and opinions that arise in them while we are sleeping, and authorize the actions of our dreams with the same approval they give to those of the day, why do we not wonder whether our thought, our action, is not another state of dreaming and our waking some kind of sleep?" (Ariew and Grene trans., pp. 156–57.)

[61] In fact, Pascal has presented only the arguments of the skeptics so far in this fragment. For the arguments of the dogmatists, see fragment S142.

them. They are not for themselves; they are neutral, indifferent, in suspense as to everything, including themselves.

What then shall man do in this state? Shall he doubt everything? Doubt whether he is awake, whether he is being pinched, whether he is being burned? Doubt whether he doubts? Doubt whether he exists? We cannot go that far, and I advance as fact that there never has been a fully effective skeptic. Nature sustains our feeble reason and prevents it from ranting so wildly.

Shall he then say, on the contrary, that he certainly has the truth, when at the slightest pressure he can produce no evidence for it and is forced to let go of his grasp?

What a chimera then is man! What a surprise (*nouveauté*), what a monster, what chaos, what a subject of contradiction, what a prodigy! Judge of all things, weak (*imbécile*) earthworm; repository of truth, sink of uncertainty and error; glory and garbage of the universe!

Who will unravel this tangle? <Certainly this transcends dogmatism and skepticism and all of human philosophy. Man transcends man. Let us grant the skeptics what they have so often proclaimed: that truth is neither our quarry nor within our grasp; that it does not reside on earth but is at home in heaven, in God's bosom; and that we can know it only to the extent it pleases him to reveal it. Let us then learn our true nature from the uncreated and incarnate truth.

You cannot be a skeptic without stifling nature; you cannot be a dogmatist without repudiating reason.> Nature confounds the skeptics, and reason confounds the dogmatists. What then will you become, you who seek to discover your true condition by your natural reason? You cannot avoid one of these sects[62] nor survive in any of them.

Know then, proud man, what a paradox you are to yourself. Humble yourself, powerless reason; be silent, dumb nature; learn that man infinitely transcends man, and hear from your Master your true condition, of which you are ignorant.

Listen to God.

<Is it not as clear as day that man's condition is dual? Certainly.> For in the end, if man had never been corrupted, in his innocence he would enjoy both truth and happiness with confidence. And if man had never been other than corrupt, he would have no idea of truth or bliss. But, wretched as we are—and more so than if there had been no great-

---

[62] Pascal had written "one of these <three> sects," following Montaigne, *Essays* II, chap. 12: "Whoever seeks anything comes to this point: either he says that he has found it, or that he cannot find it, or that he is still looking for it. All of philosophy is divided into these three kinds." (Ariew and Grene trans., pp.63–64.)

ness in our condition—we have an idea of happiness and cannot reach it. We perceive an image of truth and possess only a lie. Being incapable of absolute ignorance and certain knowledge, it is obvious that we once had a degree of perfection from which we have unhappily fallen.

It is, however, astonishing that the mystery most distant from our knowledge, that of the transmission of sin, should be a thing without which we can have no knowledge of ourselves.

For without doubt there is nothing more shocking to our reason than to say that the sin of the first man has made culpable those who, being so remote from this source, seem incapable of participating in it. This transmission not only seems impossible to us, it even appears very unjust. For what is more contrary to the rules of our wretched justice than the eternal damnation of a child, incapable of will, for a sin in which he seems to have so little part that was committed six thousand years before him? Certainly nothing shocks us more harshly than this doctrine. And yet without this most incomprehensible of all mysteries, we are incomprehensible to ourselves. The knot of our condition takes its twists and turns in this abyss, so that man is more unintelligible without this mystery than this mystery is unintelligible to man.

<Thus it seems that God, wanting to reserve for himself alone the right to teach us about ourselves and to render the difficulty of our existence unintelligible to ourselves, has concealed the knot so high—or rather we should say so low—that we were quite incapable of reaching it. As a result, it is not through the proud exertions of our reason, but through its simple submission, that we can truly know ourselves.

These foundations, solidly established on the inviolable authority of religion, let us know that there are two equally constant truths of faith. One is that man in the state of creation or in the state of grace is raised above all nature, made in some way similar to God and sharing in divinity. The other is that in the state of corruption and sin, he is fallen from the first state and made similar to the beasts. These two propositions are equally firm and certain.

Scripture plainly declares this to us, when it says in some places: *My delights are to be with the sons of men*.[63] *I will pour out my spirit upon all flesh*.[64] *You are gods*. Etc.;[65] and in other places, *All flesh is grass*.[66] *Man*

---

[63] *Deliciae meae esse cum filiis hominum*. Proverbs 8:31.

[64] *Effundam spiritum meum super omnem carnem*. Joel 2:28.

[65] *Dii estis*. Psalms 82:6.

[66] *Omnis caro faenum*. Isaiah 40:6.

has been compared with the beasts that perish and has become similar to them.[67] *I said in my heart about the sons of men.* —*Eccl.* 3.[68]

Thus it seems clear that through grace man is rendered similar to God, participating in his divinity, and that without grace he is considered similar to the brute beasts.>

[9] Diversion[69]

"If man were happy, the less diverted the happier he   S165/L132
would be, like the Saints and God." — "Yes, but is not happiness the ability to be amused by diversion?" — "No, because that comes from elsewhere and from outside, and thus it is dependent, and subject to be disturbed by a thousand accidents, which cause inevitable distress."

Despite these miseries, he wants to be happy, wants only   S166/L134
to be happy, and cannot want not to be so. But how will he go about it? The best way would be to render himself immortal, but since he cannot do this, he has decided to prevent himself from thinking about it.

As men have not been able to cure death, wretchedness,   S166/L133
ignorance, they have decided, in order to be happy, not to think about these things.[70]

I feel that I might not have existed, for my self consists in   S167/L135
my thoughts. Thus I, who think, would not have existed, if my mother had been killed before I had been given life. Therefore, I am not a necessary being. I am also neither eternal nor infinite. But I quite see that there is in nature a necessary, eternal, and infinite being.

Diversion   S168/L136

When I have thought about the various activities of men, the dangers and pains they face at court or in war, which give rise to so many quarrels, passions, bold and often bad ventures, etc., I have often said that man's unhappiness arises from one thing alone: that he cannot remain quietly in his room. A man who has enough to live on would not go to sea or lay a siege, if he knew how to enjoy staying at home. Men would never buy commissions in the army at such expense, unless they

---

[67] *Homo assimilatus est jumentis insipientibus, et similis factus est illis.* Psalms 49:12, 13.

[68] *Dixi in corde meo de filiis hominum.* Ecclesiastes 3:18.

[69] "Diversion" suggests entertainment, but to divert literally means: "to turn away" or "to mislead."

[70] See Montaigne, *Essays* I, chap. 20: "The goal of our career is death. [. . .] The remedy of the common herd is not to think about it." (Frame trans., pp. 57–58.)

found it unbearable not to leave town. They would not seek conversation and the entertainment of games, except that they do not enjoy staying at home. Etc.

But, upon further consideration, after finding the cause of all our unhappiness, I wanted to discover the reason for it and discovered a truly cogent one in the natural unhappiness of our weak and mortal condition, so wretched that nothing can console us when we think about it closely.

Whatever situation we assume for ourselves, with all the goods that can belong to us, royalty is the finest position in the world. However, let us imagine a king with all the advantages pertaining to his rank. If he is without diversion, left to ponder and reflect on what he is, this languishing felicity will not sustain him. He will necessarily come to think about the threats facing him, revolts that may occur, and, in the end, inevitable death and disease. As a result, if he is without what is called diversion, he is unhappy, even unhappier than the least of his subjects playing and diverting himself.

That is why play and the conversation of women, war, and high offices are so sought after. Not that in fact they bring happiness, or that we imagine true bliss to consist in money won at games or in the hares that are hunted; we would not accept these if they were given to us. We do not seek that easy and peaceful life that allows us to think about our unhappy condition, nor the dangers of war, nor the burdens of office, but the bustle that turns our thoughts away and diverts us. — Reason why we prefer the hunt to the kill.[71]

That is why men so love noise and activity. That is why jail is such a horrible punishment. That is why the pleasure of solitude is incomprehensible. In fact, the greatest source of happiness in being a king is that people constantly try to divert him and to procure for him every kind of pleasure. The king is surrounded by people who think only of diverting the king and of preventing him from thinking about himself. For, though he is king, he is unhappy if he thinks about himself.

This is all men have been able to devise to make themselves happy. Those who philosophize about it, and who think people are quite unreasonable to spend a whole day chasing a hare they would not have bought, scarcely know our nature. The hare does not save us from the sight of death and the miseries distracting us, but the hunt does.

A. And thus, when we reproach them for seeking so eagerly something that cannot satisfy them, their proper reply, if they thought it

---

[71] Marginal note. See also Montaigne, *Essays* II, chap. 12: "We should not find it strange if hunters despairing of their prey have not stopped enjoying the chase." (Ariew and Grene trans., p. 72.)

through, should be that they sought only a violent and vigorous occupation that turned them away from thinking about themselves, and therefore chose an alluring object to charm and strongly attract them. This would leave their opponents without a reply. But they do not reply in this way because they do not know themselves. They do not know that it is the hunt and not the kill that they seek. They imagine that, if they reached their goal, they would then enjoy resting and would not feel the insatiable nature of cupidity. They sincerely believe they seek rest and in fact seek only activity. They have a secret instinct to seek external diversion and occupation, coming from their feeling of constant wretchedness. And they have another secret instinct, a remnant of the greatness of our original nature, telling them that happiness resides only in rest and not in tumultuous activity. From these two contrary instincts they form a confused plan, hidden in the depths of their soul, leading them to seek rest through activity. They always think that the satisfaction they are missing will come to them once they overcome the difficulties they are facing and can open the door to rest.

All our life passes in this way. We seek rest in a struggle against some obstacles. And when we have overcome these, rest proves unbearable because of the boredom it produces. We have to escape from it and beg for excitement. For we think either of our miseries or of those threatening us. And even if we should feel safe enough from all sides, boredom of its own accord would not fail to rise from the depths of our heart, where it is naturally rooted, and to fill our mind with poison.

The advice given to Pyrrhus, to take the rest he was seeking with so much effort, was not without difficulty.[72]

Dancing: you have to think about where to put your feet.

A gentleman sincerely believes that hunting is a great sport and a regal sport, but his huntsman is not of this opinion.

———

B. Thus man is so unhappy that he would be bored even if he had no cause for boredom out of his own temperament (*complexion*). And he is so empty that, though he has a thousand reasons for boredom, the least thing, such as pushing a billiard ball with a cue, is enough to amuse him.

———

---

[72] See Montaigne, *Essays* I, chap. 42 (Frame trans., p. 196; Screech trans., p. 298). Pyrrhus was asked why he wanted to conquer Italy, then Gaul, then Spain. His ultimate answer was that he would rest after conquering the world. To this, Cyneas, his counselor, replied that he could rest now and spare himself such effort.

C. But, you will say, what is his object in all this? To brag to his friends the next day that he played better than somebody else. In the same way, others sweat in their rooms to show the learned they have solved a problem in algebra that had not as yet been solved. Many more expose themselves to extreme danger (just as foolishly, in my opinion) to brag afterward that they have captured a town. Others kill themselves observing all these things, not to become wiser, but just to show that they know them; and these are the most foolish of the bunch, because they are foolish knowingly, while one can think the others would no longer be so if they had the knowledge.

———

A man lives his life free from boredom, playing every day for a small amount. Give him every morning the money he can win that day, on the condition that he does not play: you make him unhappy. You may say perhaps that he seeks the entertainment of play and not the winnings. Make him, then, play for nothing. He will not get excited about it and will be bored. It is not, therefore, only the amusement he seeks. A weak and passionless amusement will bore him. He must get excited about it and trick himself into imagining that he would be happy to win what he would not accept on the condition of not playing. He must fashion for himself an object of passion to excite his desire, his anger, his fear for the fashioned object, like children who become frightened by the face they have darkened.[73]

———

How does it happen that this man who lost his only son a few months ago and who, bothered by lawsuits and quarrels, was so troubled this morning, now no longer thinks of them? Do not be surprised. He is quite busy looking for the path taken by the boar his dogs have been pursuing so avidly for the last six hours. He needs nothing more. However full of sadness a man may be, if you can prevail upon him to take up some diversion, he is happy for that time. And however happy he may be, he will soon be sad and wretched if he is not diverted and occupied by some passion or amusement that prevents boredom from overcoming him. Without diversion there is no joy. With diversion there is no sadness. This also constitutes the happiness of persons of

———

[73] The image comes from Montaigne, *Essays* II, chap. 12: "It is too bad that we trick ourselves with our own monkey business and inventions [. . .] as children are frightened by the very face of their playmates whom they have daubed and darkened." (Ariew and Grene trans., p. 91.)

high rank, in that they have a number of people to divert them and the power to maintain themselves in this state.

D. Consider this: what is it to be superintendent, chancellor, prime minister, but to have a position in which a great number of people come each morning from every quarter, so as not to leave any of them an hour a day when they can think about themselves? And when they are in disgrace and sent back to their country houses, where they lack neither wealth nor servants to cater to their needs, they do not fail to be wretched and desolate, because no one prevents them from thinking about themselves.

Diversion   S169/L137

Is not royal dignity sufficiently great in itself to make its possessor happy by the mere sight of what he is? Must he be diverted from this thought like ordinary people? I quite see that it makes a man happy to be diverted from thinking about his domestic woes by filling his thoughts with the concern to dance well. But will it be the same with a king, and will he be happier in the pursuit of these idle amusements than in considering his greatness? And what more satisfactory object could be presented to his mind? Would it not spoil his delight to occupy his soul with the thought of how to adjust his steps to the rhythm of a tune, or how to place a bar skillfully, instead of leaving him to enjoy quietly the contemplation of the majestic glory surrounding him? Let us test this. Let us leave a king all alone to reflect on himself at his leisure, without anything to satisfy his senses, without any care in his mind, without company, and we will see that a king without diversion is a man full of miseries. So this is carefully avoided; there never fail to be a great number of people near the retinues of kings, people who see to it that diversion follows the kings' affairs of state, watching over their leisure to supply them with pleasures and games, so that they have no empty moments. In other words, they are surrounded by people who take wonderful care to insure that the king is not alone and able to think about himself, knowing well that he will be miserable, though he is king, if he does think about it.

In all this I am not talking of Christian kings as Christians, but only as kings.

Diversion   S170/L138

Death is easier to bear without thinking about it than the thought of death without danger.

Diversion   S171/L139

From childhood men are entrusted with the care of their honor, their property, their friends, and even with the property and honor of their friends. They are burdened with duties, the study of languages, and exercises. And they are made to understand that they cannot be happy unless their health, their honor, their fortune, and those of their friends are in good shape, and that they will become unhappy if anything is lacking. So, they are given cares and duties that torment them from the break of day. This, you will say, is a strange way to make them happy. Could we do anything more to make them miserable? Indeed, what could we do? Were we to relieve them of all these cares, they would then see themselves and think about what they are, where they came from, where they are going. So, it is not possible to occupy and divert them too much. This is why, after we have set up so many duties for them, if they have any time for relaxation, we advise them to use it on diversion and play and always to keep fully occupied.

How hollow and full of garbage is the heart of man.

[10] Philosophers

Even if Epictetus saw the path perfectly, he only said to   S172/L140
men, "You follow the wrong one." He shows that there is another, but he does not lead to it. It is the path of wanting what God wants. Jesus Christ alone leads to it: *I am the way, the truth.*[74]

The vices of Zeno himself.[75]   S173/L140

Philosophers   S174/L141

A fine thing to cry to a man who does not know himself,
that he should come to God of himself! And a fine thing to say this to a man who does know himself!

Philosophers   S175/L142

They believe that God alone is worthy of love and admiration, and have wished to be loved and admired by men. And they do not know their own corruption. If they feel themselves full of love and admiration for him and this is their greatest joy, very well, let them think well of themselves. But if they are ill disposed, if they have no other inclination than to establish themselves in men's esteem, and if their whole perfection lies only in persuading men without compulsion to find their happiness in loving them, I would say that such perfection is horrible. Why, they have known God, and their sole desire has not been that men should love him, but that men should stop at them! They have wanted to be the object of men's intended happiness.

---

[74] *Via, veritas.* John 14:6.

[75] Zeno of Cittium, founder of Stoicism; the vices may be an allusion to his homosexuality, referred to by Montaigne, *Essays* III, chap. 10 (Frame trans., p. 777) and elsewhere.

Philosophers   S176/L143

We are full of things that move us outward.

Our instinct makes us feel that our happiness must be sought outside ourselves. Our passions push us outward, even when no objects excite them. External objects tempt us of themselves and call to us, even when we are not thinking about them. And so philosophers say in vain: "Withdraw into yourselves; there you will find your good." We do not believe them. And those who do believe them are the emptiest and the most foolish.

What the Stoics propose is so difficult and so worthless.   S177/L144

The Stoics claim that all those who are not at the high degree of wisdom are equally foolish and vicious, as those who are two inches under water.[76]

The three kinds of concupiscence have created three   S178/L145 sects, and philosophers have done no more than to follow one of these three kinds of concupiscence.[77]

Stoics   S179/L146

They conclude that we can always do what we can sometimes do, and that, since the desire for glory makes those whom it possesses do a particular thing well, others can also do it well.

These are feverish impulses that health cannot imitate.

Epictetus concludes that, since there are consistent Christians, every man can easily be so.[78]

[11] The Supreme Good

Dispute about the supreme good.   S180/L147
*So that you are content with yourself
and the goods born from you.*[79]

There is a contradiction, because in the end they advise suicide. Oh! What a happy life, of which we rid ourselves like the plague!

Part two   S181/L148
That man without faith can know
neither the true good nor justice.

---

[76] In *Essays* II, chap. 2, Montaigne rejects the Stoic doctrine that all vices are the same in that they are vices.

[77] See fragment S761 for the three kinds of concupiscence.

[78] Epictetus, *Discourses* 4.7.

[79] *Ut sis contentus temetipso et ex te nascentibus bonis.* Seneca, *Epistles*, xx. 8.

All men seek to be happy. This is without exception, whatever different means they use. They all strive toward this end. What makes some go to war, and others avoid it, is the same desire in both, accompanied by different perspectives. The will never takes the slightest step except toward this object. This is the motive of every action of every man, even of those who go hang themselves.

And yet, after such a great number of years, no one without faith has ever reached the point at which everyone constantly aims. All complain: princes, subjects, nobles, commoners, old, young, strong, weak, learned, ignorant, healthy, sick, from all countries, all times, all ages, and all conditions.

A test so long, so continuous, and so uniform, should certainly convince us of our inability to reach the good through our own efforts. But examples teach us little. No likeness is ever so perfect that there is not some slight difference; as a result, we expect that our hopes will not be disappointed on this occasion as they were on the other. And so, since the present never satisfies us, experience tricks us and leads us from misfortune to misfortune until death, which is its eternal climax.

What then does this craving and inability cry to us, if not that there once was a true happiness in man, of which there now remains only the mark and empty trace? He tries vainly to fill it with everything around him, seeking from things absent the help he does not receive from things present. But they are all inadequate, because only an infinite and immutable object—that is, God himself—can fill this infinite abyss.

He alone is man's true good. And since man has forsaken him, it is strange that nothing in nature has been capable of taking his place: stars, heavens, earth, elements, plants, cabbages, leeks, animals, insects, calves, serpents, fever, pestilence, war, famine, vices, adultery, incest. And since man has lost the true good, everything can seem equally good to him, even his own destruction, though it is so contrary to God, reason, and nature, all at once.

Some seek the good in authority, others in curiosities and in the sciences, others in pleasure.

Others, who are in fact closer to it, have considered it necessary that this universal good all men desire should not lie in any of the particular things able to be possessed only by one person. When shared, these cause their possessors more distress over the part they lack than pleasure over the part they enjoy. They have realized that the true good must be such that everyone can possess it at once, without diminution and without envy, and that no one can lose it against his will. And their reason is that this desire, since it is natural to man, because it is necessarily in everything and he cannot be without it, they therefore conclude . . .

[12] A. P. R.

A. P. R. Beginning   S182/L149
After having explained the incomprehensibility

Man's greatness and wretchedness are so evident that the true religion must necessarily teach us both that there is a great principle of greatness and a great principle of wretchedness in man.

It must then account for these astonishing oppositions.

To make man happy, it must show him that God exists; that we are required to love him; that our true bliss is to be in him and our sole ill to be separated from him. It must recognize that we are full of darkness preventing us from knowing and loving him, and that thus, as our duty requires us to love God and as our concupiscence turns us away from him, we are full of inequities. It must account for this opposition we have to God and to our own good. It must teach us the remedies for these infirmities and the means to obtain the remedies. Let us examine all the religions of the world on these points and see whether there is any other than Christianity that satisfies them.

Shall it be the philosophers, who propose the good within us as our good? Is this the true good? Have they found the remedy for our ills? Does placing man as the equal with God cure his presumption? Have those who made us equal to the beasts, or the Mohammedans who offered us earthly pleasures as our good, even in eternity,[80] have they produced a remedy for our concupiscence?

What religion, then, will teach us to cure pride and concupiscence? What religion, at last, will teach us our good, our duties, the weakness turning us away from them, the cause of this weakness, the remedies to cure it, and the means of obtaining these remedies? All the other religions have been unable to do so. Let us see what God's wisdom will do.

"O men," it says, "expect neither truth nor consolation from humans. It is I who made you and who alone can teach you what you are.

But you are no longer in the state in which I made you. I created man holy, innocent, perfect. I filled him with light and understanding. I showed him my glory and my wonders. Man's eye then beheld God's majesty. He was not then in the darkness that blinds him, nor subject to mortality and the miseries that afflict him. But he could not sustain so much glory without falling into presumption. He wanted to fashion himself his own center, independent of my help. He withdrew from my

---

[80] Montaigne, *Essays* II, chap. 12: "Mohammed promises his people a carpeted paradise, paved with gold and jewels, peopled with girls of great beauty, with wines and rare food." (Ariew and Grene trans., p. 79.)

dominion, making himself my equal in his desire to find his felicity within himself, and I abandoned him to himself. Setting into revolt the creatures that were subject to him, I made them his enemies, so that man now has become like the beasts and so estranged from me that there barely remains in him a confused vision of his author. So much has all his knowledge been extinguished or troubled! The senses, independent of reason and often its master, have led him in pursuit of pleasure. All creatures either torment or tempt him, and dominate him either by subduing him with their strength or by charming him with their sweetness, a more terrible and more harmful tyranny.

That is the state men are in today. They retain a weak instinct for the happiness of their first nature, and are plunged into the misery of their blindness and concupiscence, which has become their second nature.

From this principle I am disclosing to you, you can recognize the cause of so many oppositions that have astonished all men and divided them into such different beliefs. Observe now all the impulses of greatness and of glory that the experience of so many miseries cannot stifle, and see whether their cause must not be in another nature."

A. P. R. For tomorrow.

Prosopopaea[81]

"It is in vain, O men, that you seek within yourselves the remedy for your miseries. All your enlightenment can only bring you to realize that you will find neither truth nor good within yourselves.

The philosophers promised you that and could not deliver it.

They know neither what your true good is nor what your true state is. <I alone can teach you what your true good is and [what your true state is]. I teach these things to those who listen to me, and the Books I put in the hands of men reveal them very clearly. But I did not want this knowledge to be so open. I teach men about what can make them happy: why do you refuse to listen to me?

Do not look for satisfaction on earth; do not hope for anything from humans. Your good is only in God, and supreme felicity lies in knowing God, in being united to him forever in eternity. Your duty is to love him with all your heart. He created you.> How could they have provided remedies for your ills, which they did not even know? Your main maladies are the pride that takes you away from God and the concupiscence that binds you to the earth; and they have done nothing but entertain at least one of these maladies. If they gave you God as an end, it was only to cater to your pride; they made you think you are like him

---

[81] A rhetorical term, designating the personification or impersonation of an absent or imaginary speaker—here the personification of God's wisdom.

and of a similar nature. And those who saw the vanity of this claim threw you over another precipice, by giving you to understand that your nature was like that of the beasts, leading you to seek your good in the concupiscence shared by the animals.

This is not the way to cure you of your inequities, which these wise men never knew. I alone can make you understand what you are." Etc.

<"I do not ask you for blind faith.">

Adam, Jesus Christ.

――――

If you are united to God, it is through grace, not nature.

――――

If you are humbled, it is through penitence, not nature.

――――

Thus this dual capacity:

――――

You are not in the state of your creation.

――――

These two states being available, it is impossible for you not to recognize them.

Follow your impulses, observe yourself, and see if you do not find the living characteristics of these two natures.

――――

Could so many contradictions be found in a simple subject?

――――

Incomprehensible

Not all that is incomprehensible fails to exist. Infinite number, an infinite space equal to the finite.

――――

Incredible that God should unite himself to us.

This consideration derives solely from the perspective of our vileness. But if you are quite sincere about it, follow it as far as I do and recognize that we are indeed so vile that we are incapable of knowing by ourselves whether his mercy cannot make us worthy of him. For I would like to know by what right this animal, who recognizes himself to be so weak, measures God's mercy and puts in limits suggested by his own fancy. He has so little knowledge of what God is that he does not know what he himself is. Disturbed by the perspective of his own state, he dares to say that God cannot make him capable of communicating with him. But I would ask him if God demands anything else from him than his knowledge and love, and why he believes that God cannot make himself known and loved by him, given that he is naturally capable of love and knowledge. No doubt he knows at least that he exists and loves something. Therefore, if he sees something in the darkness around him, and if he finds some object of love among the things on earth, why, if God imparts to him some inklings of his essence, will he not be capable of knowing and loving God in whatever manner it pleases him to communicate himself to us? There is then without doubt an intolerable presumption in such arguments, although they appear founded on an apparent humility, which is neither sincere nor reasonable if it does not make us admit that, not knowing of ourselves what we are, we can only learn it from God.

———

"I do not intend you to submit your belief to me without reason, and I do not claim to subdue you by tyranny. I also do not claim to give you a reason for everything. To reconcile these oppositions, I intend to make you see clearly by convincing proofs, by marks of the divine in me that will convince you of what I am; and to establish my authority by marvels and proofs you cannot reject. You will then believe the things I teach, finding no ground for rejecting them, other than that you cannot by yourself tell whether they are true or not.

God wanted to redeem men and open salvation to those who seek it. But men make themselves so unworthy that it is right for God to refuse to some, because of their implacability, what he grants to others by a mercy not due to them.

If he had wanted to overcome the obstinacy of the most hardened, he could have done so by revealing himself so manifestly that they could not doubt the truth of his essence, as he will appear on the final day, with such bursts of lightning and such convulsions of nature that the resurrected dead and the most blind will see him.

This is not how he has wanted to appear in the sweetness of his coming, because, as so many men make themselves unworthy of his mercy, he has wanted to leave them in the privation of the good they do not want. It was not, then, right that he should appear in a manner manifestly divine and completely capable of convincing all men. But it was also not right that he should come in a manner so hidden that those who sincerely seek him could not know him. He has wanted to make himself perfectly knowable by them. Thus wanting to appear openly to those who seek him with all their heart and hidden from those who flee him with all their heart, God has tempered

[A. P. R. for tomorrow.   2

tempered the knowledge of himself by giving signs of himself that are visible to those who seek him, and not by those who do not seek him.

There is enough light for those who desire only to see and enough darkness for those of a contrary disposition.][82]

[13] Beginning

Unbelievers who profess to follow reason must be   S183/L150
uncommonly strong in reason.

What do they say then?

"Do we not see," they say, "beasts living and dying like men, and Turks like Christians? They have their ceremonies, their prophets, their doctors, their saints, their priests, like us," etc.

Is this contrary to Scripture? Does it not say all of this?

If you barely care to know the truth, this is enough to leave you at peace. But if you desire to know it with all your heart, it is not sufficiently considered in detail. It would be enough for a philosophical question, but here, where everything is at stake . . .

And yet, after a light reflection of this kind, we amuse ourselves, etc. Let us inquire into this religion: even if it does not account for this obscurity, perhaps it will teach us about it.

We are foolish to rely on the company of our peers,   S184/L151
wretched like us, powerless like us. They will not help us. We will die alone.

We must therefore act as if we were alone. And then would we build fine houses, etc.? We would seek the truth without hesitation. And, if we refuse to do so, we show that we esteem men's esteem more than the search for truth.

Between us and hell or heaven, there is only life in the in-   S185/L152
terval, the most fragile thing in the world.

What do you promise in the end, in addition to certain   S186/L153
pain, but ten years of self-love (for ten years is the portion), trying hard to please without succeeding?

---

[82] Pascal must have decided to put the conclusion of this fragment in the bundle called "Foundations" (see fragment S274). The copyist included it here as well to complete the passage, but left the marginal note indicating that "The conclusion is to be found in the chapter 'Foundations of Religion.'"

Options   S187/L154

We must live differently in the world, depending on these
different assumptions:

Whether we could always exist in it.

Whether it is certain we will not exist in it for long and uncertain if
we will exist in it for one hour.

This last assumption is ours.

Heart.   S187/L155

Instinct.

Principles.

Pity the atheists who are seeking.[83] For are they not   S188/L156
unhappy enough? Speak against those who boast about it.

Atheism shows strength of mind,[84]   S189/L157
but only up to a certain degree.

As for choosing sides, you must take the trouble to seek   S190/L158
the truth, because if you die without worshiping the true
principle, you are lost. "But," you say, "if he had wanted me to worship
him, he would have left me some signs of his will." He has done so, but
you neglect them. Seek them, then; it is well worth it.

If we ought to give up eight days of life, we ought to give   S191/L159
up a hundred years.

There are only three kinds of people: those who serve   S192/L160
God, having found him; those who are busy seeking him, not
having found him; those who live without seeking or finding him. The
first are reasonable and happy, the last are foolish and unhappy; those in
the middle are unhappy and reasonable.

Atheists must say things that are perfectly clear. Now, it is   S193/L161
not perfectly clear that the soul is material.

Begin by pitying unbelievers; they are unhappy enough in   S194/L162
their condition.

We should revile them only if it is helpful. But this does them harm.

A man is in prison, not knowing whether his sentence has   S195/L163
been passed, with only an hour to find out, this hour being
sufficient to obtain its repeal if he knew that it had been passed. It

---

[83] Atheists who are seeking might seem strange, except that atheism had a broader meaning.
One could call a believer in the wrong kind of God, such as a Jew or Protestant, an atheist.

[84] Another word for atheist or unbeliever would be *esprit fort*; thus, strength of mind, or
force d'esprit, is a play on words.

would be unnatural if he spent the hour not finding out whether his sentence had been passed, but playing piquet.

So it is beyond nature that man, etc. This is to weigh down the hand of God.

Thus, not only does the zeal of those who seek him prove God, but also the blindness of those who do not seek him.

Beginning   S196/L164

Prison.

———

I find it good that we do not further examine Copernicus' opinion, but this:

———

It matters to all of life to know whether the soul is mortal or immortal.

The final act is bloody, however fine the rest of the play.   S197/L165 In the end they throw some earth over our head, and that is it forever.

We run carelessly into the precipice after we have put   S198/L166 something in front of us to prevent us from seeing it.

[14] Submission and Use of Reason in which True Christianity Consists   L167

How I hate these stupidities: of not believing in the   S199/L168 Eucharist, etc.

If the Gospel is true, if Jesus Christ is God, where is the difficulty?

I would not be a Christian without the miracles, said   S200/L169 Saint Augustine.[85]

Submission   S201/L170

We must <have these three qualities: skeptic, geometer, Christian. Submission. Doubt. And they fit together> know when to doubt, when to affirm, when to submit. Whoever does not do so fails to understand the force of reason. There are some who fall short of these three principles, either by affirming everything as demonstrable, lacking knowledge about demonstration; or by doubting everything, lacking knowledge about when to submit; or by submitting to everything, lacking knowledge about when to judge.

---

[85] In *The City of God* (xxii. 7), Augustine writes that the human mind cannot accept such mysteries of Christianity as the Resurrection without the power of miracles confirming them.

They received the word with much readiness and searched   S202/L171
the Scriptures daily for whether those things were so.[86]

The way of God, who disposes all things kindly, is to   S203/L172
implant religion into minds through reason and into hearts
through grace. But wanting to implant it into minds and hearts with
force and threats is not implanting religion, but terror, *terror rather than
religion.*[87]

If we submit everything to reason, our religion will have   S204/L173
nothing mysterious and supernatural.

If we offend the principles of reason, our religion will be absurd and
ridiculous.

Saint Augustine. Reason would never submit, if it did not   S205/L174
judge that there are occasions when it should submit.[88]

It is therefore right for it to submit when it judges that it should submit.

It will be one of the curses of the damned to see that they   S206/L175
will be condemned by their own reason, by which they
claimed to condemn the Christian religion.

Those who do not love the truth take as pretext the   S207/L176
arguments and the multitude of those who deny it, and so
their error arises only from their dislike of truth or charity. Thus they
have no excuse.

Contradiction is a poor sign of truth.   S208/L177
Many certain things are contradicted.
Many false things pass without contradiction.
Contradiction is not a sign of falsity, nor is the absence of contradic-
tion a sign of truth.

See the two kinds of men under the title "Perpetuity."[89]   S209/L178

There are few true Christians. I say this even as regards   S210/L179
faith. There are many who believe, but out of superstition.
There are many who do not believe, but out of irreligion. Few are in
between.

———

[86] *Susceperunt verbum cum omni aviditate, scrutantes Scripturas, si ita se haberent,* Acts
17. 11.

[87] *terrorem potius quam religionem.*

[88] Augustine, *Letters,* Letter 120 and elsewhere.

[89] See fragment S318, in chap. 22, Perpetuity.

I do not include in this those whose conduct is truly pious, nor all those who believe from a feeling of the heart.

Jesus Christ performed miracles, then the apostles, and   S211/L180
the early saints in great number, because it was miracles that
alone bore witness, and the prophecies had not yet been fulfilled, but were being fulfilled. It was foretold that the Messiah would convert the nations. How could this prophecy be fulfilled without the conversion of the nations? And how could the nations be converted to the Messiah, if they did not see this final effect of the prophecies that prove him? Therefore, until he had died, risen again, and converted the nations, everything was not fulfilled, and so miracles were needed throughout that time. Now they are no longer needed against the Jews and unbelievers, since the fulfilled prophecies constitute a lasting miracle.

Piety is different from superstition.   S212/L181

———

To carry piety to the point of superstition is to destroy it.

———

The heretics reproach us for this superstitious submission. This is doing what they reproach us for.

———

Impiety of not believing in the Eucharist because it is not seen.

———

Superstition of believing some propositions, etc.

———

Faith, etc.
There is nothing so consistent with reason as this denial of   S213/L182
reason.

Two excesses   S214/L183

Excluding reason, admitting only reason.

We would not have sinned in not believing in Jesus   S215/L184
Christ, lacking miracles.

"See whether I am lying."[90]   S216/L184

Faith truly says what the senses do not say, but not the   S217/L185
contrary of what they see. It is above, not against them.

---

[90] *Videte an mentiar.* Job 6:28

You abuse the belief people have in the church and cause   S218/L186
them to be deceived.

Having to reproach the world for being too docile is not   S219/L187
an unusual thing. It is a natural vice, like incredulity, and
just as pernicious. Superstition.

Reason's final step is to recognize that there is an infinity   S220/L188
of things beyond it. It is merely feeble if it does not go as far
as realizing this.

———

But if natural things are beyond it, what will we say of supernatural
ones?

[15] Excellence of this Way of Proving God

God through Jesus Christ.   S221/L189
We know God only through Jesus Christ. Without this
mediator, all communication with God is cut off; through Jesus Christ
we know God. All those who have claimed to know God and to prove
him without Jesus Christ have had only ineffective proofs. But to prove
Jesus Christ we have the prophecies, which are solid and palpable
proofs. And these prophecies, being fulfilled and proven true by the
event, indicate the certainty of these truths and entail the proof of
Christ's divinity. In him and through him, we therefore know God.
Apart from him and without Scripture, without original sin, without a
necessary mediator who was promised and came, we cannot absolutely
prove God, nor teach right doctrine and right morality. But through
Jesus Christ and in Jesus Christ, we prove God and teach morality and
doctrine. Jesus Christ is therefore the true God of men.

But we know our wretchedness at the same time, for this God is none
other than the redeemer of our wretchedness. Thus we can only know
God well by knowing our iniquities. Those who have known God without knowing their wretchedness have not glorified him, but themselves.
*Seeing that the world did not know him through wisdom, it pleased God
to save, through the foolishness of preaching, those who believe.*[91]

Preface. The metaphysical proofs of God are so remote   S222/L190
from men's reasoning and so complicated that they make
little impression. And when they are of service to some, it is only for the

———

[91] *Quia* [. . .] *non cognovit per sapientiam* [. . .] *placuit Deo per stultitiam praedicationis
salvos facere.* I Corinthians 1:21

instant during which they see this demonstration. But an hour later they fear they have been mistaken.

———

What they have found through their curiosity, they have lost through their pride.[92]

It[93] is the result of knowing God without Jesus Christ,   S223/L190
which is communicating without a mediator with the God
known without a mediator.

Instead, those who have known God through a mediator know their own wretchedness.

It is not only impossible, but also useless to know God   S224/L191
without Jesus Christ. They have not gotten farther from him,
but closer. They have not humbled themselves, but *the better one is, the worse one becomes, if one ascribes this goodness to oneself.*[94]

Knowledge of God without knowledge of our wretched-   S225/L192
ness makes for pride.

Knowledge of our wretchedness without knowledge of God makes for despair. Knowledge of Jesus Christ is central, because in him we find both God and our wretchedness.

[16] Transition from the Knowledge of Man to That of God

Prejudice leading to error.   S226/L193

It is deplorable to see everybody deliberating only about
the means, never the end. Everyone thinks of how he will do with his position in life, but as for the choice of position, as of country, the luck of the draw gives it to us.

It is a pity to see so many Turks, heretics, and unbelievers following their fathers' footsteps simply because they have been prejudiced to think it is the best way. And this determines each person to his position, of locksmith, soldier, etc.

———

[92] *Quod curiositate cognoverunt superbia amiserunt.* Saint Augustine, *Sermon* 141, lines 1–2.

[93] Referring to the subject of the previous sentence in fragment S222: namely *superbia*, or pride.

[94] *Quo quisque optimus est, pessimus, si hoc ipsum, quod optimus est, adscribat sibi.* Saint Bernard, *Sermones in Cantica Canticorum*, lxxxiv.

In this way savages care nothing for Provence.[95]

Why have limits been placed on my knowledge, my   S227/L194
height, my life, which is set at a hundred years rather than a
thousand? What reason did nature have for doing so and choosing this
midpoint, rather than another, from all of infinity, when there is no
more reason to choose one thing over another, since nothing is more
tempting than anything else?

<Since we cannot be universal by knowing everything   S228/L195
that can be known about everything, we should know a little
about everything. For it is truly finer to know something about everything than everything about something. This universality is finest. If we
can have both, better still. But if we must choose, we should choose the
former. The world senses this and does so, for the world is often a good
judge.

———

My fancy makes me hate someone who makes croaking   S228/L196
noises and breathes hard while eating.

———

Fancy has great weight. Is there any profit in yielding to this weight
because it is natural? No, rather in resisting it.

———

Nothing shows men's vanity better than considering the   S228/L197
cause and effects of love, for the whole universe is changed by
it. Cleopatra's nose.>

H. 5.[96]   S229/L198

When I see man's blindness and wretchedness, when I
consider the whole silent universe and man left to himself without light,
as though lost in this corner of the universe, not knowing who put him
there, what he has come to do, what will become of him at death, incapable of any understanding, I become frightened, like someone
brought in his sleep to a frightening desert island who wakes up with no
knowledge[97] or means of escape. And then I marvel that we do not fall

---

[95] This is an allusion to Montaigne, *Essays* I, chap. 23: "It is by the mediation of custom
that everyone is content with the place in which nature has planted him: the savages of
Scotland care nothing for Touraine" (Frame trans., p. 84, note; Screech trans., p. 130,
note).

[96] The notation is possibly what remains of a connected series of fragments on man (H:
l'Homme): S229, H. 5; S230, H. 9; S231: H. 3; and perhaps S111, [H.] 13.

[97] Pascal had written "with no knowledge <of where he is>," then crossed the words out.

into despair in so wretched a state. I see other people around me of a similar nature. I ask them whether they are better informed than I am. They tell me they are not. Then these wretched lost souls look around and see some pleasant objects to which they give themselves and become attached. As for me, I have not been able to become attached, and, considering how much more likely it is that there is something other than what I see, I have sought out whether this God has not left some sign of himself.

I see many contrary religions, and so all of them false but one. Each of them wants to be believed on its own authority and threatens unbelievers. I do not therefore believe them on that account. Anyone can say this. Anyone can call himself a prophet. But I see Christianity, where I find prophecies, and this is not something anyone can do.

H. Man's disproportion S230/L199

9. <Here is where natural knowledge leads us: if it is not true, there is no truth in man; and if it is true, he finds in it a great source of humiliation, forced to humble himself one way or another.

And since he cannot subsist without believing this knowledge, before entering into greater explorations of nature, I want him to consider nature both seriously and at leisure just once, and also to reflect upon himself and to judge, in a comparison of these two objects, whether any proportion holds between them.>

Let man then contemplate the whole of nature in its lofty and full majesty, and let him avert his view from the lowly objects around him. Let him behold that brilliant light set like an eternal lamp to illuminate the universe. Let the earth seem to him like a point in comparison with the vast orbit described by that star. And let him be amazed that this vast orbit is itself but a very small point in comparison with the one described by the stars rolling around the firmament. But if our gaze stops here, let our imagination pass beyond. It will sooner tire of conceiving things than nature of producing them. This whole visible world is only an imperceptible trace in the amplitude of nature.[98] No idea approaches it. However much we may inflate our conceptions beyond these imaginable spaces, we give birth only to atoms with respect to the reality of things. It is an infinite sphere whose center is everywhere and circumference nowhere. In the end, the greatest perceptible sign of God's omnipotence is that our imagination loses itself in this thought.

---

[98] Compare with Montaigne, *Essays* I, chap. 26: "But whoever represents himself, as in a painting, this great image of our mother Nature in her full majesty . . . whoever finds himself there, and not just himself, but a whole kingdom, as a trace made with a fine point, that man alone estimates things according to their true proportions," (Frame trans., p. 116).

Let man, returning to himself, consider what he is with respect to what exists. Let him regard himself as lost in this remote corner of nature, and from the little cell in which he finds himself lodged, I mean the universe, let him learn to estimate the just value of the earth, kingdoms, cities, and himself.

What is a man in the infinite?

But to present him with another equally astonishing prodigy, let him examine the most delicate things he knows. A mite with its miniscule body shows him incomparably more minute parts, legs with joints, veins in its legs, blood in its veins, humors in this blood, drops in the humors, vapors in these drops. Let him divide these last things again until he exhausts his powers of conception, and let the final object to which he can now arrive be the object of our discourse. Perhaps he will think that this is nature's extremity of smallness.

I want to make him see a new abyss in there. I want to depict for him not just the visible universe, but the immensity of nature we can conceive inside the boundaries of this compact atom. Let him see there an infinity of universes, each with its firmament, its planets, its earth, in the same proportion as in the visible world; and on this earth animals, and finally mites, where he will find again what he saw before, and find still in the others the same thing without end and without cessation. Let him lose himself in wonders as astonishing in their minuteness as the others are in their extent! For who will not marvel that our body, imperceptible a little while ago in the universe, itself imperceptible inside the totality, should now be a colossus, a world, or rather a whole, with respect to the nothingness beyond our reach?

Whoever considers himself in this way will be afraid of himself, and, seeing himself supported by the size nature has given him between these two abysses of the infinite and nothingness, he will tremble at these marvels. I believe that, as his curiosity changes into admiration, he will be more disposed to contemplate them in silence than to examine them with presumption. For, in the end, what is man in nature? A nothing compared to the infinite, an everything compared to the nothing, a midpoint between nothing and everything, infinitely removed from understanding the extremes: the end of things and their principle[99] are hopelessly hidden from him in an impenetrable secret. <What then will he be able to conceive? He is> equally incapable of seeing the nothingness from which he derives and the infinite in which he is engulfed.

---

[99] Principle (*principe*) here and below means starting point or foundation of things, referring to one of the two extremities, the other being the end of things.

What will he do then, but perceive [some] appearance from the middle of things, in an eternal despair at knowing neither their principle nor their end? All things come from nothingness and are swept toward the infinite. Who will follow these astonishing proceedings? The author of these wonders understands them. No one else can.

Having failed to contemplate these infinites, men have boldly rushed into the examination of nature, as though they bore some proportion to it.

It is strange that they have wanted to understand the principle of things and in this way come to know everything, a presumption as infinite as their object. For there is no doubt we cannot form such a design without presumption or without infinite capacity, like nature.

If we are knowledgeable, we understand that, since nature has engraved its image and that of its author on all things, they almost all share its double infinity. Thus we see that all the sciences are infinite in the scope of their inquiry. For who can doubt that geometry, for example, has an infinite infinity of propositions to demonstrate? These too are infinite in the multiplicity and subtlety of their principles. For who cannot see that those proposed as ultimate are not self-supporting, but depend on others that, depending on others for their support, never allow anything to be final?

But we treat as ultimate those appearing to be so to reason, as in material things we call a point indivisible when our senses no longer perceive anything beyond it, although by its nature it is infinitely divisible.

Of these two infinites of science, that of greatness is more observable, which is why few people have claimed to know all things. "I will speak about all things," said Democritus.[100] <But apart from the fact that it is a small matter simply to speak about it without proof and knowledge, it is nevertheless impossible to do so. The infinite number of things is so hidden from us that what is expressible in speech or thoughts is only an invisible trace of it. Hence the absurdity, vanity, and ignorance of the title of some books: *Of Everything Knowable*.[101]

We see immediately that arithmetic by itself offers innumerable properties, as does each science.>

But the infinitely small is much less visible. Philosophers have more readily claimed they have reached it, and here is where all have stumbled. It has given rise to such common titles as *Of the Principles of Things, Of the Principles of Philosophy*, and the like, as pretentious in

---

[100] See Montaigne, *Essays* II, chap. 12: "Equally impudent is this promise of Democritus' book: 'I am going to speak of all things.'" (Ariew and Grene trans., p. 51.)

[101] *De omni scibili*, title given by Pico della Mirandola to one of his proposed 900 theses, in 1486.

fact, though less so in appearance, as this other one offensive to our eyes: *Of Everything Knowable*.[102]

We naturally believe we are far more capable of reaching the center of things than of embracing their circumference. The visible extent of the world visibly surpasses us. But since we surpass the small things, we believe we are more capable of possessing them, and yet it takes no less capacity to reach nothingness than totality. Infinite capacity is required for both. It seems to me that whoever had understood the ultimate principles of things could also have reached knowledge of the infinite. The one depends on the other, and one leads to the other. These extremities touch and reunite by dint of their separation from one another, and find each other in God and God alone.

Let us, then, understand our condition: we are something and we are not everything. Such being as we have removes us from knowledge of first principles, which arise out of nothingness. And the smallness of our being conceals from us the sight of the infinite.

Our intellect holds the same rank in the order of intelligible things as our body occupies in the extension of nature.

Limited as we are in every respect, this condition of holding the midpoint between two extremes is apparent in all our faculties. Our senses perceive nothing extreme. Too much noise deafens us; too much light dazzles, too great a distance or proximity hinders our view. A great length or great brevity obscures the discourse; too much truth confounds us. I know people who cannot understand that four from zero leaves zero. First principles are too self-evident for us. Too much pleasure disagrees with us, too much harmony is annoying in music, and too much kindness irritates us. We want to have the means to repay our debt with interest. *Kindness is agreeable as long as it seems possible to repay the debt; when it goes beyond that, gratitude makes way for hatred.*[103] We feel neither extreme heat nor extreme cold. Qualities in excess are harmful to us and cannot be perceived: we no longer feel but suffer them. Extreme youth and extreme ages disturb the mind, as do too much and too little learning. In short, extremes are for us as though they did not exist, nor we for them. They escape us, or we them.

---

[102] *De omni scibili*. The two other titles given by Pascal are *Des principes de choses* and *Des principes de la philosophie*. The first is possibly a reference to a work by John Duns Scotus, *De rerum principio*; the second is a reference to Descartes' *Principia philosophiae* (1644; French language ed., *Les principes de la philosophie*, 1647).

[103] *Beneficia eo usque laeta sunt dum videntur exsolvi posse; ubi multum antevenere, pro gratia odium redditur.* Tacitus, *Annals*, 4. Montaigne quotes this also in *Essays* III, chap. 8 (Frame trans., p. 718; Screech trans., p. 1065).

This is our true state. It is what makes us incapable of certain knowledge or absolute ignorance. We float on a vast ocean, ever uncertain and adrift, blown this way or that. Whenever we think we have some point to which we can cling and fasten ourselves, it shakes free and leaves us behind. And if we follow it, it eludes our grasp, slides away, and escapes forever. Nothing stays still for us. This is our natural condition and yet the one farthest from our inclination. We burn with desire to find firm ground and an ultimate secure base on which to build a tower reaching up to the infinite. But our whole foundation cracks, and the earth opens up into abysses.

Let us, therefore, not seek certainty and stability. Our reason is always deceived by inconstant appearances; nothing can affix the finite between the two infinites that both enclose and escape it.

Once this is well understood, I think we will remain at rest, each of us in the state where nature has placed us.

Since this midpoint allotted to us is always distant from the extremes, what does it matter if someone has slightly more knowledge of things? If he has, and he goes a little farther with it, is he not still infinitely remote from the end? And is not the duration of our life equally insignificant in relation to eternity, even if it lasts ten years longer?

From the perspective of these infinites, all finites are equal, and I see no reason for fixing our imagination on one rather than on another. The only comparison we make of ourselves to the finite is painful to us.

If man studied himself foremost, he would see how incapable he is of going further. How could a part know the whole? But perhaps he will aspire to know at least the parts to which he bears some proportion. But the parts of the world are all so related and so linked to one another that I believe it impossible to know one without the other and without the whole.

Man, for example, is related to everything he knows. He needs place to hold him, time to endure, motion to live, elements to constitute him, warmth and food to nourish him, air to breathe. He sees light; he feels bodies. In short, everything falls under his purview. To understand man, then, we must know why he needs air to live, and, to understand air, we must know how it is related to man's life, etc.

Flame cannot subsist without air. Therefore, to understand the one, we must understand the other.

All things, then, are caused and causing, supporting and dependent, mediate and immediate; and all support one another in a natural, though imperceptible chain linking together things most distant and different. So, I hold it is as impossible to know the parts without knowing the whole as to know the whole without knowing the particular parts.

<The eternity of things in themselves or in God must always astonish our brief duration.

The fixed and constant immobility of nature, compared with the continual change going on within us, must have the same effect.>

And what completes our inability to know things is that they are simple in themselves and we are composed of two natures, opposite and different in kind, soul and body. For it is impossible for the part of us that reasons to be other than spiritual. And anyone claiming we are simply corporeal would be excluding us far more from knowledge of things, since there is nothing so inconceivable as saying that matter knows itself. It is not possible for us to know how it would know itself.

Thus, if we are simple, material, we can know nothing at all. And if we are composed of mind and matter, we cannot have perfect knowledge of simple things whether spiritual or corporeal, <since the instrument that brings about this knowledge is spiritual in part. And how would we understand spiritual substances, having a body that weighs us down and drags us toward the earth?>

This is why almost all philosophers confuse their ideas of things and speak of corporeal things in spiritual terms, and of spiritual things in corporeal terms. For they say boldly that bodies have a tendency to fall; that they seek after their center; that they flee from destruction; that they fear the void; that they have inclinations, sympathies, antipathies—all things pertaining only to minds. And in speaking of minds, they consider them as in a place, and attribute to them motion from one place to another—things pertaining only to bodies.

Instead of receiving the ideas of these things in their purity, we taint them with our own qualities, and stamp our composite being on all the simple things we contemplate.

Who would not think, seeing us compose everything of mind and body, that this mixture would be quite intelligible to us? Yet it is what we understand the least. Man is to himself the most prodigious object of nature, for he cannot conceive what body is, still less what mind is, and least of all how a body can be united to a mind. This is the culmination of his difficulties, and yet it is his very being. *The way the spirit is united to the body cannot be understood by man, and yet it is man.*[104]

<This is a part of the reason why man is so ineffectual in understanding nature. It is infinite in two ways; he is finite and limited. It endures and maintains itself perpetually; he is transient and mortal.

---

[104] *Modus quo corporibus adhaerent spiritus comprehendi ab hominibus non potest, et hoc tamen homo est*; Saint Augustine, *City of God*, xxi. 10.

Particular things change and transform every instant; he only sees them in passing. Things have their principle and their end; he conceives neither one nor the other. They are simple, and he is composed of two different natures.>

Finally, to complete the proof of our weakness, I will conclude with these two considerations.

H. 3.   B231/L200

Man is only a reed, the weakest thing in nature, but he is a thinking reed. The whole universe does not need to take up arms to crush him; a vapor, a drop of water, is enough to kill him. But if the universe were to crush him, man would still be nobler than what killed him, because he knows he is dying and the advantage the universe has over him. The universe knows nothing of this.

All our dignity consists, then, in thought. It is from this   S232/L200
that we must raise ourselves, and not from space and duration, which we could not fill.

Let us labor, then, to think well. This is the principle of morality.

The eternal silence of these infinite spaces frightens me.   S233/L201

Take comfort. It is not from yourself that you should   S234/L202
expect it; rather, you should expect it by expecting nothing
from yourself.

[17] Nature Is Corrupt [and] Falsity of Other Religions

Falsity of other religions   S235/L203

Mahomet without authority.

His reasons, therefore, must have been very powerful, since they had only their own strength.

What does he say, then? That we must believe him.

Falsity of other religions   S236/L204

They have no witnesses. These do.

God challenges other religions to produce such signs. Isaiah 43.9–44.8.[105]

If there is a single principle of everything, a single end of   S237/L205
everything— everything through him, everything for him—
then the true religion must teach us to worship only him, and to love
only him. But as we find ourselves unable to worship what we do not
know, or to love anything other than ourselves, the religion instructing

---

[105] Pascal translates these passages in fragment S735.

us about these duties must instruct us about our inadequacies as well. And it must also tell us the remedies. It tells us that through one man everything was lost and the bond broken between God and us, and that through one man the bond is repaired.

We are born so contrary to this love of God, and it is so necessary that we must be born guilty, or God would be unjust.

They have seen the thing; they have not seen the cause.[106]   S238/L206

Against Mahomet   S239/L207

The Koran is not more of Mahomet than the Gospel is of Saint Matthew, for many authors quote it from century to century. Even its enemies, Celsus and Porphyry, never denied it.[107]

The Koran says Saint Matthew was a good man. Therefore he was a false prophet, either for calling good men wicked or for disagreeing with what they said about Jesus Christ.

Without this divine knowledge, what could men do but   S240/L208 become elated by the inner feeling of their past greatness that remains in them or dejected at the sight of their present weakness? For, not seeing the whole truth, they could not attain perfect virtue. Some considering nature as incorrupt, the others as irreparable, they were not able to escape either pride or apathy,[108] the two sources of all vices, since their only choices were to give in through cowardice or to escape through pride. For if they knew man's excellence, they were ignorant of his corruption; as a result, they easily avoided apathy, but became lost in pride. And if they recognized the infirmity of nature, they were ignorant of its dignity; as a result, they could easily avoid vanity, but did so by falling into despair.

From this arise the different sects of Stoics and Epicureans, the dogmatists and Academics, etc.

Only the Christian religion has been able to cure these two vices, not by using one to expel the other according to the wisdom of the world, but by expelling both through the simplicity of the Gospel. For it teaches the righteous, whom it exalts even to participation in divinity itself, that in this sublime state they still carry the source of all corruption, rendering them throughout their lives subject to error, wretchedness,

---

[106] *Rem viderunt, causam non viderunt.* Saint Augustine, *Contra Pelagium*, iv.

[107] Celsus and Porphyry are third-century opponents of Christianity; thus what they did not deny is Saint Matthew's *Gospel*.

[108] Pascal's term, *paresse*, is usually translated as sloth. *Paresse* can mean laziness, but Pascal's concept is closer to resignation, the counterpart of pride (*orgueil*). *Paresse* and *orgueil* result from man's wretchedness or greatness and are the foundations for Stoicism and Epicureanism. See also fragment 637.

death, and sin. And it proclaims to the greatest unbelievers that they are capable of their Redeemer's grace. So, having those it renders just tremble and consoling those it condemns, it tempers fear with hope so well through that double capacity common to all for grace and sin, that it humbles infinitely more than reason alone, but without despair. And it exalts infinitely more than natural pride, but without inflating us, making it evident in this way that, since it alone is exempt from error and vice, the duty of instructing and correcting men belongs to it alone.

Who, then, can refuse to believe and worship such heavenly illumination? For is it not clearer than day that we sense within ourselves indelible marks of excellence? And is it not equally true that we experience every hour the results of our deplorable condition?

What does this chaos and monstrous confusion proclaim to us, but the truth of these two states, with a voice so powerful that it is impossible to resist it?

Difference between Jesus Christ and Mahomet   S241/L209

Mahomet not foretold. Jesus Christ foretold.

Mahomet by killing. Jesus Christ by having his followers killed.

Mahomet by forbidding reading, the apostles by ordering reading.

In fact, the two are so opposite that, if Mahomet took the   S242/L209
path of succeeding in a human way, Jesus Christ took that of
perishing in a human way. And instead of concluding that, since Mahomet succeeded, Jesus Christ could well have succeeded, we must conclude that, since Mahomet succeeded, Jesus Christ had to perish.

All men naturally hate one another. We have used   S243/L210
concupiscence as best as we could to serve the public good.
But this is only a pretense and a false image of charity. For at bottom it is only hate.

We have established and derived from concupiscence   S244/L211
admirable rules of policy, morality, and justice.

But, in the end, this vile foundation of man, this *evil component*,[109]
is only covered up, not removed.

Jesus Christ is a God we approach without pride, and   S245/L212
before whom we humble ourselves without despair.

Deserving blows more than kisses, I do not fear because I   S246/L213
love.[110]

---

[109] *figmentum malum*. Genesis 8:21. See fragment S309.

[110] *Dignior plagis quam osculis non timeo quia amo.* Saint Bernard, *Sermones in Cantica Canticorum*, lxxxiv.

The true religion must have as mark the obligation to love   S247/L214
its God. This is quite right, and yet none has ordered it. Ours
has.

It must also have understood concupiscence and weakness. Ours has.

It must have brought remedies for them. One is prayer. No other religion has required of God to love and follow him.

After having perceived all of man's nature, for a religion to   S248/L215
be true, it must have known our nature.[111] It must have
known its greatness and smallness, and the reason for both. What religion but Christianity has known this?

The true religion teaches our duties, our weaknesses,   S249/L216
pride, and concupiscence, and the remedies, humility,
mortification.

Some figures are clear and demonstrative, but others   S250/L217
seem somewhat far-fetched, convincing only those who are
already persuaded. They are like the Apocalyptics.[112] But the difference
is that they have none that are indubitable, so that nothing is so wrong
as when they point out that theirs are as well founded as some of ours.
For they have none so demonstrative as some of ours. The cases, therefore, are not equal. We must not treat as equal and confuse these things
when they seem to agree on one point, while differing so much on another. Clarity, when it is divine, requires us to revere obscurity.

I would not have Mahomet judged by what is obscure and   S251/L218
can pass as mysterious, but by what is clear, such as his paradise and the rest. In that he is ridiculous. And since what is clear is
ridiculous, it is not right to take his obscurities as mysteries. It is not the
same with Scripture. I agree that in it there are obscurities as strange as
Mahomet's, but in it are admirably clear passages and manifest, fulfilled
prophecies. The cases, therefore, are not equal. We must not treat as
equal and confuse things resembling each other only in their obscurity,
and not in the clarity that requires us to revere the obscurity.

Other religions, such heathen ones, are more popular, for   S252/L219
they are wholly external, but they are not for clever people. A
purely intellectual religion would be better suited to the clever, but it
would not serve the common people. The Christian religion alone is proportionate to all, being a mixture of external and internal. It elevates the

---

[111] Pascal is developing the theme announced in fragment S238.

[112] Referring to those who base their predictions on the book of Revelations. See also fragment S478.

people to the internal and humbles the proud to the external; it is not perfect without both, for the people must understand the spirit of the letter, and the clever must submit their spirit to the letter.[113]

No other religion has proposed that we should hate   S253/L220
ourselves. No other religion, then, can please those who hate
themselves and who seek a being truly worthy of love. And these, if they had never heard of the religion of a humiliated God, would embrace it at once.

[18] To Make Religion Attractive

Jesus Christ for everyone.   S254/L221

Moses for one people.

The Jews blessed in Abraham. *I will bless those who bless you*, but all nations are blessed in his seed.[114]

It is a light thing, etc. Isaiah.[115]

A light to enlighten the gentile.[116]

He has not dealt in this way with any nation,[117] said David, in speaking of the Law. But, in speaking of Jesus Christ, we must say *He has dealt in this way with all nations; it is a light thing*, etc. Isaiah.[118]

Thus it is for Jesus Christ to be universal. The Church itself offers the sacrifice only for the faithful.[119] Jesus Christ offered that of the cross for everyone.

Carnal Jews and heathens have their miseries and so do   S255/L222
Christians. There is no Redeemer for the heathens, for they
do not even hope for one. There is no Redeemer for the Jews; they hope for him in vain. There is a Redeemer only for the Christians.

See Perpetuity[120]

---

[113] This fragment can be better understood by reference to Pierre Charron, *De la sagesse* II, chap. 5, sec. 14: "Christianity, like a midpoint, has tempered everything, the sensible and external with the insensible and internal, serving God with mind and with body."

[114] Genesis 12:3, 22:18.

[115] *Parum est ut.* Isaiah 49:6.

[116] *Lumen ad revelationem gentium.* Luke 2:32

[117] *Non fecit taliter omni nationi.* Psalms 147:20.

[118] *Fecit taliter omni nationi; parum est ut, etc.*

[119] The sacrifice is a reference to the sacrament of the Eucharist.

[120] Chap. 22.

[19] Foundations of Religion and Reply to Objections

To the chapter on Foundations must be added what is in   S256/L223
Figurative Types regarding the cause of figures. Why [was]
Jesus Christ predicted in his first coming? Why predicted in an obscure
way?

Unbelievers are the most credulous. They believe the   S257/L224
miracles of Vespasian[121] in order not to believe those of
Moses.

As Jesus Christ remained unknown among men, so his   S258/L225
truth remains without external difference in the midst of ordinary opinions. So the Eucharist in the midst of ordinary bread.

———

All faith consists in Jesus Christ and Adam, and all moral-   S258/L226
ity in concupiscence and grace.

What do they have to say against resurrection and against   S259/L227
a Virgin giving birth? Which is more difficult, to produce a
man or animal, or to reproduce one? And if they had never seen a
species of animals, could they guess whether they are produced without
intercourse from one another?

What do the prophets say of Jesus Christ? That he will   S260/L228
manifestly be God? No. But that he is *a truly hidden God*,
that he will not be recognized, that no one will think he is the one, that
he will be a stumbling stone upon which many will fall, etc.[122]
Let us, then, no longer be criticized for our lack of clarity, since we
proclaim it ourselves. But, they say, there are obscurities, and without
them, we would not have stumbled over Jesus Christ. And this is one of
the formal intentions of the prophets. *Harden* [their heart].[123]

What men were able to apprehend by their greatest   S261/L229
insights, this religion has taught its children.

Not all that is incomprehensible fails to exist.   S262/L230

<If we would say that man is too slight to merit com-   S263/L231
munication with God, we must be very great to judge of this.>

---

[121] Montaigne, in *Essays* III, chap. 8, refers to Tacitus, who reports that Vespasian "cured
a blind woman in Alexandria by anointing her eyes with his saliva, and I know not what
other miracles," (Frame trans., p. 720; Screech trans., p. 1068).

[122] See fragment S734, quoting the pertinent passages from Isaiah.

[123] *Excaeca*. Isaiah 6:10.

We understand nothing of God's works, unless we take as S264/L232 a principle that he wanted to blind some people and enlighten others.

Jesus Christ does not deny he is from Nazareth, so as to S265/L233 leave the wicked in their blindness, nor that he is Joseph's son.

God wants to dispose the will more than the mind. Perfect S266/L234 clarity would serve the mind and harm the will.

Humble your pride.

Jesus Christ came to blind those who see clearly and give S267/L235 sight to the blind, heal the sick and let the healthy die; to call sinners to repent and justify them and leave the righteous in their sins; to fill the hungry and *send away empty the rich*.[124]

Blind, enlighten   S268/L236

Saint Augustine, Montaigne, Sebond.

There is enough light to enlighten the chosen and enough darkness to humble them. There is enough darkness to blind the reprobate and enough clarity to condemn them and leave them without excuse.

———

Jesus Christ's genealogy in the Old Testament is intermingled with so many other useless ones that it cannot be discerned. If Moses had recorded only Jesus Christ's ancestors, it would have been too perceptible. If he had not indicated Jesus Christ's, it would not have been perceptible enough. But, after all, anyone looking closely easily discerns Jesus Christ's genealogy through Tamar, Ruth, etc.

———

Those who ordered these sacrifices knew they were useless, and those who declared they were useless did not stop performing them.

———

If God had allowed only one religion, it would have been too easily recognizable. But looking at it more closely, we easily discern the true one in this confusion.

———

Principle: Moses was a clever man. Therefore, if he was governed by his intellect, he must have put nothing down that would go directly counter to the intellect.

---

[124] Luke 1:53.

Thus all the very obvious weaknesses are strengths — for example, the two genealogies of Saint Matthew and Saint Luke. What can be clearer than that this was not done in concert?

If Jesus Christ had come only to sanctify, all of Scripture S269/L237 and all things would tend toward this, and it would be quite easy to convince unbelievers. If Jesus Christ had come only to blind, his whole behavior would be obscure and we would have no way to convince unbelievers. But since he came *to be a sanctuary and a stumbling stone*,[125] as Isaiah says, we cannot convince unbelievers and they cannot convince us. But by this very fact we do convince them, since we say that in his whole behavior there is nothing that convinces in one way or another.

Figures
S270/L238

Wanting to deprive his people of perishable goods, God made the Jewish people to show that this was not through a lack of power.

Man is not worthy of God, but he is not incapable of S271/L239 being made worthy.

It is unworthy of God to unite himself to wretched man, but it is not unworthy of God to draw man out of his wretchedness.

Proof
S272/L240

Prophecy with its fulfillment.

What preceded and what followed Jesus Christ.

Source of oppositions. S273/L241

A God humiliated, to the point of death on the cross. Two natures in Jesus Christ. Two comings. Two states of man's nature. A Messiah triumphing over death through his own death.[126]

A. P. R. for tomorrow
S274/L149

[Wanting to appear openly to those who seek him with all their heart and hidden from those who flee him with all their heart, God has] tempered the knowledge of himself by giving signs of himself that are visible to those who seek him, and not by those who do not seek him.

There is enough light for those who desire only to see and enough darkness for those of a contrary disposition.[127]

That God wanted to be hidden. S275/L242

If there were only one religion, God would be overly manifest.

---

[125] *In sanctificationem et in scandalum.* Isaiah 8:14.

[126] Hebrews 2:14. See also fragment S285.

[127] See fragment S182.

If there were martyrs only in our religion, the same.

————

God being thus hidden, any religion that does not say God is hidden is not true. And any religion that does not explain it is not instructive. Our religion does all this. ***Truly you are a hidden God***.[128]

Heathen religion has no foundation <today. They say it   S276/L243
once had a foundation in the oracles that spoke. But what are
the books to assure us of this? Are they so worthy of faith because of their authors' virtue? Have they been so carefully preserved that we can be sure they have not been corrupted?>

The Mohammedan religion has the Koran and Mahomet for foundation. But this prophet, who should have been the world's last hope, was he foretold? And what sign does he have that every man who would call himself a prophet does not also have? What miracles does he himself say he has performed? What mystery did he teach, according to his own tradition? What morality and what happiness?

The Jewish religion must be regarded differently in the tradition of their saints and in popular tradition. Its morality and happiness are ridiculous in popular tradition, but admirable in that of their saints. Its foundation is admirable. It is the oldest book in the world and the most authentic, and whereas Mahomet, to preserve his, forbade people to read it, Moses, to preserve his, ordered everyone to read it. And it is the same for all religions, for Christianity is quite different in its Sacred Books and in those of the casuists.

Our religion is so divine that another divine religion is merely its foundation.

Objection of atheists   S277/L244

"But we have no illumination."

[20] That the Law Was Figurative   L245

Figure   S278/L246

The Jewish and Egyptian peoples visibly foretold by the
two individuals whom Moses met, the Egyptian beating the Jew, Moses avenging him and killing the Egyptian, and the Jew being ungrateful.[129]

————

---

[128] ***Vere tu es Deus absconditus.*** Isaiah 45:15.

[129] Exodus 2:11–14.

Figurative things   S279/L247

Do all things according to the pattern shown to you on the mount.[130] Of which Saint Paul says that the Jews shadowed heavenly things.[131]

Figure   S280/L248

The prophets prophesied in figures, of a girdle, of burnt beard and hair, etc.[132]

Figurative things   S281/L249
The key to the cipher.

True worshipers.[133] *Behold the Lamb of God who takes away the sin of the world.*[134]

Figurative things   S282/L250

The terms sword, shield, *O most mighty.*[135]

Whoever wants to give the meaning of Scripture without   S283/L251
taking it from Scripture is the enemy of Scripture. Saint Augustine, *Of Christian Doctrine.*[136]

Two errors: 1. Taking everything literally. 2. Taking   S284/L252
everything spiritually.

Figures   S285/L253

Jesus Christ opened their minds to understand the Scriptures.

These are two great revelations: 1. *Everything happened to them in figures. True Israelite, True freedom, True bread from heaven.*[137]

2. A God humiliated even unto the cross. Christ had to suffer to enter into his glory. That he should destroy death through his death.[138] Two comings.

Speak against excessive figurative language.   S286/L254

In order to have the Messiah recognized by the good and   S287/L255
not by the wicked, God had him foretold in this way. If the manner of the Messiah had been clearly foretold, there would have

---

[130] Exodus 25:40.

[131] Hebrews 8:5.

[132] Jeremiah 13:1–11. Daniel 3:27.

[133] *Veri adoratores*; John 4:23.

[134] *Ecce agnus Dei qui tollit peccata mundi.* John 1:29.

[135] *Potentissime.* Psalms 44:4.

[136] Augustine, *De doctrina christiana* III, 28, no. 39.

[137] *Vere Israelitae.* John 1:47; *Vere liberi.* John 8:36. Also John 6:32.

[138] Hebrews 2:14.

been no obscurity, even for the wicked. If the time had been foretold obscurely, there would have been obscurity even for the good; <for their goodness of heart> would not have made them understand, for example, that the closed *mem*[139] signifies 600 years. But the time was foretold clearly and the manner in figures.

In this way, taking the promised benefits as material, the wicked go astray, despite the clear prediction of the time; and the good do not go astray.

For an understanding of the promised benefits depends on the heart, which calls good that which it loves; but an understanding of the promised time does not depend on the heart. And thus the clear prediction of the time and the obscure prediction of the benefits deceive only the wicked.

The carnal Jews understood neither the greatness nor the   S288/L256
abasement of the Messiah foretold in their prophecies. They
did not recognize him in his greatness foretold, as when he said that the Messiah would be David's lord, though his son,[140] and that he is before Abraham who has seen him.[141] They did not believe him so great as to be eternal, and likewise they did not recognize him in his abasement and death. The Messiah, they said, abides forever, and this man says he will die.[142] Therefore they believed him neither mortal nor eternal; they sought in him only a carnal greatness.

Contradiction   S289/L257

We can present a good appearance only by harmonizing
all our contrary features, and it is not enough to follow a series of compatible qualities without reconciling their opposites. To understand the meaning of an author, we must reconcile all contrary passages.

Thus, to understand Scripture, we must have a meaning in which all the contrary passages are reconciled. It is not enough to have one that fits many compatible passages, but one that reconciles even contradictory passages.

Every author has a meaning in which all the contrary passages agree, or he has no meaning at all. The latter cannot be said of Scripture and the prophets; they certainly were full of good sense. We must, then, seek for a meaning that reconciles all oppositions.

---

[139] A Hebrew letter.
[140] Matthew 22:45.
[141] John 8:56.
[142] John 12:34.

The true meaning, then, is not that of the Jews, but all contradictions are reconciled in Jesus Christ.

The Jews could not reconcile the end of the kings and princes predicted by Hosea with the prophecy of Jacob.[143]

If we take the law, the sacrifices, and the kingdom for realities, we cannot reconcile all the passages. It necessarily follows, then, that they are only figures. We cannot even reconcile passages by the same author, in the same book, or sometimes in the same chapter; this indicates clearly what the author meant. As when Ezekiel, chap. 20, says that we will live by God's commandments and we will not live by them.

It was not permitted to sacrifice outside of Jerusalem, the   S290/L258
place the Lord had chosen, or even to eat the tithes else-
where. Deuteronomy 12:5, etc.; Deuteronomy 14:23, etc.; 15:20; 16:2, 7, 11, 15.

———

Hosea foretold that they would be without a king, without a prince, without sacrifice, etc., and without idols. This is now fulfilled, since no lawful sacrifice can be made outside Jerusalem.

Figure   S290/L259

If the law and sacrifices are the truth, they must please
God and not displease him. If they are figures, they must both please and displease.

Now all through Scripture they both please and displease. It is said that the Law will be changed; that the sacrifice will be changed; that they will be without a king, without princes, and without sacrifices; that a new covenant will be made; that the law will be renewed; that the precepts they have received are not good; that their sacrifices are abominable; that God did not ask for them.

It is said, on the contrary, that the law will last forever; that this covenant will be eternal; that sacrifice will be eternal; that the scepter will never leave from among them, because it must not leave until the coming of the eternal king.

Do all these passages indicate what is real? No. Do they then also indicate what is figurative? No, but that it is either real or figurative. But the first passages, by excluding what is real, indicate that they are only figurative.

All these passages together cannot be said of reality. All can be said figuratively. Therefore they are not said of reality, but figuratively.

---

[143] Hosea 3:4 and Genesis 49:10. See fragments S290, S294, and S719.

The Lamb was slain from the beginning of the world.[144] *Perpetual sacrifice.*[145]

A portrait brings absence and presence, pleasure and   S291/L260
displeasure. Reality excludes absence and displeasure.

_____

Figures

To know whether the Law and sacrifices are reality or figurative, we must see whether the prophets, in speaking of these things, thought and looked no further, so that they saw only the old covenant. Or whether they saw in them something else of which they were the representation. For in a portrait we see the thing figured. For this we need only examine what they say about it.

When they say it will be eternal, do they refer to this covenant that they say will be changed? And the same for the sacrifices, etc.

_____

A cipher has two meanings. When we come upon an important letter whose meaning is clear, but where it is said that the meaning is veiled and obscure, hidden in such a way that we might see the letter without seeing it, and understand it without understanding it, what must we think but that the cipher has a double meaning? And the more so if we find obvious oppositions in the literal meaning? The prophets clearly said that Israel would always be loved by God and that the law would be eternal. And they said their meaning would not be understood and that it was veiled.

How much, then, should we esteem those who solve the cipher and teach us to understand the hidden meaning, especially if the principles they derive from it are completely natural and clear? This is what Jesus Christ and the apostles did. They broke the seal. He lifted the veil and revealed the spirit. Through this they taught us that the enemies of man are his passions; that the Redeemer would be spiritual and his reign spiritual; that there would be two comings, one in misery to humble the proud, the other in glory to exalt the humble; that Jesus Christ would be both God and man.

The time of the first coming foretold, not the time of the   S292/L261
second, because the first needed to be hidden and the
second brilliant and so manifest that even his enemies had to recognize

_____

[144] *Agnus occisus est ab origine mundi.* Revelations 13:8.
[145] *Juge sacrificium.* Daniel 12:11 and elsewhere.

him. But, as he had to come in obscurity and be known only by those who probed the Scriptures . . .

What could the Jews, his enemies, do?   S293/L262

If they receive him, they prove him by their reception, for then those entrusted with anticipating the Messiah receive him; and if they reject him, they prove him by their rejection.

Oppositions.   S294/L263

The scepter until the Messiah. *Without a king or a prince.*[146]

Eternal Law, changed.[147]

Eternal covenant, a new covenant.[148]

Good laws, *bad precepts*. Ezekiel, 20.[149]

The Jews were accustomed to great and glorious miracles.   S295/L264
And so, having had the great deeds of the Red Sea and land of Canaan as an epitome of the great things to be done by the Messiah, they therefore expected something glorious, of which the miracles of Moses were only the sample.

A figure carries absence and presence, pleasure and   S296/L265
displeasure.

———

A cipher has a double meaning, one clear and one about which it is said the meaning is hidden.

We might perhaps think that, when the prophets foretold   S297/L266
that the scepter would not leave Judah until the eternal King came, they were speaking to flatter the people and Herod would prove their prophecy false. But to show that this is not what they meant and, on the contrary, that they knew well this temporal kingdom must cease, they said that they would be without a king and without a prince, and for a long time. Hosea.

                         Figures   S298/L267
Once this secret is revealed, it is impossible not to see it.
Let us read the Old Testament in this light and see if the sacrifices were real, if Abraham's lineage was the true cause of God's friendship, and if the Promised Land was the true place of rest. No. Then they are figures.

---

[146] See fragment S719 and Hosea 3:4.

[147] See Leviticus 7:34 and fragment S693.

[148] See fragment S651 and Jeremiah 31:31.

[149] See many passages in Deuteronomy and Ezechiel 20.

Let us in the same way examine all those ordained ceremonies, all the commandments not directed toward charity, and we will see that they are figures.

All these sacrifices and ceremonies were therefore figures or nonsense. Now some things are too clear and lofty to be thought nonsense.

Know whether the prophets restricted their view in the Old Testament or saw other things in it.

Figures   S299/L268

The letter kills.[150]
Everything happened in figures.
Christ needed to suffer.
A God humiliated. Here is the cipher Saint Paul gives us.

Circumcision of the heart, true fasting, true sacrifice, true temple. The prophets indicated that all these must be spiritual.[151]
Not the meat that perishes, but the one that does not perish.[152]

"You shall be *free indeed.*"[153] Therefore the other freedom is only a figure of freedom.

I am the true bread from heaven.[154]
When David foretold that the Messiah would deliver his   S300/L269
people from their enemies, we may believe that, according to
the carnal perspective, these would be the Egyptians, and then I cannot show that the prophecy was fulfilled. But we may also well believe that the enemies would be iniquities, for in fact the Egyptians are not enemies, but iniquities are.
The word "enemies," therefore, is equivocal. But if he says elsewhere, as he does, that he will deliver his people from their sins,[155] as do

------

[150] II Corinthians 3:6.
[151] See fragment S693.
[152] John 6:27.
[153] John 8:36.
[154] John 6:32.
[155] Psalm 129:8.

Isaiah and others,[156] the equivocation is removed, and the double meaning of enemies is reduced to the simple meaning of iniquities. For if he had sins in his mind, he could well denote them by enemies; but if he thought of enemies, he could not designate them by iniquities.

Now, Moses, David, and Isaiah used the same terms. Who can say, then, that they did not have the same meaning and that David's meaning, which is plainly iniquities when he spoke of enemies, was not the same as that of Moses speaking of enemies?

———

Daniel (9) prays for the people to be delivered from the captivity of their enemies. But he was thinking about sins, and to show this, he says that Gabriel came to tell him that his prayer was heard, and that there were only seventy more weeks to wait. After this the people would be freed from iniquity, sin would come to an end, and the Redeemer, the Holy of Holies, would bring **eternal** justice—not the justice of the law, but the eternal one.

———

There are some who see clearly that man has no other enemy but the concupiscence that turns him away from God, and not [armies]; no other good but God, and not a rich land. Let those who believe that man's good lies in his flesh, and evil in what turns him away from sensual pleasures, gorge themselves and die of it. But those who seek God with all their hearts, who are unhappy only at being deprived of the sight of him, who desire only to possess him and have as enemies only those who turn them away from him, who are grieved at seeing themselves surrounded and dominated by such enemies, take comfort. I bring them happy news. There is a liberator for them. I will show him to them. I will show them there is a God for them. I will not show him to others. I will show that a Messiah was promised for deliverance from enemies, and that one has come for deliverance from iniquities, but not from enemies.

Figures   S301/L270

The Jews had grown old in these earthly thoughts: that God loved their father Abraham, his flesh and what came from it; that because of this he caused them to multiply and distinguished them from all other peoples, without allowing them to intermingle; that when

---

[156] Isaiah 43:25; Daniel 9:21–24.

they were languishing in Egypt, he brought them out with all these great signs of his favor; that he fed them with manna in the desert; that he led them into a very rich land; that he gave them kings and a well-built temple to offer up beasts before him and be purified by the shedding of their blood; and that, at last, he was to send them the Messiah to make them masters of all the world. And he foretold the time of his coming.

The world having grown old in these carnal errors, Jesus Christ came at the time foretold, but not with the expected blaze of glory. And thus they did not think that he was the one. After his death, Saint Paul came to teach men that all these things had happened figuratively; that the kingdom of God did not consist in the flesh, but in the spirit; that the enemies of men were not the Babylonians, but their passions; that God did not delight in temples made by hands, but in a pure and humble heart; that circumcision of the body was useless, but that of the heart was needed; that Moses had not given them the bread from heaven, etc.[157]

———

God did not want to reveal these things to people unworthy of them, and yet he wanted to produce them so that they might be believed. Thus he foretold the time clearly and sometimes expressed them clearly, but very often in figures, so that those who loved figurative things might consider them (I do not say they would do this well) and those who loved the things figured should see them there.

———

Everything that does not lead to charity is figurative.

———

The sole object of Scripture is charity.[158]

———

Everything that does not lead to the sole end is a figure of it. For, since there is but one end, everything not leading to it in explicit terms is figurative.

———

God thus diversifies that sole precept of charity to satisfy our curiosity, which seeks diversity, through that diversity which always leads us to our one necessity. For, *one thing alone is necessary*[159] and we love diversity.

---

[157] I Corinthians 10:11; Romans 4; Romans 8:14–25; Hebrews 9:24; Romans 2:28–29.

[158] Augustine, *Christian doctrine* III, 10. 15–16.

[159] Luke 10:42.

And God satisfies both needs by these diversities that lead to this one necessity.

————

The Jews loved figurative things so much and so fully expected them that they failed to recognize the real thing when it came in the time and manner foretold.

————

The Rabbis take the breasts of the Spouse as a figure,[160] like everything that does not express their only end, that of temporal goods.

————

And Christians even take the Eucharist as a figure of the glory toward which they aim.

Jesus Christ did nothing but teach men that they loved   B302/L271
themselves, that they were slaves, blind, sick, wretched, and
sinners; that he needed to deliver, enlighten, beatify, and heal them; that this would be done through their self-hate and by following him through his misery and death on the cross.

Figures   S303/L272

When the word of God, which is true, is literally false, it is spiritually true. *Sit at my right hand*[161] is literally false, so it is spiritually true.

In these expressions, God is spoken of in human terms. And this means nothing else but that the intention that men have in giving a seat at their right hand, God will have also. It then indicates God's intention, not his manner of carrying this out.

Thus when it is said, *God has received the odor of your perfumes, and will give you a rich land in recompense,*[162] it is equivalent to saying that God will have the same intention toward you that a man would have, who, pleased with your perfumes, would give you a rich land in recompense, because you have the same intention toward him as a man has toward the person to whom he presents perfumes.

So also with *the Lord's anger,*[163] *a jealous God,* etc. For, as the things of God are inexpressible, they cannot be said otherwise, and the Church still uses them today: *For he has strengthened the bars,*[164] etc.

---

[160] Song of Solomon 4:5.

[161] *Sede a dextris meis.* Psalms 109:1.

[162] Genesis 8:21, 27:27–28.

[163] *Iratus est.* Isaiah 5:25.

[164] *Quia confortavit seras.* Psalms 147:13.

It is not permissible to attribute meanings to Scripture it has not revealed to us that it has. Thus, saying that the closed *mem*[165] of Isaiah signifies 600, this is not revealed. It is not said that the final *tsade* and
defective *he* signify mysteries. Then it is not permissible to say so. And
still less to say that this is the method of the philosopher's stone. But we
say that the literal meaning is not the true one, because the prophets
themselves said so.

Those who find it hard to believe seek an excuse in that   S304/L273
the Jews did not believe: "If it was so clear," they say, "why
did they not believe?" And they almost want them to have believed, so
that they would not be held back by the example of their refusal. But
their very refusal is the foundation of our faith. We would be much less
inclined if they were on our side, and would then have a greater pretext.

It is admirable to have made the Jews great lovers of the things foretold, and great enemies of their fulfillment.

Proof of the two Testaments at once   S305/L274

To prove the two with one stroke, we need only see
whether the prophecies of the one are fulfilled in the other.

To examine the prophecies, we must understand them.

For if we believe they have only one meaning, it is certain that the
Messiah has not come. But if they have two meanings, it is certain that
he has come in Jesus Christ.

The whole question is then to know if they have two meanings.

Here are the proofs given by Jesus Christ and the apostles
that Scripture has two meanings.

1. Proof by Scripture itself.
2. Proof by the Rabbis. Moses Maimonides says that it has two aspects,
   proved.[166] And that the prophets foretold only Jesus Christ.
3. Proof by the Cabala.[167]
4. Proof by the mystical interpretation the Rabbis themselves give to
   Scripture.

---

[165] *Mem, tsade,* and *he* are Hebrew letters. *Mem* has a closed and open form. *Tsade* also
has two forms, initial and final. *He* is said to be defective (*deficientes*) when it is not written as a final letter.

[166] Moses Maimonides, *Guide of the Perplexed.*

[167] Cabala refers to Jewish mystical writings from the 2nd century on.

5. Proof by the Rabbis' principles that there are two meanings.

That there are two comings of the Messiah, glorious or abject, according to what they merit.

That the prophets foretold only the Messiah.

[That] the Law is not eternal but must change with the Messiah.

That then they will no longer remember the Red Sea.

That the Jews and the Gentiles will be intermingled.[168]

A. Figures   S306/L275

Isaiah 51: the Red Sea, image of the Redemption.

———

So that you may know that the Son of man has power on earth to forgive sins [. . .] *I say to you: Arise.*[169]

Wanting to show that he could form a people holy with an invisible holiness and fill them with an eternal glory, God made visible things. Since nature is an image of grace, he made in the blessings of nature what he would in those of grace, so that we might judge that he could make the invisible ones, given that he made the visible ones so well.

Therefore he saved the people from the Flood, caused them to be born from Abraham, redeemed them from the midst of their enemies, and set them at rest.

God's object was not to save them from the Flood and cause a whole people to be born from Abraham just to lead them to a rich land.

And even grace is only a figure of glory, for it is not the ultimate end. It was prefigured by the Law, and it itself prefigures [glory], but it is both its figure and its principle or cause.

———

The ordinary life of men is like that of the saints. They all seek satisfaction and differ only as to the object in which they locate it. They call those who hinder them their enemies, etc. Thus God has shown the power he has for conferring invisible blessings by showing the power he has over visible ones.

---

[168] Pascal had added then crossed out: "6. Proof by the key Jesus Christ and the apostles give us."

[169] *Ut sciatis quod Filius hominis habet potestatem remittendi peccata, tibi dico: Surge.* Mark 2:10, 11.

Two people are telling inane stories, one with a double   S307/L276
meaning in a cabalistic framework and another with a single
meaning. If an uninitiated person were to hear them both talking in this
manner, he would judge them alike. But if afterward, in the rest of their
conversation, the first having said angelic things and the other invariably
dull commonplaces, he would judge that the first spoke in mysteries,
but not the other. The first has shown sufficiently that he is incapable of
such inanities and capable of being mysterious, the other that he is incapable of mystery and capable of inanity.

The Old Testament is a cipher.

[21] Rabbinism

Chronology of Rabbinism.   S308/L277
The page references are from the book *Pugio*.[170]

Page 27. R. Hakadosh,
    author of the *Mishna* or vocal law,
    or second law, year 200.

Commentaries on
the *Mishna*
$\left\{ \begin{array}{l} \text{The one } Siphra \\ \text{<which is a commentary} \\ \text{on the } Mishna\text{>} \\ Baraitot \\ Talmud\ of\ Jerusalem^{171} \\ Tosephta \end{array} \right\}$
year 340

Bereshith Rabbah by R. Hoshaiah Rabbah,
commentary on the *Mishna*.
Bereshith Rabbah, Bar Nachoni,
    are subtle, pleasant, historical, and theological discourses. The same
author wrote books called *Rabboth*.

-----

[170] These are Pascal's notes on the 1651 edition, by Joseph de Voisin, of the book *Pugio Fidei* by the 13th-century Dominican Ramón Martí.

[171] *Talmud Hierosol*, here and below.

A hundred years after the *Talmud of Jerusalem*, the *Babylonian Talmud* was written by R. Ashi, by the universal consent of all the Jews, who are necessarily required to observe everything contained in it: 440.

The addition of R. Ashi is called the *Gemara*, meaning the commentary on the *Mishna*.

And the *Talmud* comprises both the *Mishna* and the *Gemara*.

Of original sin

S309/L278

Ample tradition of original sin according to the Jews.

On the saying in Genesis 8[:21]: *The composition of man's heart is evil from his youth.*

R. Moses Hadarshan: This evil leaven is placed in man from the moment of his creation.

Massechet Sukkah: This evil leaven has seven names in Scripture. It is called evil, foreskin, unclean, enemy, scandal, heart of stone, north wind: all this signifies the wickedness hidden and impressed in the heart of man. *Midrash Tehillim* says the same thing, and that God will deliver man's good nature from his bad.

This wickedness is renewed every day against man, as it is written in Psalm 37[:32–33]: *The wicked watches the righteous and seeks to slay him, but the Lord will not abandon him.*

This wickedness tempts the heart of man in this life and will accuse him in the other.

All of this is found in the *Talmud*.

Midrash Tehillim on Psalm 4[:5]: *Stand in awe and do not sin.* Stand in awe and frighten your concupiscence and it will not lead you into sin. And on Psalm 36[:1]: *The wicked has said in his heart: there is no fear of God before me.* In other words, the natural wickedness of man has said that to the wicked.

Midrash el Kohelet: *The poor and wise child is better than the old and foolish king who cannot foresee the future.*[172] The child is virtue, and the king is man's wickedness. It is called king because all the members obey it and old because it is in the human heart from childhood to old age, and foolish because it leads man into the way of perdition, which he does not foresee.

The same thing is in *Midrash Tehillim*.

Bereshith Rabbah on Psalm 35[:10]: *Lord, all my bones will bless you, who delivers the poor from the tyrant.* And is there a greater tyrant than the evil leaven?

---

[172] Ecclesiastes 4:13.

And on Proverbs 25[:21]: *If your enemy is hungry, give him bread to eat.* In other words, if the evil leaven is hungry, give him the bread of wisdom of which it is spoken in Proverbs 9[:5]. And if he is thirsty, give him the water of which it is spoken in Isaiah 55[:1].

Midrash Tehillim says the same thing and that Scripture in that passage, speaking of our enemy, means the evil leaven, and that, by [giving] him this bread and water, we shall heap coals of fire on his head.

Midrash el Kohelet on Ecclesiastes 9[:13–18]: *A great king besieged a little city.* This great king is the evil leaven; the great bulwarks surrounding it are temptations. And a poor wise man has been found who delivered it—namely, virtue.

And on Psalm 41[:1]: *Blessed is he who considers the poor.*

And on Psalm 78[:39]: *The spirit passes away and does not come again.*[173] This has led some to argue erroneously against the immortality of the soul, but its meaning is that this spirit is the evil leaven that accompanies man until death and will not return at the resurrection.

And on Psalm 103[:15–16]. The same thing.

And on Psalm 16.

Principles of the Rabbis: two Messiahs.   S310/L278

[22] Perpetuity

From a single statement of David or of Moses, such as   S311/L279
"God will circumcise their hearts,"[174] we can understand
their way of thinking. All their other expressions may be ambiguous and may cast doubt on whether they are philosophers or Christians, but in the end a single statement of this kind should determine all the others, just as a single statement of Epictetus determines all the others to the opposite meaning. Ambiguity exists until then, but not afterward.

States would perish if their laws did not often give way to   S312/L280
necessity. But religion has never tolerated or practiced this.
So, either these compromises or some miracles are needed.

There is nothing strange in being preserved by giving way, but this is not, strictly speaking, preservation. Moreover, all states wholly perish in the end; none has endured a thousand years. But the fact that this religion has always been preserved and is inflexible . . . this is divine.

---

[173] Pascal's word is *l'esprit*, playing on the ambiguity of the word, which can also mean breath. The King James Bible gives the passage as "A wind that passeth away and cometh not again."

[174] Deuteronomy 30:6.

Perpetuity   S313/L281

This religion consists in the belief that man has fallen
from a state of glory and communion with God into a state of sorrow,
penitence, and estrangement from God, but that after this life we will
be restored by a Messiah who was to come. It has always existed on
earth. All things have passed, and this one, for which all things are, has
endured.

In the first age of the world, men were led into all kinds of debauchery,
and yet there were saints, such as Enoch, Lamech, and others, who
waited patiently for the Christ promised ever since the beginning of the
world. Noah saw men's wickedness at its highest degree and had the merit
in his own person to save the world, through the hope for the Messiah,
whom he prefigured. Abraham was surrounded by idolaters when God
made known to him the mystery of the Messiah, whom he hailed from
afar. Abomination spread over all the earth in the time of Isaac and
Jacob, but these saints lived in their faith. And Jacob, blessing his children as he was dying, cried out in a rapture that caused him to interrupt
what he was saying: *I await, O my Lord, the savior you have promised —
Salutare tuum expectabo, Domine.*[175]

The Egyptians were infected with idolatry and magic; even the people
of God were led astray by their example. Yet Moses and others saw him
whom they did not see, and worshiped him, as they looked to the eternal gifts he was preparing for them.

The Greeks and Romans subsequently erected false deities. The
poets created a hundred different theologies. The philosophers separated into a thousand different sects. And yet, in the heart of Judaea,
there were always chosen men foretelling the coming of this Messiah,
who was known only to them. He came at last in the fullness of time,
and since then we have witnessed the birth of so many schisms and
heresies, so many states overthrown, so many changes in all things; yet
this Church, which worships him who always has been worshiped, has
continued without interruption. It is wonderful, incomparable, and altogether divine that this religion, which has always endured, has continually been under attack. It was on the eve of universal destruction a
thousand times, and every time it was in that state, God restored it by extraordinary strokes of his power. What is astonishing is that it was preserved without yielding or bending to the will of tyrants, for it would not

---

[175] Pascal repeats the phrase in Latin for emphasis: "I have waited for your salvation, O
Lord." Genesis 49:18.

be strange for a state to endure when its laws are sometimes made to yield to necessity. But for that, **see the circle in Montaigne.**[176]

Perpetuity   S314/L282

The Messiah has always been believed in. The tradition of Adam was still fresh in Noah and in Moses. The prophets have foretold him ever since, while always foretelling other things, which, being fulfilled from time to time in the sight of men, showed the truth of their mission and consequently that of promises they made concerning the Messiah. Jesus Christ performed miracles, as did the apostles, converting all the heathens; in this way, with the fulfillment of all the prophecies, the Messiah has been proven forever.

The six ages, the six fathers of the six ages, the six wonders   S315/L283
at the start of the six ages, the six dawns at the start of the six ages.

The only religion contrary to nature,[177] to common sense,   S316/L284
and to our pleasures, is the only one that has always existed.

If the ancient Church was in error, the Church has fallen.   S317/L285
If the Church should be in error today, it is not the same thing, because it has always the higher principle of the ancient Church's tradition of faith. And so this submission and conformity to the ancient Church prevail and correct everything. But the ancient Church did not presuppose the future Church and did not consider it, as we presuppose and consider the ancient Church.

Two kinds of men in each religion   S318/L286
Among heathens, those who worship beasts, and others who worship the one God in natural religion.

Among Jews, carnal and spiritual men, the Christians of the old Law.
Among Christians, coarse men, the Jews of the new Law.

Carnal Jews awaited a carnal Messiah, and coarse Christians believe that the Messiah has dispensed them from loving God. True Jews and true Christians worship a Messiah who makes them love God.

Whoever judges of the Jewish religion through the coarse   S319/L287
men will misunderstand it. This can be seen in the Holy Books, and in the tradition of the prophets, who made it clear enough that they did not interpret the Law literally. Thus our religion is divine

---

[176] Probably a passage that Pascal had circled in his copy of Montaigne's *Essays*, perhaps the end of *Essays* 1, chap. 23, where Montaigne says "fortune . . . sometimes presents us with such urgent necessity that the laws must make some room for it." (Frame trans., p. 89; Screech trans., p. 138.) See fragments S312 and S313.

[177] Nature understood as our second nature—that is, our fallen state; see fragment S509.

in the Gospel, in the apostles, and in tradition, but it is absurd in those who misuse it.

The Messiah, according to the carnal Jews, was to be a great temporal prince. Jesus Christ, according to carnal Christians, came to dispense us from loving God and to give us sacraments that are fully efficacious without our help. Neither of these is the Christian religion or the Jewish religion.

True Jews and true Christians have always awaited a Messiah who would make them love God and, through this love, triumph over their enemies.[178]

Moses (Deuteronomy 30) promises that God will   S320/L288
circumcise their hearts to make them capable of loving him.

The carnal Jews hold the middle place between   S321/L289
Christians and heathens. Heathens do not know God and
love only earthly things. Jews know the true God, and love only earthly things. Christians know the true God and do not love earthly things. Jews and heathens love the same goods; Jews and Christians know the same God.

Jews were of two kinds: the first had only heathen sensibilities; the other had Christian sensibilities.

[23] Proofs of Moses

Another circle[179]   S322/L290

The longevity of the patriarchs, instead of causing the loss
of past events, served, on the contrary, to preserve them. For the reason why we are sometimes not sufficiently knowledgeable about the history of our ancestors is that we have barely lived with them, and often they died before we reached the age of reason. Now, when men lived so long, children lived a long time with their fathers. They spent a long time conversing with them. And what else could they talk about, except the history of their ancestors? For all history was reduced to that, since they had no studies, sciences, or arts, which make up a large part of daily conversation. We see also that, in these days, tribes took particular care to preserve their genealogies.

---

[178] That is, their sins; see fragment S300.

[179] Again this is possibly a passage that Pascal had circled in his copy of Montaigne's *Essays* (see fragment S313), this time perhaps *Essays* 2, chap. 18: "What satisfaction I would have in hearing someone relating in this way the manners, look, expression, ordinary talk, and fortunes of my ancestors! How attentive I would be!" (Frame trans., p. 503; Screech trans., p. 754.)

This religion, so great in miracles—holy, pious, ir-   S323/L291
reproachable, learned, and great witnesses; martyrs; established kings (David); Isaiah, a prince of the blood—so great in knowledge, after having displayed all its miracles and all its wisdom, rejects it
all and says that it has neither wisdom nor signs, only the cross and
foolishness.[180]

For those who have earned your belief by these signs and this wisdom, and who have proved their character to you, declare to you that
none of this can change us and make us capable of knowing and loving
God, other than the virtue contained in the foolishness of the cross,
without wisdom or signs, and not the signs without this virtue. Thus our
religion is foolish with respect to its efficient cause and wise with respect
to its wisdom, which prepares for it.

Proofs of Moses   S324/L292

Why should Moses make men's lives so long, with so few
generations?

Because it is not the length of years, but the multitude of generations
that makes things obscure.

For truth is altered only by the change of men.

And yet he puts the two most memorable things ever imagined,
namely, the Creation and the Flood, so close they can be touched.

———

If we ought to give up eight days, we ought to give up a   S324/L293
whole life.

Proofs of Moses   S325/L294

When the prophets were there to maintain the Law, the
people were negligent. But once there were no more prophets, zeal
prevailed.

Josephus hides the shame of his nation.   S326/L295
Moses does not hide his own shame nor . . .[181]
Would that all people were prophets.[182]
He was weary of the people.[183]

---

[180] Paul, I Corinthians 1:18.

[181] Moses does not hide the fact that the Jews venerated the golden calf, something the
Jewish historian Josephus does not mention.

[182] *Quis mihi det ut omnes prophetent?* Numbers 11:29.

[183] Numbers 11:14. The King James Bible gives this as: "I am not able to bear all this
people alone."

Shem, who saw Lamech, who saw Adam, also saw Jacob,   S327/L296
who saw those who saw Moses.[184] Therefore the Flood and
the Creation are true. This is conclusive among certain people who understand it properly.

Zeal of the Jewish people for their Law, especially after   S328/L297
there were no more prophets.

[24] Proofs of Jesus Christ

Order. Against the objection that Scripture has no order.   S329/L298
The heart has its order; the mind has its own, which consists of principle and demonstration. The heart has another. We do not
prove that we should be loved by displaying in order the causes of love.
That would be absurd.

———

Jesus Christ and Saint Paul use the rule of charity, not of the mind,
for they wanted to impassion, not to instruct.

The same with Saint Augustine. This order consists mainly in elabo-
rations on each point relating to the end, so as to indicate it always.

The Gospel only speaks of the Virgin's virginity up to the   S330/L299
time of Jesus Christ's birth. All with reference to Jesus Christ.

Jesus Christ is so obscure (according to what the world   S331/L300
calls obscure) that historians, writing only of important
matters of state, barely noticed him.

Holiness   S332/L301

I will pour out my spirit.[185] All nations were given to unbelief and concupiscence; the whole world became fervent with love.
Princes abandoned their greatness; maidens suffered martyrdom.
Where did this strength come from? The Messiah had come. These
were the effect and signs of his coming.

The combinations of miracles.   S333/L302

An artisan who speaks of wealth, a lawyer who speaks of   S334/L303
war, of royalty, etc. But the rich speak well of wealth, the king
speaks impersonally of a great gift he has just made, and God speaks
rightly of God.

---

[184] Pascal elaborates upon this in fragment S741.

[185] *Effundam spiritum meum.* Joel. 2:28.

Proofs of Jesus Christ   S335/L304
Why was the book of Ruth preserved?
Why the story of Tamar?

Proofs of Jesus Christ   S336/L305
Captivity, with the assurance of deliverance within seventy
years, was not real captivity. But now they are captives without any hope.

God promised them that, even though he would scatter them to the
ends of the earth, nevertheless, if they were faithful to his Law, he would
bring them together again.[186] They are very faithful to it and remain
oppressed.

Testing whether he was God, the Jews showed he was   S337/L306
man.

The Church has had as much difficulty in showing Jesus   S338/L307
Christ was man, to those who denied it, as in showing he was
God. And the semblances were equally great.

The infinite distance between bodies and minds is a   S339/L308
figure of the infinitely more infinite distance between minds
and charity, for charity is supernatural.

———

All the glory of greatness has no luster for people who are engaged in
the pursuits of the mind.

———

The greatness of intelligent men is invisible to kings, to the rich, to
leaders, to all these great men of the flesh.

———

The greatness of wisdom, which is nothing if not of God, is invisible
to carnal or intelligent men. These are three different orders. Of kind.

———

Great geniuses have their power, their splendor, their greatness, their
victory, and their luster, and do not need carnal greatness, which has no
relevance for them. They are recognized, not with the eyes, but with the
mind. This is sufficient.

———

Saints have their power, their splendor, their victory, their luster, and
do not need carnal or intellectual greatness, which have no relevance at
all for them, since they neither add nor subtract anything. They are

---

[186] Deuteronomy 28:1–13.

recognized by God and the angels, and not by bodies or curious minds. God is enough for them.

———

Archimedes, without splendor, would be given the same veneration. He fought no battles visible to the eyes, but he gave his discoveries to all minds. And how he has dazzled those minds!

———

Jesus Christ, without goods and without external show of knowledge, has his own order of holiness. He made no discoveries; he did not reign. But he was humble, patient, holy, holy, holy to God, terrible to devils, without any sin. With what great pomp and magnificent splendor did he come to the eyes of the heart, which perceive wisdom!

———

It would have been useless for Archimedes to act the prince in his books on geometry, even though he was one.

———

It would have been useless for Our Lord Jesus Christ to come as a king, in order to shine in his reign of holiness. But he truly came with the splendor of his own order.

———

It is most absurd to be shocked by Jesus Christ's lowliness, as if this lowliness were of the same order as the greatness he came to reveal.

Let us consider this greatness in his life, his passion, his obscurity, his death, his choice of disciples, their desertion, his secret resurrection, and the rest. We will see it to be so great that we would have no reason for being offended by a lowliness that is not there.

———

But there are those who can only admire carnal greatness, as if there were no such thing as intellectual greatness. And others who only admire intellectual greatness, as if there were not infinitely higher greatness in wisdom.

———

All bodies, the firmament, the stars, the earth and its kingdoms, are not worth the least of minds. For mind knows all of these, and itself, and bodies know nothing.

———

All bodies together and all minds together and all their productions are not worth the least impulse of charity. This belongs to an infinitely higher order.

From all bodies together we cannot succeed in obtaining a single small thought; this is impossible and of a different order. From all bodies and minds we cannot derive a single impulse of true charity; this is impossible and of a different, supernatural order.

Proofs of Jesus Christ   S340/L309

Jesus Christ said great things so simply that he seems not
to have thought about them, and yet so clearly that we easily see what he thought about them. This clarity joined to this simplicity is wonderful.

Proofs of Jesus Christ   S341/L310

The hypothesis that the apostles were impostors is quite
absurd. Let us follow this through. Imagine those twelve men assembled after the death of Jesus Christ, plotting to say that he has risen from the dead! They attack in this way all the powers that be. The heart of man is strangely inclined to fickleness, to change, to promises, to gains. In whatever small way one of them might have repudiated his story because of these attractions, or still more because of the fear of prisons, tortures, and death, all of them would have been lost.

Follow this thought!

It is stunning and worthy of peculiar attention to see the   S342/L311
Jewish people surviving for so many years and to see them
perpetually wretched. But it is necessary, as a proof of Jesus Christ, both that they should survive to prove him and that they should be wretched because they crucified him. And although to be wretched and to survive are contraries, yet they survive always, in spite of their wretchedness.

> *Read the prophecies.*   S343/L312
> *See what has been accomplished.*
> *Cultivate what is left to be accomplished.*[187]

Canonical   S344/L313

The heretics at the beginning of the Church serve to
prove the canonical books.

When Nebuchadnezzar led away the people, for fear they   S345/L314
should believe that the scepter had been removed from
Judah, God told them beforehand they would not be there for long: they would be there and they would be restored.[188]

---

[187] *Prodita lege. / Impleta cerne. / Implenda collige.*
[188] Jeremiah 25:8–13.

They were always consoled by the prophets; their kings continued.

But the second destruction is without promise of restoration, without prophets, without kings, without consolation, without hope, because the scepter has been taken away forever.

Moses teaches about the Trinity, original sin, the Messiah,   S346/L315
from the start.

———

David a great witness.

Good, merciful king, beautiful soul, good, powerful mind; he predicts, and his miracle comes to pass. This is infinite.[189]

———

He had only to say that he was the Messiah, if he had been vain; for the prophecies are clearer about him than about Jesus Christ.

———

And the same with Saint John.[190]

Who taught the evangelists the qualities of a perfectly   S347/L316
heroic soul such that they could depict it so perfectly in Jesus
Christ? Why do they make him weak in his agony? Do they not know how to depict a resolute death? Yes, for the same Saint Luke depicts Saint Stephen's death[191] as stronger than that of Jesus Christ.

They make him, then, capable of fear before the necessity of dying has come, and afterward altogether strong.

But when they make him so troubled, it is when he troubles himself. And when men trouble him, he is altogether strong.

The zeal of the Jews for their law and their temple.   S348/L317
Josephus and Philo Judaeus, *Ad Caium*.[192]

———

What other people had such zeal? It was necessary for them to have it.

———

---

[189] The phrase "miracle comes to pass. This is infinite." is missing from Sellier's edition, but is present in the *Recueil original*.

[190] John the Baptist.

[191] Acts 7:58–60.

[192] Philo Judaeus, *De Legatione ad Caium*, 14ff.

<Figures>

Jesus Christ foretold as to the time and state of the world. The nobleman that would be taken from his thigh,[193] and the fourth monarchy.[194]

———

How lucky we are to have this light amid this darkness!

———

How fine it is to see with the eyes of faith Darius and Cyrus, Alexander, the Romans, Pompey and Herod acting unwittingly for the glory of the Gospel!

The apparent discrepancy of the Gospels.[195] S349/L318

The synagogue preceded the church; the Jews, the S350/L319
Christians. The prophets foretold the Christians; Saint John,
Jesus Christ.

Macrobius. On the innocents killed by Herod.[196] S351/L320

Any man can do what Mahomet has done, for he S352/L321
performed no miracles; he was not foretold. No man can do
what Christ has done.

The apostles were either deceived or deceivers. Both S353/L322
alternatives are difficult, because it is not possible to accept a
man as having been raised from the dead.

———

While Jesus Christ was with them, he could sustain them. But afterward, if he did not appear to them, who made them act?

[25] Prophecies

Jews and heathens ruined by Jesus Christ: S354/L323
All nations will come and worship him.[197]
It is a light thing, etc., Isaiah.[198]

---

[193] A literal translation of Genesis 49:10: *Non auferetur sceptrum de Juda, et **dux de femore ejus***, which is given in the King James Bible as "The scepter shall not depart from Judah, nor a lawgiver from between his feet."

[194] Daniel 7:23.

[195] See the end of fragment S268.

[196] See fragment S623.

[197] *Omnes gentes venient et adorabunt eum.* Psalms 22:27.

[198] *Parum est ut*, etc. Isaiah 49:6. See fragment S254.

Ask of me.[199]
All kings will adore him.[200]
False witnesses.[201]
He gives his cheek to the one who smites him.[202]
They gave me gall for my meat.[203]

That idolatry would be overthrown then,[204] that this   S355/L324
Messiah would cast down all idols and bring men to worship
the true God.

That the temples of the idols would be cast down and that among all
nations and in all the places of the world, a pure sacrifice, not that of animals, would be offered to him.[205]

That he would teach men the perfect path.[206]   S356/L325
And there has never come, before or after him, any man
who has taught anything divine close to this.

That he would be king of the Jews and Gentiles.[207] And   S357/L324
here is this king of the Jews and Gentiles, oppressed by both
who conspire to kill him, ruling over both, and destroying the worship
of Moses in Jerusalem, its center, where he creates his first Church; and
also the worship of idols in Rome, its center, where he creates his main
Church.

And what crowns all this is prophecy, so that it should not   S358/L326
be said that it was done by chance.

Anyone with only eight days to live will not discover that the best
wager is to believe that all of this is not a stroke of chance.

Now, if the passions had no hold on us, eight days and a hundred
years would amount to the same thing.[208]

---

[199] *Postula a me.* Psalms 2:8.

[200] *Adorabunt eum omnes reges.* Psalms 72:11.

[201] *Testes iniqui.* Psalms 35:11.

[202] *Dabit maxillam percutienti.* Lamentations 3:30.

[203] *Dederunt fel in escam.* Psalms 69:21.

[204] Ezechiel 30:13.

[205] Malachi 1:11.

[206] Isaiah 2:3.

[207] Psalms 72:11.

[208] See fragments S5, S191, and S324.

After many persons had gone before, Jesus Christ at last   S359/L327
came to say: "Here am I and this is the time. What the
prophets said was to come in the fullness of time, I tell you my apostles
will accomplish. The Jews will be cast out, Jerusalem will soon be destroyed, and the heathens will enter into the knowledge of God (Celsus
laughed at this). My apostles will accomplish this after you have slain
the heir to the vineyard."[209]

And then the apostles said to the Jews: "You will be accursed." And to
the heathens: "You will enter into the knowledge of God." And then this
came to pass.

Then *they will no longer teach their neighbor, saying,*   S360/L328
"Here is the Lord," **for God will make himself known to all**.[210]

Your sons will prophesy.[211] I will put my spirit and my fear **in your
heart**.[212]

This is all the same thing.

To prophesy is to speak of God, not from external proofs, but from an
internal and **immediate** feeling.

That Jesus Christ would be small in his beginning and   S361/L329
then grow. Daniel's little stone.[213]

————

If I had never heard of the Messiah at all, nevertheless, after seeing
fulfilled such wonderful predictions of the course of the world, I should
see that this was divine. And if I knew that these same Books foretold a
Messiah, I would be sure that he should come; and seeing that they set
the time before the destruction of the second temple, I should say that
he had come.

Prophecies   S362/L330

Conversion of the Egyptians.
Isaiah (19. 19).
An altar in Egypt to the true God.

At the time of the Messiah, the people were divided.   S363/L331
Spiritual men embraced the Messiah; coarse men remained to serve as witnesses for him.

---

[209] Mark 12:6.
[210] Jeremiah 31:34.
[211] Joel 2:28.
[212] Jeremiah 32:40.
[213] Daniel 2:34–35. See the beginning of fragment S720.

Prophecies   S364/L332

If a single man had written a book predicting the time and
manner of Jesus Christ's coming, and Jesus Christ had come in conformity to these prophecies, this would carry infinite weight.

But there is much more here. There is a succession of men coming
for 4,000 years, one after the other, constantly and without variation, to
foretell this same advent. It is an entire people who proclaim it and who
survive for 4,000 years to testify as a body to their certainty of it, something from which they cannot be diverted by whatever threats and persecutions are made against them. This is of another order of
importance.

Prophecies   S365/L333

The time foretold by the state of the Jewish people, by the
state of the heathen people, by the state of the temple, by the number of
years.

Hosea 3.   S366/L334

———

Isaiah 42, 48. *I foretold it long since* so that they might know that it
was I, 54, 60, 61, last chapter.

———

Jaddus to Alexander.[214]

It takes boldness to predict the same thing in so many   S367/L336
ways. The four idolatrous or heathen monarchies, the end of
the kingdom of Judah, and the seventy weeks, all had to happen at the
same time. And all this before the second temple was destroyed.

The prophecies are the greatest proof of Jesus Christ. It is   S368/L335
also for them that God made most provision, for the event
that fulfilled them is a miracle subsisting from the birth of the Church
to the end. Thus God raised up prophets for 1,600 years, and, for 400
years afterward, scattered all these prophecies with all the Jews, who
brought them to all parts of the world. This was the preparation for the
birth of Jesus Christ. As his Gospel had to be believed by the entire
world, it was not only necessary that there be prophecies to make people
believe it, but these prophecies needed also to be throughout the whole
world to have the whole world embrace it.

---

[214] According to the Jewish historian Josephus, the High Priest Jaddus opposed Alexander
the Great, who consequently worshipped the God of the Jews.

Herod believed [himself] the Messiah. He had taken   S369/L337
away the scepter from Judah, but he was not of Judah. This
gave rise to a considerable sect.

And Bar Kochba and another accepted by the Jews. And the rumor
that was everywhere at that time.

Suetonius, Tacitus, Josephus.[215]

How was the Messiah to be, since through him the scepter was to be
eternally in Judah, and at his coming the scepter was to be taken away
from Judah?

So that in seeing they should not see and in hearing they should not
understand,[216] nothing could have been more effective.

Curse of the Greeks against those who calculate the periods of
time.[217]

Predictions   S370/L338

That in the fourth monarchy, before the destruction of
the second temple, before the Jews lost their dominion in the seventieth
week of Daniel, while the second temple continued, the heathens
would be instructed and brought to the knowledge of the God worshiped by the Jews. That those who loved him would be delivered from
their enemies and filled with his fear and love.

And it came to pass that in the fourth monarchy, before the destruction of the second temple, etc., the crowd of heathens worshiped God
and led an angelic life.

Maidens dedicate their virginity and life to God; men renounce all
pleasures. That which Plato could render acceptable only to a few
chosen men so educated, a secret influence renders acceptable to a
hundred thousand ignorant men, by virtue of a few words.

---

[215] Bar Kochba attacked Rome (from 132 to 135), was proclaimed Messiah and King, but
died in battle. This is referred to by Suetonius, *Life of Claudius*, 25; and Tacitus, *Annals*, 15.

[216] Isaiah 6:9.

[217] Pascal wrote "Greeks" by mistake. He is referring to a passage in *Pugio fidei* in which
a Rabbi prohibits the Jews from calculating the date of the Messiah's coming. The curse is
that those who calculate the periods of time should die—*Expirent ipsi qui supputant ter-
minos*. For more on the *Pugio fidei*, see fragments S308 and S309.

The rich abandon their wealth; children abandon their fathers' opulent homes for the austerity of the desert. See **Philo Judaeus.**

What is all this? It is what was foretold such a long time ago. For 2,000 years, no heathen has worshiped the God of the Jews, and at the time foretold, the crowd of heathens worships this only God, temples are destroyed, and even kings make submission to the cross. What is all this? It is the Spirit of God spreading on the earth.

No heathen believed from the time of Moses to that of Jesus Christ, according to the Rabbis themselves. The crowd of heathens after Jesus Christ believes in the books of Moses, keeps them in essence and spirit, and only rejects what is useless.

Since the prophets had given various signs that were all to   S371/L339
occur at the coming of the Messiah, all these signs had to
occur at the same time. So, the fourth monarchy had to have come when the seventy weeks of Daniel ended, and the scepter had then to be removed from Judah. And all this occurred without any difficulty. And then the Messiah had to come. And then Jesus Christ came, calling himself the Messiah. And all this again was without difficulty. And this shows clearly the truth of the prophecies.

We have no king but Caesar.[218] Therefore Jesus Christ was   S372/L340
the Messiah, since they had no longer any king but a
stranger, and they did not want any other.

Prophecies   S373/L341

The seventy weeks of Daniel are ambiguous in regard to
when they begin, because of the terms of the prophecy, and in regard to when they end, because of the differences among chronologists. But all this difference only amounts to 200 years.

Prophecies   S374/L342

The scepter was not interrupted by the captivity in Babylon, because the return was prompt and foretold.[219]

Prophecies   S375/L343

The great Pan is dead.[220]

What can we have except reverence for a man who   S376/L344
foretells clearly things that come to pass, who declares his in-
tention both to blind and to enlighten, and who mixes in obscurities among the clear things that come to pass?

---

[218] *Non habemus regem nisi Caesarem.* John 19:15.

[219] See fragment S345.

[220] Plutarch, *De defectu*, 17.

It is a light thing.[221] Isaiah. Vocation of the Gentiles.   S377/L345

Predictions   S378/L346

It was foretold that, in the time of the Messiah, he would come to establish a new covenant that would make them forget the exodus from Egypt—Jeremiah 23:5, Isaiah 43:16—that would put his law not in externals, but in the heart; that he would put his fear, which had only been on the outside, in the middle of the heart. Who does not see the Christian law in all this?

Prophecies   S379/L347

That the Jews would reject Jesus Christ and that they would be rejected of God for that reason. That the chosen vine would bring forth only sour grapes.[222] That the chosen people would be unfaithful, ungrateful, and unbelieving, *populum non credentem et contradicentem.*[223]

28:28: That God would strike them with blindness, and they would grope at high noon like blind men.[224]

And that a forerunner would come before him.[225]

The eternal reign of David's race: II Chronicles [7:18]. By   S380/L348
all the prophecies, and with an oath. And is not fulfilled temporally. Jeremiah 33:20.

[26] Particular Figures

Particular Figures   S381/L349

A double law, double tables of the law, a double temple, a double captivity.

<Japhet begins the genealogy.>   S382/L350

———

Joseph crosses his arms, and prefers the younger.[226]

---

[221] *Parum est ut.* Isaiah 49:6. See fragment S254.

[222] Isaiah 5:1–7. The King James Bible says "wild grapes."

[223] Romans 10:21. Pascal repeats the description in Latin for emphasis; the King James Bible has it as "a disobedient and gainsaying people."

[224] Deuteronomy 28:28.

[225] Malachi 3:1.

[226] Genesis 48:13–14. Pascal wrote Joseph by mistake; the blessing is by Jacob. Pascal translates the text in fragment S719.

[27] Christian Morality

Christianity is strange. It requires man to recognize that   S383/L351
he is vile, and even abominable, and requires him to want to
be like God. Without such a counterweight, this elevation would make
him horribly vain, or this abasement would make him horribly abject.

Wretchedness provokes despair.   S384/L352
Pride provokes presumption.
The Incarnation shows man the greatness of his wretchedness
through the greatness of the remedy that was required.

Not an abasement that makes us incapable of good, nor a   S385/L353
holiness exempt from evil.

There is no doctrine more appropriate to man than the   S386/L354
one that teaches him his double capacity for receiving and
losing grace, because of the double peril to which he is always exposed,
of despair or pride.

Of all that is on earth, he partakes only of the pains, not of   S387/L355
the pleasures. He loves his neighbors, but his charity does
not keep itself within these bounds and extends to his enemies, and
then to those of God.

What difference is there between a soldier and a   S388/L356
Carthusian monk with respect to obedience? For both are
equally obedient and dependent and engaged in equally painful exercises. But the soldier always hopes to become a master and never does,
for even captains and princes are always slaves and dependents; still he
always hopes for it and strives to attain it. Instead, the Carthusian monk
vows never to be anything but dependent. So, they do not differ in their
perpetual servitude, which they both possess, but in the hope the one always has and the other never has.

No one is happy like a true Christian, or so reasonable, or   S389/L357
virtuous, or loveable.

With how little pride does a Christian believe himself   S390/L358
united to God! With how little abjection does he make
himself equal to earthworms! A fine way to receive life and death, good
and evil!

The examples of the unselfish deaths of Lacedaemonians   S391/L359
and others scarcely touch us. For what does this matter to us?

But the example of the death of martyrs touches us, for they are our
members. We have a common bond with them. Their resolution can inform ours, not only by example, but because it has perhaps deserved ours.

There is nothing of this in the examples of the heathens. We have no bond with them. As we do not become rich by seeing a stranger who is rich, but by seeing our father or husband who is so.

Morality S392/L360

Since God made the heavens and the earth, which do not feel the happiness of their existence, he wanted to make beings who would understand it and compose a body of thinking members. For our members do not feel the happiness of their union, of their wonderful arrangement (*intelligence*), of the care taken by nature to infuse them with spirits and to make them grow and endure. How happy they would be if they felt this, if they saw it! But they would need to have intelligence to know it and good will to consent to that of the universal soul. But if, having received intelligence, they used it to retain nourishment for themselves without allowing it to proceed to the other members, they would not only be wrong, but wretched, and would hate themselves rather than love themselves, since their blessedness, as well as their duty, consists in consenting to the conduct of the whole soul to which they belong, which loves them better than they love themselves.

Are you less a slave for being loved and favored by your   S393/L361
master? You are indeed well off, slave; your master favors you. He will soon beat you.

The will itself can never be satisfied, even if it had power   S394/L362
over everything it wanted. But we are satisfied the moment we give it up. Without it we cannot be discontented; with it we cannot be content.

They let concupiscence act freely and rein in scruples,   S395/L363
whereas they should do the contrary.

It is superstitious to put one's hope in formalities, but it is   S396/L364
arrogant to be unwilling to submit to them.

Experience shows us an enormous difference between   S397/L365
religious devotion and goodness.

Two kinds of men in each religion S398/L366
See Perpetuity

Superstition, concupiscence.   S399/L366

Not at all formalists S400/L367

When Saint Peter and the apostles deliberated about abolishing circumcision, where it was a question of going against God's law, they did not look to the prophets, but simply to the reception of the Holy Spirit in the person of the uncircumcised.

They judged it more certain that God approves of those he fills with his Spirit, rather than that the law must be obeyed.

———

They knew that the intent of the Law was only the Holy Spirit, and that thus, since it was certainly received without circumcision, circumcision was not **necessary**.[227]

Members   S401/L368
Begin with this

To regulate the love we owe to ourselves, we must imagine a body full of thinking members, for we are members of the whole, and must see how each member should love itself, etc.

———

Republic   S401/L369

The Christian, and even the Jewish, republic has had only God for ruler, as Philo Judaeus notes, *On Monarchy*.

When they fought, it was only for God, and their main hope was in God alone; they considered their towns as belonging to God alone and maintained them for God. I Chronicles 19. 13.

To make the members happy, they must have one will and   S402/L370
have it conform to the body.

Let us imagine a body full of thinking members!   S403/L371

To be a member is to have life, existence, and motion   S404/L372
only for the body and through the spirit of the body. The separated member, no longer seeing the body to which it belongs, has only a perishing and moribund existence. Yet it believes itself a whole, and, not seeing the body on which it depends, it believes it depends only on itself and wants to make itself its own center and body. But not having in itself any principle of life, it only goes astray and becomes astonished at the uncertainty of its existence, properly aware that it is not a body, and still not seeing that it is a member of a body. In the end, when it comes to know itself, it is as if it has returned home and no longer loves itself except for the body. It deplores its past wanderings.

It cannot by its nature love another thing except for itself and to subject it to itself, because each thing loves itself more than anything else.

---

[227] Acts 15.

But, in loving the body, it loves itself, because it only exists in it, through it, and for it. *He who adheres to God is one spirit.*[228]

The body loves the hand, and, if it had a will, the hand would love itself in the same way as the soul loves it. All love that goes further is wrong.

Adhering to God is one spirit.[229] We love ourselves because we are members of Jesus Christ. We love Jesus Christ because he is the body of which we are members. All is one. One is in the other. Like the Three Persons [of the Trinity].

We must love only God and hate only ourselves.   S405/L373

If the foot had never known that it belonged to the body and that there was a body on which it depended, if it had only known and loved itself, and if it came to know that it belonged to a body on which it depended, what regret, what shame it would feel for its past life, for having been useless to the body that infused it with life, a body that would have annihilated it if it had rejected it and separated itself, as the foot separated itself from the body! What prayers would be said so that it might be kept! And with what submission it would allow itself to be governed by the will that rules the body, to the point of consenting to be lopped off, if necessary. Otherwise it would lose its status as member. For every member must be quite willing to perish for the body, for which alone everything exists.

If the feet and hands had a will of their own, they would   S406/L374
never be in their order except by submitting this particular
will to the primary will governing the whole body. Outside of this, they are in disorder and misfortune. But in wanting only the good of the body, they accomplish their own good.

Philosophers have consecrated the vices by placing them   S407/L375
in God himself. Christians have consecrated the virtues.

Two laws suffice to rule the whole Christian Republic   S408/L376
better than all political laws.[230]

---

[228] *Qui adhaeret Deo unus spiritus est.* I Corinthians 6:17.

[229] *Adhaerens Deo unus spiritus est.* Ibid.

[230] That is, to love God and one's neighbor. Matthew 22:35.

[28] Conclusion

How far it is from the knowledge of God to the love of   S409/L377
him.

"If I had seen a miracle," they say, "I would be converted."   S410/L378
How can they be sure they would do that of which they are
ignorant? They imagine that this conversion consists in a worship of
God like some communion and conversation they represent to themselves. True conversion consists in self-annihilation before that universal Being whom we have so often irritated and who can legitimately
destroy us at any time, in recognizing that we can do nothing without
him and have deserved nothing from him but his disfavor. It consists in
knowing there is an insurmountable opposition between God and us,
and that without a mediator there can be no communion with him.

Miracles do not serve to convert, but to condemn. Part I,   S411/L379
quest. 113, art. 10, ad 2.[231]

Do not be surprised to see simple people believe without   S412/L380
reasoning about it: God makes them love him and hate
themselves; he inclines their heart to believe. We will never believe
with an effective belief based on faith unless God inclines our heart.
And we will believe as soon as he inclines it.

And this is what David understood well. *Incline my heart, O Lord,
unto,* etc.[232]

Those who believe without having read the Testaments   S413/L381
do so because they have an entirely holy inward disposition
and what they hear about our religion resonates with it. They feel that a
God has created them. They want to love only God; they want to hate
only themselves. They feel they do not have this power in themselves,
that they are incapable of going to God, and that if God does not come
to them, they are incapable of any communication with him. And they
hear it said in our religion that we must love only God and hate only
ourselves, but that, as we are all corrupt and incapable of God, God
made himself man to unite himself with us. Nothing more is needed to
convince men who have this disposition in their heart and who have
this knowledge of their duty and their incapacity.

---

[231] Thomas Aquinas, *Summa Theologica.*
[232] *Inclina cor meum, Deus, in.* Psalms 119:36.

Knowledge of God   S414/L382

Those we see to be Christians without knowledge of the
prophecies and proofs judge as well as those who have that knowledge.
They judge with the heart as others judge with the mind. God himself
inclines them to believe, and thus they are most effectively convinced.

<Someone might reply that unbelievers would say the same thing.
But my answer to that is that we have proofs that God truly inclines
those he loves to believe the Christian religion, and that unbelievers
have no proof at all of what they say. And so, although our propositions
are similar as to their terms, they differ in that the one lacks proof and
the other is very soundly proved.>

I freely admit that one of those Christians who believe without proofs
will perhaps not be capable of convincing an unbeliever who might say
the same about himself. But those who know the proofs of religion can
prove without difficulty that this believer is truly inspired by God, even
though he cannot prove it himself.

For, since God said in his prophecies (which are undoubtedly
prophetic) that in the reign of Jesus Christ he would spread his spirit
among the nations, and that the sons, daughters, and children of the
Church would prophesy;[233] it is certain that God's spirit is in them and
not in the others.

---

[233] Joel 2:28.

[II. FOLDERS SET ASIDE JUNE 1658]

[29] Against the Fable of Esdras

Against the fable of Esdras[1]

S415/L971

2 Maccabees, 2.

Josephus, *Antiquities*, 2. 1. Cyrus released the people on account of Isaiah's prophecy.

The Jews peacefully held possessions in Babylon under Cyrus. Hence they could well have had the law.

In the entire story of Esdras, Josephus does not say one word about this restoration. 4 Kings, 17:27.

If the fable of Esdras is believable, then we must believe   S416/L972
that Scripture is Holy Scripture, for this fable is based only
on the authority of those who tell that of the Seventy, which shows that Scripture is holy.[2]

Therefore, if this tale is true, we have our account; if not, we have it from elsewhere. Thus those who would like to destroy the truth of our religion, based on Moses, establish it with the same authority with which they attack it. So, through this providence it still subsists.

On Esdras

S417/L970

Fable: the books were burned with the temple. Shown
false by Maccabees: **Jeremiah gave them the law**.

Fable: that he recited all of it by heart.

Josephus and Esdras point out **that he read the book**.[3]

------

[1] The *Fourth Book of Esdras*, an apocryphal work, says that the Scriptures were burned during the exile and that Esdras reconstituted them under God's direction. Such a story would undermine the authority of the Scriptures; so Pascal is interested in showing the fable false.

[2] The Seventy (*Les Septante*) are said to have translated the Bible into Greek circa 3rd century BC.

[3] Nehemiah 8:3; Josephus, *Antiquities*, 11:5.

Baronius, *Annales* [year] 180: *Among the ancient Hebrews none can be found who maintains that the Books were destroyed and restored by Esdras, except in* Esdras IV.[4]

Fable: that he changed the letters.

Philo, in his *Life of Moses: The language and characters in which the Law was previously written remained so until the Seventy.*[5] Josephus says that the Law was in Hebrew when the Seventy translated it.

———

Under Antiochus and Vespasian, when they wanted to abolish the Books and when there was no prophet, it could not be done. And under the Babylonians, when no persecution took place and when there were so many prophets, would they have let them be burned?

———

Josephus ridicules the Greeks who would not suffer . . .

Tertullian: *He could equally have restored it from memory*   S418/L970
after it had been destroyed by the violence of the cataclysm,
just as every document of Jewish literature is generally agreed to have been restored by Esdras after the destruction of Jerusalem by the Babylonian attack. Tertullian, *De cultu feminarum*, book I, chap. 3.[6]

He says that Noah could as easily have reconstructed from memory the book of Enoch, lost in the Flood, as Esdras could have reconstructed the Scriptures lost during the captivity.

The Scriptures were destroyed when the people were the captives of Nebuchadnezzar; after seventy years the Jews returned to their country, and later, in the time of Artaxerxes, king of the Persians, Esdras, priest of the tribe of Levi, was inspired to reconstruct all the sayings of the previous prophets and to restore to the people the law once given by Moses.[7]

He claims this to prove that it is not incredible that the Seventy could have explained the Holy Scriptures with that uniformity we admire in

---

[4] *Nullus penitus Hebraeorum antiquorum reperitur qui tradiderit libros periisse et per Esdram esse restitutos, nisi in IV Esdras.*

[5] **Vita Mosis** [II]: *Illa lingua ac character quo antiquitus scripta est lex sic permansit usque ad LXX.*

[6] *Perinde potuit abolefactam eam violentia cataclysmi in spiritu rursus reformare, quemadmodum et Hierosolymis Babylonia expugnatione deletis, omne instrumentum Judaicae literaturae per Esdram constat restauratum. De cultu feminarum, I. 3.*

[7] *Theos en te epi Nabouchodonosor aichmalosia tou laou, diaphthareison ton Graphon, enepneuse 'Esdra to ierei, ek tes phules Leui tous ton progegonoton propheton pantas anataxasthai logous, kai apokatastesai to lae ten dia Mouseos nomothesian.*

them. Eusebius, *Hist.*, book 5, chap. 8. And he took this from Saint Irenaeus, book 3, chap. 25.

Saint Hilary, in his preface to the Psalms, says that Esdras put the Psalms in order.

The origin of this tradition comes from the fourteenth chapter of the fourth book of Esdras.

―――

God was glorified, and the true divine Scriptures were recognized, all of them reciting the same things in the same words and same phrases, from beginning to end, so that even the people today understood that the Scriptures had been interpreted through God's inspiration. And it is not surprising that God accomplished this through them, for the Scriptures were destroyed when the people were the captives of Nebuchadnezzar; after seventy years the Jews returned to their country, and later, in the time of Artaxerxes, king of the Persians, Esdras, priest of the tribe of Levi, was inspired to reconstruct all the sayings of the previous prophets and to re-store to the people the law once given by Moses.[8]

[30] Miracles [1]

The points about which I have to ask the Abbé de Saint-   S419/L830
Cyran[9] are mainly these. But, since I have no copy of them,
he will need to take the trouble of sending back this paper with the an-swers he is kind enough to provide.

1. Whether it is necessary, for an effect to be miraculous, that it should be beyond the powers of men, devils, angels, and all created nature?

Theologians say that miracles are either supernatural in substance, quoad substantiam, *as in the interpenetration of two bodies or when a single body is in two places at the same time; or supernatural in the man-ner of their production,* quoad modum, *as when they are produced by*

―――――――――――――――――――――――――――――――――

[8] *Deus glorificatus est, et Scripturae vere divinae creditae sunt, omnibus eandem et eisdem verbis et eisdem nominibus recitantibus ab initio usque ad finem, uti et praesentes gentes cognoscerent quoniam per inspirationem Dei interpretatae sunt Scripturae, et non esset mirabile Deum hoc in eis operatum: quando in ea captivitate populi quae facta est a Nabu-chodonosor, corruptis scripturis et post 70 annos Judaeis descendentibus in regionem suam, et post deinde temporibus Artaxerxis Persarum regis, inspiravit Esdrae sacerdoti tribus Levi praeteritorum prophetarum omnes rememorare sermones, et restituere populo eam legem quae data est per Moysen.* Eusebius, *Ecclesiastical History*, V. viii. 14. This is Pascal's ren-dering into Latin of the passage from Eusebius of which the last lines are in Greek, above.

[9] Martin de Barcos (1600–1678), nephew and successor to Jean Duvergier de Hauranne at the Abbey of Saint-Cyran. The replies of Barcos are in italics.

means not naturally capable of producing them: as when Jesus Christ healed the eyes of the blind man with mud and Saint Peter's mother-in-law by bending over her, and the woman afflicted with bleeding through her touching the hem of his robe. And most of the miracles he performed in the Gospels are of this latter kind. So too is the curing of a fever or some other illness either instantaneously or more completely than nature can bear, through touching a relic or the invocation of God's name. Thus the view of the person proposing these difficulties is right and in conformity with that of all theologians, even those of the present day.

2. Whether it is not sufficient for it to be beyond the natural powers of the means employed? My view is that any effect is miraculous when it exceeds the natural power of the means employed. Thus I call it miraculous when an illness is cured by touching a sacred relic, when a man possessed is cured by invoking the name of Jesus, etc., because these effects exceed the natural powers of the words by which we invoke God and the natural powers of a relic that cannot heal the sick or drive out devils. But I do not call driving out devils by the devil's art a miracle, for in using the power of the devil to drive out the devil, the effect does not exceed the natural power of the means employed. And thus it seemed to me that the true definition of miracles is the one I have just given.

What the devil is able to do is not a miracle, any more than what an animal is able to do, even though man cannot do it himself.

3. Whether Saint Thomas is not opposed to this definition, and is of the opinion that for an effect to be miraculous it must exceed the powers of all created nature?

Saint Thomas holds the same opinion as the others, although he divides the second kind of miracles into two categories: namely, into miracles quoad subjectum *and miracles* quoad ordinem naturae.[10] *He says that the former are those nature can produce absolutely, but not in a given subject, as when it can produce life, but not in a dead body; and that the latter are those it can produce in a given subject, but not by such means, or so promptly, etc., as when it can cure a fever or other illness—which is not actually incurable—in a moment and through a single touch.[11]*

4. Whether declared and known heretics can perform true miracles to confirm an error?

5. Whether known and declared heretics can perform such miracles as curing illnesses that are not actually incurable; whether, for example,

---

[10] *Quoad subjectum* means "as regards their subject," and *quoad ordinem naturae* means "as regards the order of nature."

[11] See Thomas Aquinas, *Summa Theologiae* I, quest. 105, art. 8.

they can cure a fever to confirm an erroneous proposition, as Father Lingendes preaches that they can.[12]

True miracles can never be performed by anyone, Catholic or heretic, holy or wicked, to confirm an error, because God would be giving his stamp of his approbation and affirmation on that error in the fashion of a false witness, or, rather, a false judge. This is certain and constant.

6. Whether declared and known heretics can perform miracles that are beyond all created nature by invoking the name of God or through a sacred relic?

They can do so to confirm a truth, and there are many examples of this throughout history.

7. Whether covert heretics—who, while not separated from the Church, yet remain in error, and do not declare themselves against the Church, so as to induce the faithful more easily into error and strengthen their side—can perform miracles going beyond the whole of nature by invoking the name of Jesus or through a sacred relic; or even whether they can perform things that merely go beyond human [powers], like the immediate cure of illnesses that are not incurable?

Covert heretics have no more power over miracles than do declared ones, since nothing is covert to God, who is the sole author and worker of miracles, whatever they are, provided they are true miracles.

8. Whether miracles performed by the name of God and through the intermediary of divine things are not the marks of the true Church, and whether all Catholics have not affirmed this against all heretics?

All Catholics agree about this, especially Jesuit authors. One has only to read Bellarmine.[13] Even when heretics have performed miracles, which has happened occasionally though rarely, these miracles were marks of the Church, because they were performed only to confirm the truth taught by the Church and not the error of the heretics.

9. Whether it has ever happened that heretics performed miracles, and of what kind are those they performed?

There are very few attested cases, but those spoken of are miraculous only quoad modum; *that is to say, natural effects produced miraculously in a manner that goes beyond the order of nature.*

10. Whether the man in the Gospel[14] who drove out devils in the name of Jesus Christ, and of whom Jesus Christ said *he who is not*

---

[12] Father Lingendes, a Jesuit, in a sermon preached at Saint-Merri on February 21, 1657, had related the miracle of the Holy Thorn to those produced by magicians and heretics.

[13] Cardinal Robert Bellarmine (1542–1621), noted Jesuit polemicist.

[14] Mark 9:38–40.

against you is for you, was the friend or enemy of Jesus Christ; and what do the interpreters of the Gospel say about it? I ask this because Father Lingendes preached that this man was opposed to Jesus Christ.

The Gospel sufficiently attests that he was not opposed to Jesus Christ, and the Fathers and nearly all the Jesuit authors maintain this.

11. Whether the Antichrist will accomplish his works in the name of Jesus Christ or in his own name?

Since, according to the Gospel, he will not come in the name of Jesus Christ, but in his own name, he will perform no miracles in the name of Jesus Christ, but in his own and against Jesus Christ, to destroy the faith and his Church. For this reason they will not be true miracles.

12. Whether the oracles were miraculous?

Miracles of the heathens and idols were no more miraculous than the other works of devils and magicians.

The second miracle can suppose the first; the first cannot   S420/L831
suppose the second.

[31] Miracles [2]

5. Miracles.   S421/L832
                          Beginning
Miracles set apart doctrine, and doctrine sets apart miracles.

———

There are false ones and true ones. There must be some sign for them to be recognized; otherwise they would be useless.

But they are not useless and are, on the contrary, fundamental.

But the rule we are given must be such that it does not destroy the proof that the true miracles give of the truth, which is the principal purpose of miracles.

———

Moses has given two rules: that the prophecy does not come to pass (Deuteronomy 18), and that miracles do not lead to idolatry (Deuteronomy 13). And Jesus Christ [gave] one.

———

If doctrine determines miracles, miracles are useless for doctrine.
If miracles determine . . .
                    Objection to the rule
Distinction of the times; one rule during the time of Moses, another rule now.

———

Any religion is false that, in its faith, does not worship one   S421/L833
God as the principle of all things and that, in its morals, does
not love one single God as the object of all things.

Reason why we do not believe   S422/L834

John 12:37:

*But though he had done so many miracles before them, yet they did
not believe in him: that the saying of Isaiah the prophet might be fulfilled. . . . He has blinded their eyes,*[15] *etc.*

Isaiah said these things when he saw his glory and spoke of him.[16]

———

For the Jews require a sign, and the Greeks seek after wisdom.
We preach Christ crucified.
But full of signs, but full of wisdom.
*You, however, preach a Christ not crucified and a religion without
miracles and without wisdom.*[17]

———

The reason we do not believe in true miracles is lack of charity. John:
But you do not believe, because you are not of my sheep.[18]
The reason we believe the false is lack of charity.
2 Thessalonians 2.

Foundation of religion

It is miracles. What then? Does God speak against miracles, against
the foundations of the faith we have in him?

———

If there is a God, faith in God must exist on earth. Now Jesus Christ's
miracles are not foretold by the Antichrist, but the Antichrist's miracles
are foretold by Jesus Christ. And so, if Jesus Christ were not the Messiah, he would have indeed led people into error. But the Antichrist can
certainly not lead people into error.

When Jesus Christ foretold the miracles of the Antichrist, did he
think he was destroying faith in his own miracles?

---

[15] *Cum autem tanta signa fecisset, non credebant in eum, ut sermo Isayae impleretur. Ex-
caecavit.*

[16] *Haec dixit Isaias, quando vidit gloriam ejus et locutus est de eo.* John 12:41.

[17] *Judaei signa petunt et Graeci sapientiam quaerunt, nos autem Jesum crucifixum.* I
Corithians 1:22, 23. *Sed plenum signis, sed plenum sapientia; vos autem Christum non
crucifixum et religionem sine miraculis et sine sapientia.*

[18] *Sed vos non creditis, quia non estis ex ovibus.* 10:26

There is no reason for believing in the Antichrist that is not a reason for believing in Jesus Christ. But there are reasons for believing in Jesus Christ that are not reasons for believing in the other.

Moses foretold Jesus Christ and bade people to follow him. Jesus Christ foretold the Antichrist and forbade people to follow him.

It was impossible in the time of Moses for people to keep faith in the Antichrist, who was unknown to them. But it is quite easy, in the time of the Antichrist, to believe in Jesus Christ, who is already known.

The prophecies, the very miracles and proofs of our   S423/L835
religion, are not of such a nature that it can be said that they
are absolutely convincing; but they are also of such a kind that it cannot be said that it is unreasonable to believe them. Thus there is both evidence and obscurity, to enlighten some and to confuse others. But the evidence is such that it exceeds, or at least equals, the evidence to the contrary, so that reason cannot persuade us not to follow it, and thus it can only be concupiscence and malice of heart. And in this way there is enough evidence to condemn, and not enough to convince; and it seem that those who follow it are motivated by grace and not reason, and that those who shun it are motivated by concupiscence and not reason.

––––––

True *disciples; an Israelite* **indeed**; *free indeed;* **true bread**.[19]

––––––

I assume that miracles are believed.

––––––

You corrupt religion either in favor of your friends or   S423/L836
against your enemies. You deal with it at your whim.

If there were no false miracles, there would be certainty.   S424/L837
If there were no rule for determining them, miracles
would be useless and there would be no reason to believe.

But there is, humanly speaking, no human certainty, only reason.

––––––

The Jews, who were called to subdue nations and kings,   S424/L838
have been the slaves of sin. And the Christians, whose calling has been to serve and be subjects, are free children.

––––––

---

[19] *Vere discipuli, vere Israelita, vere liberi, vere cibus.* Allusion to John 6:56, 1:47, 8:36, 6:32.

Judges 13:23: *If the Lord were pleased to kill us, he would not have showed us all these things.*   S424/L839

———

Hezekiah, Sennacherib.[20]

———

Jeremiah. Hananiah, the false prophet, dies in the seventh month.[21]

———

2 Maccabees 3. The temple, ready for pillage, miraculously saved. 2 Maccabees 15.

———

3 Kings 17. The widow to Elijah, who had revived her son: *By this I know that your words are true.*

———

III Kings 18. Elijah with the prophets of Baal.

———

Never, in the dispute concerning the true God and the truth of religion, has any miracle happened to support error, and not truth.

This is not the country of truth. It wanders unknown   S425/L840
among men. God has covered it with a veil, which leaves it unrecognized by those who do not hear its voice. The place is open for blasphemy, even against the truths that are at least very apparent. If the truths of the Gospel are proclaimed, the opposite is proclaimed too, and questions are obscured, so that the people cannot distinguish among them. And they ask, "What do you have to make you believed rather than others? What sign do you give? You have only words, and so have we. If you had miracles, that would be good." It is a truth that doctrine ought to be supported by miracles, one they misuse in order to blaspheme against doctrine. And if miracles happen, it is said that miracles are not enough without doctrine. And this is another truth they misuse in order to blaspheme against miracles.

———

Jesus Christ cured the man born blind and performed a number of miracles on the Sabbath day; in this way he blinded the Pharisees, who said that miracles must be judged by doctrine.

---

[20] 2 Kings 19.
[21] Jeremiah 28:14–17.

We have Moses, but this one, we do not know where he comes from.
What is remarkable is that you do not know where he comes from, and
yet he performs such miracles.[22]

Jesus Christ spoke neither against God, nor against Moses.

The Antichrist and the false prophets, foretold by both *Testaments*, will speak openly against God and against Jesus Christ.

Who is not against, who would be a covert enemy, God would not allow him to perform miracles openly.

Never, in a public dispute where the two parties profess to be for God, for Jesus Christ, for the Church, have miracles been on the side of the false Christians, and the other side left without a miracle.

He has a devil. John 10:21. And others said, *Can the devil open the eyes of the blind?*

The proofs that Jesus Christ and the apostles derive from Scripture are not demonstrative; for they say only that Moses foretold that a prophet would come, but they do not thereby prove that he is the one; and that is the whole question. These passages, therefore, serve only to show that they are not contrary to Scripture and that there appears no inconsistency, but not that there is agreement. Now this is enough: the exclusion of inconsistency together with miracles.

Jesus Christ says that the Scriptures bear witness to him.   S426/L841
But he does not show in what respect.[23]

Even the prophecies could not prove Jesus Christ during his life. And so people would not have been guilty for not believing in him before his death if miracles were not sufficient without doctrine. But those who did not believe in him when he was still alive were sinners, as he himself said, and without excuse. Therefore they must have had a demonstration that they resisted. They did not have Scripture, but only miracles. Therefore miracles suffice, when the doctrine is not contrary. And they must be believed.

-----

[22] John 9:29–30.
[23] John 5:39.

John 7:40. Dispute among Jews as among today's Christians.

Some believed in Jesus Christ; others did not believe in him because of the prophecies that said he should be born in Bethlehem. They should have considered more carefully whether he was not from there. For, as his miracles were convincing, they should have been quite sure of these supposed contradictions of his teaching with Scripture. And this obscurity did not excuse, but blinded them. Thus those who refuse to believe in present-day miracles on account of a supposed chimerical contradiction are not excused.

The Pharisees said to the people who believed in him because of his miracles: *This people, who does not know the law, is cursed. But have any of the rulers or of the Pharisees believed in him? For we know that no prophet arises out of Galilee. Nicodemus answered: Does our law judge any man before it has heard him?*

Our religion is wise and foolish. Wise, because it is the   S427/L842
most learned and the most based on miracles, prophecies,
etc. Foolish, because it is not all this that makes us belong to it. This, indeed, is sufficient to condemn those who do not belong to it, but not to make those who belong to it believe. What makes them believe is the cross, *Lest the cross be made of no effect.*[24]

And so Saint Paul, who came with wisdom and signs, said that he came neither with wisdom nor with signs: for he came to convert. But those who come only to convince can say that they come with wisdom and with signs.

There is a great difference between not being for Jesus   S427/L843
Christ and saying so, and not being for Jesus Christ but pre-
tending to be so. The former can perform miracles, not the latter. For it is clear of the former that they are opposed to the truth, but not of the latter; and thus miracles are clearer.

That we must love only one God is a thing so evident that   S427/L844
it does not need miracles to prove it.

---

[24] *Ne evacuata sit crux.* I Corithians 1:17.

The Church is in an excellent state when it is no longer   S427/L845
sustained by anything but God.

There is a reciprocal duty between God and men. We   S428/L840
must pardon this saying: *What could I have done?*[25] *Accuse
me*, said God in Isaiah.[26]

God must fulfill his promises, etc.

Men owe it to God to accept the religion he sends to them.

God owes it to men not to lead them into error.

But they would be led into error if the makers of miracles proclaimed
a doctrine that should not appear evidently false to the light of common
sense, and if a greater maker of miracles had not already cautioned
against believing them.

Thus, if there was a split in the Church, and the Arians,[27] for example, who declared themselves based on Scripture, like the Catholics,
had performed miracles, and the Catholics had not, people would have
been led into error.

―――

For as a man who announces to us God's secrets is not worthy to be
believed on his private authority, and that is why the impious doubt
him, so a man who, as a token of the communion he has with God,
raises the dead, foretells the future, parts the seas, heals the sick; there is
none so impious as not to bow down to him, and the incredulity of
Pharaoh and the Pharisees is the effect of a supernatural obstinacy.

―――

When, therefore, we see miracles and a doctrine above suspicion, altogether on one side, there is no difficulty. But when we see miracles
and a suspect doctrine on the same side, we must see then which is the
clearest. Jesus Christ was suspect.

―――

Bar-jesus blinded.[28] The power of God surpasses that of his enemies.

―――

The Jewish exorcists beaten by the devils, saying: *Jesus I know, and
Paul I know, but who are you?*[29]

---

[25] *Quid debui?* Isaiah 5:4; more fully: *Quis est quod debui ultra facere vineae meae, et non
faci ei?*

[26] Isaiah 1:18.

[27] Arians are the fourth-century heretic followers of Arius.

[28] Acts 13:11.

[29] Acts 19:13–16.

———

Miracles are for doctrine, and not doctrine for miracles.

———

If the miracles are true, can any doctrine persuade? No, for this will not come to pass. *But though an angel.*[30]

Rule

We must judge of doctrine by miracles. We must judge of miracles by doctrine. All this is true, and it does not contradict itself.

———

For we must distinguish the times.

———

How glad you are to know the general rules, thinking in this way to set up dissension and render everything useless. We shall prevent you, my father.[31] The truth is one and constant.

———

It is impossible, because of God's duty, that a man, hiding his evil doctrine and showing only a good one, saying that he conforms to God and to the Church, should perform miracles so as to instill insensibly a false and subtle doctrine. This cannot happen.

———

And still less that God, who knows the heart, should perform miracles in favor of such a person.

Jesus Christ has proved that he was the Messiah, never by   S429/L846 confirming his doctrine through Scripture or prophecies, but always through his miracles.

———

He proves by a miracle that he remits sins.[32]

Do not rejoice in your miracles, said Jesus Christ, *but because your names are written in heaven.*[33]

———

---

[30] *Si angelus.* Galatians 1:8.

[31] Pascal is most probably addressing Father Annat, Jesuit king's confessor and presumed author of *Rabat-joie des jansénistes* (August 1656).

[32] Mark 2:10–11.

[33] Luke 10:20.

If they do not believe Moses, they will not believe one raised from the dead.[34]

Nicodemus recognized by his miracles that his teaching was of God. *We know that you are a teacher who comes from God; for no man can perform these miracles that you do, unless God is with him.*[35] He does not judge miracles by doctrine, but doctrine by miracles.

The Jews had a doctrine of God as we have one of Jesus Christ: it was confirmed by miracles; they were forbidden to believe every maker of miracles; and they were further commanded to have recourse to the chief priests and to follow them. And thus, all those reasons we have for refusing to believe the makers of miracles, they had in regard to their prophets. And yet they were very culpable in rejecting the prophets because of their miracles, and Jesus Christ also; and they would not have been culpable, if they had not seen the miracles. *If I had not done, they would not have sinned.*[36] Therefore all belief rests on miracles.

Prophecy is not called miracle. As Saint Jehan speaks of the first miracle in Cana and then of what Jesus Christ says to the woman of Samaria, when he reveals to her all her hidden life, and then of how he heals the nobleman's son. And Saint Jehan calls this *the second sign.*[37]

By showing the truth, we cause it to be believed. But by showing the injustice of ministers, we do not correct it. Our thought is made secure by showing falsehood; our purse is not made secure by showing injustice.   S430/L847

Miracles and truth are necessary, because we must convince the whole man, in body and in soul.   S430/L848

Charity is not a figurative precept. It is dreadful to say that Jesus Christ, who came to replace figures in order to set up   S430/L849

---

[34] Luke 16:31.

[35] *Scimus quia venisti a Deo magister; nemo enim potest haec signa facere quae tu facis nisi Deus fuerit cum eo.* John 3:2.

[36] *Nisi fecissem, peccatum non haberent.* John 15:24

[37] John 2:11, 4:17–19, 4:54. Jehan is an old form of John.

the truth, came only to set up the figure of charity, in order to take away the existing reality that was there before.

If the light is darkness, what will the darkness be![38]

There is a great difference between tempting and leading   S431/L850 into error. God tempts, but he does not lead into error. To tempt is to provide opportunities to do certain things, if we not love God, which impose no necessity. To lead into error is to place a man under the necessity of inferring and following a falsehood.

Are you the Christ? Tell us.[39]   S432/L851
The works I do in my father's name,[40]
They bear witness of me.[41]
But you do not believe, because you are not of my sheep.[42]
My sheep hear my voice.[43]

John 6:30. *What sign do you show then, that we may see, and believe you? They do not say: What doctrine do you preach?*[44]

———

No man can perform these miracles that you do, except God.[45]
2 Maccabees 14:15
The Lord, by making manifest his presence, upholds his own portion.[46]

———

*And others, **tempting him**, sought of him a sign **from heaven**.*[47] Luke 11:16.

An evil generation seeks after a sign; and there shall no sign be given to it.[48]

---

[38] Matthew 6:23.

[39] *Si tu es Christus, dic nobis.* Luke 22:66.

[40] *Opera quae ego facio **in nomine patris mei**.*

[41] *Haec testimonium perhibent de me;* John 10:26–27.

[42] *Sed vos non creditis quia non estis ex ovibus meis.*

[43] *Oves meae vocem meam audiunt;* John 5:36.

[44] *Quod ergo tu facis signum ut videamus et credamus tibi? (Non dicunt: Quam doctrinam praedicas?)*

[45] *Nemo potest facere signa quae tu facis nisi Deus.* John 3:2.

[46] *Deus qui signis evidentibus suam portionem protegit.*

[47] *Volumus signum videre, **de coelo tentantes** eum.*

[48] *Generatio prava signum quaerit; et non dabitur.* Matthew 12:39.

And he sighed deeply in his spirit, and said, why does this generation seek after a sign?[49] (Mark 8:12). They asked for a sign with an evil intention.

And he could there do no mighty work.[50] And yet he promises them the sign of Jonah, the great and incomparable one of his resurrection.

———

Unless you see, you will not believe.[51] He does not blame them for failing to believe without there being miracles, but [for failing to believe] without themselves being spectators of them.

———

The Antichrist [will come] in signs and lying wonders,[52] says Saint Paul (2 Thessalonians 2) [. . .] *After the working of Satan, and with all deceivableness of unrighteousness in they who perish, because they did not receive the love of the truth, that they might be saved. And for this cause God shall send them strong delusion, that they should believe a lie.*[53] As in the passage of Moses: *for the Lord your God tests you to know whether you love him.*[54]

———

Behold, I have told you before. Therefore you behold![55]

In the *Old Testament*: when you will be turned from God.   S433/L852
In the *New*: when you will be turned from Jesus Christ.

———

These are the cases indicated for withholding particular miracles from faith. We must not propose any other case.

———

Does it follow, as a result, that they would have the right to withhold belief in all the prophets who came to them? No. They would have sinned in not rejecting those who denied God, and would have sinned in rejecting those who did not deny God.

---

[49] *Et ingemiscens ait: Quid generatio ista signum quaerit?*

[50] *Et non poterat facere.* Mark 6:5.

[51] *Nisi videritis [. . .] non creditis.* John 4:48.

[52] *Antichrist in signis mendacibus.*

[53] *Secundum operationem Satanae, in seductione iis qui pereunt eo quod charitatem veritatis non receperunt ut salvi fierent, ideo mittet illis Deus optationes erroris ut credant mendacio.* II Thessalonians 2:9–11.

[54] *Tentat enim vos Deus, utrum diligatis eum.* Deuteronomy 13:3.

[55] *Ecce praedixi vobis: vos ergo videte.* Matthew 24:25–26.

As soon as we see a miracle, then, we must either assent to it or have received peculiar marks to the contrary. We must see whether it denies God, or Jesus Christ, or the Church.

To reproach Miton for not being moved.[56]   S433/L853
Since God will reproach him.

Though you do not believe me, believe at least the   S434/L854
miracles;[57] he refers them, as it were, to the strongest proof.

It had been told to the Jews, as well as to Christians, that they should not always believe the prophets. But yet the Pharisees and scribes made much of his miracles and tried to show them false or brought about by the devil, since they had to be convinced if they recognized that they came from God.

Today we need not be troubled to make this distinction. Still, it is very easy to do. Those who deny neither God nor Jesus Christ perform no miracles that are not certain.

There is no man who, having performed a miracle in my name, can soon after speak evil of me.[58]

But we do not have to draw this distinction.

Here is a sacred relic. Here is a thorn from the crown of the Savior of the world, over whom the prince of this world has no power, working miracles by the very power of this blood that was shed for us. Here God himself chooses this house in order to display conspicuously his power in it.

These are not men who perform miracles by an unknown and doubtful power (*vertu*), requiring us to make a difficult decision. It is God himself. It is the instrument of the passion of his only son, who, being in many places, chooses this one, and draws people from all quarters to receive this miraculous relief for their weaknesses.

---

[56] Daniel Miton or Mitton (1618–1690) was one of Pascal's wordly friends and the author of *Pensées sur l'honnêteté* and *La description de l'honnête homme.*

[57] John 10:38.

[58] *Nemo facit virtutem in nomine meo, et cito possit de me male loqui;* Mark 9:39.

John 6:26: *Not because you saw the miracles, but because* S435/L855
you were filled.[59]

Those who follow Jesus Christ because of his miracles honor his power in all the miracles it produces.

But those who, professing to follow him because of his miracles, follow him in fact only because he comforts them and satisfies them with worldly goods, dishonor his miracles, when miracles threaten their own comforts.

John 9: *This man is not of God, because he does not keep the Sabbath day. Others said: How can a man who is a sinner perform such miracles?*[60] Which is the clearer?

This is the house of God, for he brought about peculiar miracles in it. Others: This is not the house of God, for they do not believe there that the five propositions are in Jansenius. Which is the clearer?

What do you say of him? He said he is a prophet. If this man were not of God, he could do nothing.[61]

Oppositions. S436/L856

Abel, Cain.[62] / Moses, Magicians.[63] / Elijah, false prophets.[64]

Jeremiah, Hananiah.[65] / Micah, false prophets.[66] / Jesus Christ, Pharisees.[67] / Saint Paul, Bar-jesus.[68] /

Apostles, exorcists.[69] / Christians and unbelievers. /

Catholics and heretics. / Elijah, Enoch, Antichrist.[70] /

---

[59] *Non quia vidisti signum, sed quia [. . .] saturati estis.*

[60] *Non est hic homo a Deo, quia sabbatum non custodit. Alii: Quomodo potest homo peccator haec signa facere?*

[61] *Tu quid dicis? Dico quia propheta est. [. . .] Nisi esset hic a Deo, non poterat facere quidquam.* John 9:17, 33.

[62] Genesis 4.

[63] Exodus 8.

[64] 1 Kings 18.

[65] Jeremiah 28.

[66] 1 Kings 22.

[67] Luke 5; John 9; et passim.

[68] Acts 13.

[69] Acts 19.

[70] Apocalypse 11.

The truth always prevails in miracles. The two crosses.[71]

Jeremiah 23:32. The *miracles* of the false prophets. In the   S437/L857
Hebrew and Vatable, they are the *tricks*.

Miracle does not always signify miracles. I Kings 14:15; *miracle*
signifies *fear*, and is so in the Hebrew.

The same clearly in Job 33:7.

And also Isaiah 21:4; Jeremiah 44:22.

———

Portentum signifies *simulacrum*, Jeremiah 50:38; and it is so in the
Hebrew and Vatable.

———

Isaiah 8:18. Jesus Christ says that he and his [disciples] will be in
miracles.

———

The Church has three kinds of enemies: the Jews, who   S437/L858
have never been part of its body; the heretics, who have with-
drawn from it; and the bad Christians, who tear it from within. These
three kinds of different adversaries usually attack it in different ways. But
here they are attacking it in one and the same way. As they are all
without miracles, and as the Church has always had some miracles
against them, they have all had the same interest in evading them, and
they all make use of this excuse: that doctrine must not be judged by
miracles, but miracles by doctrine. There were two sides among those
who listened to Jesus Christ: those who followed his teaching because
of his miracles; others who said . . . There were two sides in the time of
Calvin. There are now the Jesuits, etc.

[32] Miracles [3]

Unjust persecutors of those whom God visibly protects.   S438/L859

———

If they reproach you for your excesses, they are speaking like the
heretics.

———

If they say that the grace of Jesus Christ distinguishes us, they are
heretics.

———

[71] Since two crosses were discovered, miracles are needed to determine which of the two
was Christ's.

———

If miracles occur, it is the sign of their heresy.

———

It is said, believe in the Church; but it is not said, believe in miracles, because the latter is natural, and not the former. One needed a precept, but not the other.

———

Ezekiel.
It is said: Here are God's people who speak thus.

———

Hezekiah.
The synagogue was a figure,[72] and thus it did not perish; and it was merely a figure, and so it has perished. It was a figure containing the truth, and thus it has lasted until it no longer had the truth.

My reverend father, *all this happened in figures.*[73] Other religions perish; this one does not perish.

Miracles are more important than you think. They have served at the foundation and will serve for the continuation of the Church until the Antichrist, until the end. The two witnesses.

———

In the *Old Testament* as in the *New*, miracles are performed by the touching of figures, by salvation, or useless thing, if only to show that we must submit to creatures.

Figure of the sacraments.

In all times, either people have spoken of the true God, or the true God has spoken to men.   S439/L860

———

The two foundations; one internal, the other external; grace, miracles, both supernatural.   S439/L861

———

The wretched people who have obliged us to speak of the fundamentals of religion.   S439/L862

———

Montaigne against miracles.   S439/L863

———

[72] That is, a figure of the Church; see fragment S476.
[73] 1 Corinthians 10:11.

Montaigne for miracles.

Sinners purified without penitence, the righteous sanc-   S439/L864
tified without charity; all Christians without the grace of
Jesus Christ, God without power over the will of men, a predestination
without mystery. A savior without certainty!

Miracles are no longer necessary because we have already   S439/L865
had them. But when we no longer listen to tradition; when
the Pope alone is proposed to us; when he has been manipulated, and
thus the true source of truth, which is tradition, has been excluded; and
the Pope, who is its guardian, has become biased; the truth is no longer
free to appear. Then, as men no longer speak of truth, truth itself must
speak to men. This is what happened in the time of Arius.
    Miracles under Diocletian.
    And under Arius.
                              Perpetuity   S440/L866
Is your character based on Escobar?[74]

Perhaps you have reasons for not condeming them.
    It is enough that you should approve of what I tell you about it.

Would the Pope be dishonored by receiving his enlight-   S440/L867
enment from God and tradition? And is it not dishonoring
him to separate him from this holy union?
    Tertullian: *The Church will never be reformed.*[75]   S440/L868
    Grace is indeed needed to turn a man into a saint. And he   S440/L869
who doubts it does not know what is a saint, or a man.

---

[74] Escobar y Mendoza, Spanish Jesuit (1589–1669), author of *Liber theologiae moralis*
(Lyon, 1644), whose laxity is denounced by Pascal in the *Provincial Letters*.
[75] *Nunquam Ecclesia reformabitur.*

The heretics have always attacked these three signs,   S440/L870
which they do not possess.

Perpetuity.   S440/L871
Molina.[76]
Novelty.

Miracles   S440/L872

How I hate those who pretend to doubt miracles!
Montaigne speaks rightly of them in two places.[77]

We see how prudent he is in the first; and yet, in the second, he believes and ridicules the unbelievers.

However it may be, the Church is without proof if they are right.

Either God has confounded the false miracles or foretold   S440/L873
them.

And in both cases he has raised himself above what is "supernatural
with respect to us," and has raised us to it.

The Church teaches, and God inspires, both infallibly.   S440/L874
The work of the Church serves only as a preparation for
grace or damnation. What it does is enough for damnation, not for
inspiration.

Every kingdom divided.[78] For Jesus Christ acted against   S440/L875
the devil, and destroyed his empire over the heart, of which
exorcism is the figure, in order to establish the kingdom of God. And
thus he adds, *If with the finger of God, the kingdom of God is come upon
you.*[79]

If the devil favored the doctrine that destroys him, he would be divided [against himself], as Jesus Christ said. If God favored the doctrine
that destroys the Church, he would be [so] divided. *When a
strong man armed keeps his goods, his goods are in peace.*   S440/L876

Will *yes and no*[80] be accepted in faith itself as well as in   S441/L877
morals, if it is so inseparable in actions?

<Saint Hilary. Wretched people who oblige us to speak of miracles!>
When Saint Xavier works miracles.

---

[76] Luis de Molina (1536–1600), Jesuit author of *De Concordia* (1588), about free will and grace.

[77] *Essays* III, chap. 11, and I, chap. 27.

[78] *Omne regnum divisum.* Matthew 12:25; Luke 11:17.

[79] *Si in digito Dei* [. . .] *regnum Dei ad Vos.* Luke 11:20.

[80] *Est et non est.*

Unjust judges, do not make up laws on the spur of the moment; judge by those already established, and established by yourselves. *Woe unto them who decree unrighteous decrees.*[81]

In order to weaken your adversaries, you disarm the whole Church.

Continuous miracles, false.

If they say they are obedient to the Pope, it is hypocrisy.

If they are ready to subscribe to all the articles, it is not enough.

If they say our salvation depends upon God, they are heretics.

If they say we must not kill for an apple, they attack the morality of Catholics.

If miracles are made among them, it is not a sign of holiness, but, on the contrary, a symptom of heresy.

The way in which the Church has survived is that truth was not challenged; or, if it was, the Pope was there, and, if not he, the Church.

First objection: An angel from heaven.[82]

B442/L878

Truth must not be judged by miracles, but miracles by truth.

Therefore miracles are useless.

But they are of use and we must not be opposed to the truth.

Therefore what Father Lingende has said, that "God will not permit a miracle to lead into error . . ."

When there shall be a controversy in the same Church, miracle will decide.

Second objection:
"But the Antichrist will produce signs."[83]

The Pharaoh's magicians did not entice people into error.

Thus we cannot say to Jesus Christ about the Antichrist, "You have led me into error." For the Antichrist will produce them against Jesus Christ, and thus they cannot lead into error.

Either God will not permit false miracles, or he will bring about greater ones.

———

<Jesus Christ has existed since the beginning of the world. This is greater than all the miracles of the Antichrist.>

---

[81] *Vae qui conditis leges iniquas.* Isaiah 10:1.

[82] Galatians 1:8. See fragment S419/L830.

[83] 2 Thessalonians 2:9. See fragment S432/L851.

If in the same Church a miracle happened on the side of those in error, people would be led into error.

Schism is visible; miracle is visible. But schism is more a sign of error than a miracle is a sign of the truth. Therefore miracle cannot lead into error.

But, apart from schism, error is not as visible as miracle. Therefore miracle could lead into error.

Where is your God?[84] Miracles reveal him, and are an illumination.

<Men [are] by nature roofers and of every trade, except in   S442/L879
their rooms.>

The five propositions condemned, but no miracle. For   S443/L881
the truth was not attacked. But the Sorbonne, but the [Papal]
bull . . .

It is impossible for those who love God with all their heart to fail to recognize the Church; so evident is it.

It is impossible for those who do not love God to be convinced of the Church.

Miracles have such force that it was necessary for God to warn men not to think about them in opposition to him—so clear it is that there is a God. Otherwise miracles would have been able to disturb men.

And thus, far from these passages (Deuteronomy 13) arguing against the authority of the miracles, nothing more indicates their power. Likewise for the Antichrist. *To seduce, if it were possible, even the chosen.*[85]

Atheists   S444/L882

What reason do they have for saying that we cannot rise
from the dead? What is more difficult, to be born or to rise again? That what has never been should be, or that what has been should be again? Is it more difficult to come into existence than to return to it? Habit makes the one seem easy to us; lack of habit makes the other impossible. A popular way of judging!

---

[84] *Ubi est Deus tuus?* Psalm 41.

[85] Matthew 24:24.

Why cannot a virgin bear a child? Does not a hen produce eggs without a cock? What distinguishes these outwardly from the others, and who has told us that a hen may not form this germ as well as a cock?

There is such disproportion between the worth he   S444/L883
imagines himself to have and his stupidity that it is hard to
believe he should so grossly mistake himself.

After so many other signs of piety, they are still perse-   S444/L884
cuted, which is the clearest sign of piety.

It is good that they should commit injustices, lest it might   S445/L885
appear that the Molinists have acted justly. And so they must
not be spared; they are worthy of committing them.

Skeptic for opinionated.   S445/L886

Descartes useless and uncertain.   S445/L887

No one calls another a courtier apart from those who are   S445/L888
not, the same for pedant and provincial. And I would wager
it was the printer who put the word in the title of *Letters to a Provincial*.

Thoughts   S445/L889
In all things I have sought rest.[86]
If our condition were truly happy, we would not need to divert our-
selves from thinking of it in order to make ourselves happy.

All of men's occupations involve the possession of some   S445/L890
good. But they have neither the title to possess it justly nor
the strength to possess it securely. It is the same with knowledge and
pleasures. We have neither the truth nor the good.

---

[86] *In omnibus requiem quaesivi.* Ecclesiasticus 24:11.

Miracle   S445/L891

It is an effect that exceeds the natural power of the means
employed. And what is not a miracle is an effect that does not exceed
the natural power of the means employed. Thus those who heal by invocation of the devil do not work a miracle, because that does not exceed the natural power of the devil. But . . .[87]

Abraham and Gideon: signs above revelation.   S446/L892

The Jews blinded themselves by judging miracles by the
Scripture.

God has never left *his true worshipers.*

I prefer to follow Jesus Christ than any other, because he has miracle, prophecy, doctrine, perpetuity, etc.

The Donatists.[88] No miracle that requires one to say it is the devil.

The more we particularize God, Jesus Christ, the Church . . .

Blindness of Scripture   S447/L893

Scripture, said the Jews, says that we shall not know where
Christ will come from (John 7:27 and 12:34). *Scripture says that Christ
abides forever, and he said that he should die.* Therefore, says Saint John,
*they did not believe him, though he had performed so many miracles, that
the word of Isaiah might be fulfilled:* **he has blinded them**, etc.

The three signs of religion: perpetuity, a holy life,   S448/L894
miracles. They[89] destroy perpetuity by probability, a holy life
by their morals, miracles by destroying either their truth or importance.
If we believed them, the Church would have nothing to do with perpetuity, holiness, and miracles.

———

The heretics deny them, or deny their importance. They do the
same. But we would be lacking in sincerity to deny them, or have lost
our senses to deny their importance.

———

Religion is proportionate to all kinds of minds. The first   S448/L895
go no further than its first institution, and this religion is such
that its institution alone is enough to prove its truth. Others go as far

———

[87] See fragment S419/L830.

[88] Schismatics fought against by Saint Augustine.

[89] The Jesuits.

back as to the apostles. The more learned go as far back as the beginning of the world. Angels see it better still, and from farther back.

———

My God! How foolish this talk is! Would God have   S448/L896
created the world in order to damn it? Would he ask so much
from people so weak? Etc. Skepticism is the cure for these ills, and will
beat down this vanity.[90]

———

Humbling [my] heart, Saint Paul.[91] This is the Christian   S448/L897
character. *Alba has nonimated you, I no longer know you*,
Corneille.[92] This is the character of inhumanity. The character of humanity is the opposite.

———

No one has ever suffered martyrdom for the miracles he   S448/L899
claims to have seen; for, in the case of those the Turks tradi-
tionally believe, human folly goes perhaps as far as martyrdom, but not
for those that have been seen.

———

The Jansenists resemble the heretics in their reform of   S448/L900
customs, but you resemble them in the evil [you do].

———

Those who wrote that in Latin talk in French.   S448/L898

———

The harm having been done by putting them into French, con-
demning them should have done some good.

———

There is a single heresy explained differently in the schools and in
the world.

---

[90] See Montaigne, *Essays* II, chap. 12 (Ariew and Grene trans., p. 11): "The means that I
take to beat back this frenzy, and which seems to me most appropriate, is to crush and
trample under foot human vanity and pride; to make them feel the inanity, the vanity and
nothingness of man, to snatch from their hands the miserable weapons of their reason; to
make them bow their heads and bite the dust beneath the authority and reverence of divine majesty."

[91] *Comminuentes cor*, Acts 21:13.

[92] *Horace*, II. iii.

Miracles distinguish between things that are in doubt: B449/L.901
between Jewish and heathen peoples, between Jewish and
Christian, Catholic and heretic, slandered and slandering, between the
two crosses.

But miracles would be useless to heretics, for the Church, given authority by miracles that have already gained credence, tells us that they
lack the true faith. There is no doubt that they lack it, since the
Church's first miracles preclude faith in theirs. Thus miracle is set
against miracle. And both the first and greatest miracles are on the side
of the Church.

————

These nuns, astonished at what is said—that they are on   S449/L.902
the road to perdition, that their confessors are leading them
to Geneva, suggesting to them that Jesus Christ is not in the Eucharist,
nor on the right hand of the Father—know all this to be false. They
therefore offer themselves to God in this state: *See whether the way of
iniquity is in me*.[93] What happens then? This place, which is said to be
the devil's temple, God makes it his own temple. It is said that children
should be taken away from it; God heals them there. It is said to be the
arsenal of hell; God makes it the sanctuary of his grace. Finally, they are
threatened with all the fury and vengeance of heaven, and God fills
them with his favors. You would have to have lost your senses to conclude from this that they are therefore on the road to perdition.

We have, no doubt, the same signs as Saint Athanasius had.

The foolish idea you have of your Company's impor-   S450/L.904
tance has made you institute these horrible methods. It is
perfectly evident that this is what made you adopt the method of
calumny, since you blame my slightest deceptions as horrible while excusing them in yourselves; because you regard me as an individual and
yourselves as the **Imago**.[94]

It truly seems as if what you praise is folly by the foolish, like the
privilege of not being damned.[95]

Does it encourage your children to condemn them when they serve
the Church?

———

[93] *Vide si via iniquitatis in me est.*

[94] This is a reference to *Imago primi saeculi Societatis Jesu* (1640), a volume celebrating
Jesuit activities during the society's first hundred years.

[95] The *Imago* asserts that no Jesuit will be damned.

———

It is a device of the devil for diverting elsewhere the arms with which these people[96] would attack heresies.

———

You are bad politicians.

———

Skepticism.

Everything here is partly true, partly false. Essential truth is not like that; it is wholly pure and wholly true. This mixture dishonors and destroys it. Nothing is purely true, and thus nothing is true in the sense of pure truth. You will say it is true that homicide is wrong. Yes, for we know well evil and falsehood. But what will you say is good? Chastity? I deny it, for the world would come to an end. Marriage? No, continence is better. Not to kill? No, for disorders would be horrible, and the wicked would kill all the good. To kill? No, for that destroys nature. We possess neither truth nor goodness except in part and mingled with evil and falsehood.

———

The story of the man blind from birth.[97]   S450/L903

———

What does Saint Paul say? Does he continually refer to the prophecies? No, but to his miracle.[98]

———

What does Jesus Christ say? Does he refer to the prophecies? No. His death had not fulfilled them. But he says: *If I had not done.*[99] *Believe the works.*[100]

———

Two supernatural foundations of our wholly supernatural religion: the one visible, the other invisible.

Miracles with grace, miracles without grace.

The synagogue, treated with love as a figure of the Church, and with hatred, because it was only a figure, was restored, being about to collapse, when it stood well with God, and thus a figure.

---

[96] The theologians of Port-Royal.

[97] John 9.

[98] 2 Corinthians 12:12.

[99] *Si non fecissem.* John 15:24.

[100] John 10:38.

———

Miracles prove the power God has over our hearts by the one he exercises over our bodies.

The Church has never approved a miracle among the heretics.

———

Miracles, a mainstay of religion: they have set apart the Jews; they have set apart Christians, saints, the innocent, and the true believers.

———

A miracle among schismatics is not so much to be feared. For schism, which is more visible than miracle, visibly indicates their error. But, when there is no schism and error is disputed, miracle decides.

If I had not done the works that no other man did.[101]

———

These wretched people who have obliged us to speak of miracles.

———

Abraham, Gideon.
Confirm faith by miracles.

———

Judith. God speaks at last during the final oppressions.

———

If the cooling of charity leaves the Church almost without *true worshipers*, miracles will rouse them. These are the final efforts of grace.

If a miracle happened among the Jesuits.

When a miracle frustrates the expectation of those in whose presence it occurs, and there is a disproportion between the state of their faith and the instrument of the miracle, then it ought to induce them to change, but, etc. Otherwise, there would be as much reason for saying that, if the Eucharist raised a dead man, one should become a Calvinist rather than remain a Catholic. But when it crowns the expectation, and those who hoped that God would bless the remedies see themselves cured without remedies . . .

———

The impious

No sign has ever occurred on the part of the devil without a more powerful sign on the part of God.

　At least without such an occurrence having been foretold.

---

[101] *Si non fecissem quae alius non fecit.* John 15:24.

Probability. They have some true principles, but they   S451/L906
abuse them. Now, the abuse of truth ought to be as much
punished as the introduction of falsehood.

As if there were two hells, one for sins against charity, the other,
against justice.

Aperitive virtue of a key, attractive virtue of a hook.   S451/L907

Superstition and concupiscence.   S451/L908

Scruples, evil desires, evil fear.

Fear, not the one that comes from believing in God, but from doubting whether he exists or not. Good fear comes from faith, false fear
comes from doubt; good fear is attached to hope, because it is born of
faith and one hopes in the God in whom one believes; false fear is attached to despair, because one fears the God in whom one has put no
faith. Some fear to lose him, others fear to find him.

<Dishonest people, without faith, without honor, with-   S451/L909
out truth, duplicitous in heart, duplicitous in speech, and resembling, as it was once reproached, that amphibious animal in the
fable, remaining ambiguously neither fish nor fowl.>

When it is said that Jesus Christ did not die for all, you are   S451/L912
abusing a fault in men, who at once apply to themselves this
exception, which favors despair instead of turning them from it to favor
hope.

For we thus accustom ourselves to internal virtues by these external
habits.

It is important to kings and princes to be esteemed for   S451/L909
their piety. And for this they must confess themselves to you.

Port-Royal is worth as much as Voltigerod.

To the extent that your procedure is just from this perspective, it is
unjust with respect to Christian piety.

Figures standing for the totality of the Redemption, such   S451/L910
as the sun illuminating everything, indicate only totality; but
figures standing for exclusions, such as the Jews chosen to the exclusion
of the Gentiles, indicate exclusion.

Jesus Christ Redeemer of all. Yes, for he has offered, like a   S451/L911
man who has ransomed all those who were willing to come
to him. Those who died on the way are unfortunate. But, as for him, he
offered them redemption. That holds good in this example, where the
one who ransoms and the one who prevents death are two persons, but
not for Jesus Christ, who does both. No, for Jesus Christ, in his quality
of redeemer, is not perhaps master of all, and thus, insofar as it is in
him, he is redeemer of all.

[33] **Miscellaneous Thoughts** [1]

When words are repeated in a discourse and, in trying to   S452/L515
correct them, we find them so appropriate that we would be
spoiling the discourse to do so, we must leave them, for this is the sign of
it. And here we are dealing with envy, which is blind and does not realize that such repetition is not a defect here. For there is no general rule.

———

We like certainty, we like the Pope to be infallible in faith   S452/L516
and for grave doctors to be so in morals, in order to be re-
assured.

———

If Saint Augustine came at the present time and had as   S452/L517
little authority as his defenders, he would accomplish nothing. God directs his Church well, by having sent him earlier with authority.

———

Skepticism   S452/L518

Extreme intelligence is accused of madness, as is its extreme deficiency. Nothing but the mean is good: the majority has instituted this and sinks its teeth into anyone who deviates from whichever
end by any amount. I will not be stubborn about this; I quite consent to
be put there in the middle, and refuse to be placed at the lower end, not
because it is low, but because it is an end, for I would likewise refuse to
be placed at the top. To leave the mean is to abandon humanity.

The greatness of the human soul consists in knowing how to keep in
the mean. Greatness does not consist in deviating from it, but rather in
not deviating from it.

<Nature does not. . . .   S453/L519

Nature has placed us so well in the middle that if we
change one side of the balance, we change the other also: ***animals
run.***[102]

This leads me to believe that there are mechanisms in our head so
arranged that whoever touches one touches its opposite, as well.

———

[102] *Je faisons, zoa trekei.*

I have spent much of my life believing that there was such   S453/L520
a thing as justice, and in this I was not mistaken, for there is
such a thing, to the extent that God has willed to reveal it to us. But I did
not understand it in this way, and this is where I was mistaken, for I believed that our justice was essentially just, and that I had the means to
know and judge it. But I have so often found myself making unsound
judgments that in the end I have come to distrust myself, and then others. I have seen all nations and all men change. And thus, after many
changes of judgment regarding true justice, I have recognized that our
nature was nothing but continual change, and I have not changed
since. And if I changed, I would be confirming my opinion. The skeptic
Arcesilaus, who became a dogmatist again.[103]

———

It may be that there are true demonstrations, but this is   S453/L521
not certain. Thus this only shows that it is not certain that
everything is uncertain. To the glory of skepticism.

———

How does it happen that this man, so distressed at the   S453/L522
death of his wife and his only son, bothered by some great
quarrel, is not sad at this moment and is so visibly free from all these
painful and disquieting thoughts? We should not be surprised: he has
just had a ball served to him and he must return it to his fellow player.
He is concentrating on catching it as it falls from the roof, to win the
point.[104] How do you expect him to think of his own affairs when he has
this other affair to handle? Here is something worthy of occupying this
great soul and lifting every other thought from his mind. This man, born
to know the universe, to judge all things, to govern a whole state, here he
is occupied and wholly concerned with catching a hare. And if he does
not abase himself to this and wants always to be tense, the more foolish
will he be, because he would be raising himself above humanity, and he
is only a man, after all; that is to say, capable of little and of much, of
everything and of nothing. He is neither angel nor beast, but man.[105]

---

[103] See Montaigne, *Essays* II, chap. 12 (Ariew and Grene trans., p. 139): "And Arcesilaus
said that constancy and rigidity and inflexibility of judgment were goods, but consent and
application were vices and evils. It is true that insofar as he was establishing this by a certain axiom, he was departing from Pyrrhonism."

[104] These sentences describe the serve and return in a *jeu de paume*.

[105] See Montaigne, *Essays* II, chap. 12 (Ariew and Grene trans., p. 164): " 'Oh, what a vile
and abject thing,' he[Seneca] says, 'is man, if he does not raise himself above humanity!'
There you have a good word and a useful desire, but similarly absurd."

A single thought occupies us. We cannot think of two   S453/L523
things at the same time. This is just as well for us, according
to the world, not according to God.

We must judge divine ordinances soberly, my father.[106]   S453/L524
Saint Paul in the isle of Malta.[107]>

Montaigne is wrong: custom should be followed only   S454/L525
because it is custom, and not because it is reasonable or just.
But people follow it for the sole reason that they think it just. Otherwise
they would follow it no longer, even though it is custom. For we want to
submit only to reason or justice. Lacking this, custom would pass for
tyranny, but the rule of reason and justice is no more tyrannical than
that of pleasure. These are principles natural to man.

It would, therefore, be good to obey laws and customs because they
are laws, understanding that there are none true or just to be introduced; that we know nothing of these, and so must follow the ones that
are accepted. In this way we would never abandon them. But people are
not capable of following this doctrine. And so, as they believe that truth
can be found and that it resides in laws and customs, they believe them
and take their antiquity as a proof of their truth (and not just of their authority, without truth). Thus they obey laws and customs, but are liable
to revolt once these are shown to be without value, which can be done
for all of them when looked at from a certain perspective.

Evil is easy, there are infinite forms of it, while good is   S454/L526
almost unique. But a certain kind of evil is as difficult to find
as what is called good, and often this particular evil gets passed off as
good on that account. It even takes extraordinary greatness of soul to attain to such evil, as to attain good.

If we wanted to prove the examples we take to prove other   S454/L527
things, we would take the other things to be their examples.
For, since we always believe the difficulty lies in what we want to
prove, we find examples clearer and a help to demonstration. Thus,
when we want to demonstrate something general, we must give the par-

---

[106] This refers to the title of one of Montaigne's essays: *Essays* I, chap. 32.
[107] Acts 28:1–10.

ticular rule for a case. But if we want to demonstrate a particular case, we must begin with the particular rule.[108] For we always find obscure what we want to prove, and clear what we use for the proof. For, when we propose a thing to be proved, we first imagine that it is therefore obscure, whereas what proves it is clear, and so we easily understand it.

———

I am always ill at ease with such civilities as: "I have given   S454/L528
you lots of trouble." "I am afraid I am bothering you." "I am
afraid this is too long." —We are either persuasive or irritating.

How difficult it is to propose something for another to   S454/L529
judge without affecting his judgment by the manner in
which we propose it. If you say, "I find it beautiful, I find it obscure," or the like, you either carry his imagination to that judgment or irritate it to the contrary. It is better to say nothing, and then he judges according to what it is; that is, according to what it is then and according to how other circumstances, not of our making, have affected it. But at least we will have added nothing. Unless this silence also produces an effect, according to the turn and interpretation he will be disposed to give it, or as he will conjecture from our gestures and facial expression, or tone of voice, to the extent that he can read faces. So difficult is it not to dislodge a judgment from its natural place, or, rather, so few of these are firm and stable.

All our reasoning reduces to giving in to feeling.   S455/L530

———

But fancy is similar and opposite to feeling, so that we cannot distinguish between these opposites. One person says that my feeling is fancy, another that his fancy is feeling. We must have a rule. Reason is proposed, but it is pliable in every direction.[109]

And so there is no rule.

The things that have most hold on us, as the hiding of our   S456/L531
few possessions, often amount to practically nothing. It is a
nothing that our imagination enlarges into a mountain: another turn of the imagination makes us discover this without difficulty.

———

[108] Pascal must have meant: "we must begin with the general rule."

[109] See Montaigne, *Essays* II, chap. 12 (Ariew and Grene trans., p. 127): "reason . . . is an instrument of lead and wax, ductile, pliable, and able to accommodate itself to every bias and to every standard."

Skepticism   S457/L532

I will write my thoughts here without order, but not perhaps in unplanned confusion. This is true order, and it will always indicate my aim by its very disorder.

I would be honoring my subject too much if I treated it with order,
since I want to show that it is incapable of it.

––––––

We can only imagine Plato and Aristotle in long academic   S457/L533
gowns. They were honest men like others, laughing with
their friends. And when they amused themselves writing their *Laws*
and their *Politics*, they did it as a game.[110] This was the least philosophic and least serious part of their life, the most philosophic being
living simply and quietly. If they wrote about politics, it was as if to lay
down rules for an insane asylum. And if they pretended to talk about it
as something important, it was because they knew that the madmen to
whom they were talking thought themselves kings and emperors. They
entered into their principles in order to make their madness as little
harmful as possible.

––––––

Those who judge a work without any rule stand in   S457/L534
relation to others as those with a watch in relation to others.
One says, "It has been two hours." —The other says, "It has only been
three-quarters of an hour." —I look at my watch and say to the first,
"You are bored," and to the other, "Time goes fast for you, because it has
been an hour and a half," and I laugh at those who tell me that time
passes slowly for me and that I am judging it according to my fancy.

They do not know that I am judging it according to my watch.

There are vices that take hold of us only through other   S457/L535
ones, and that, when the trunk is removed, are carried away
like branches.

God and the Apostles, foreseeing that the seeds of pride   S458/L536
would give rise to heresies, and being unwilling to give them
the opportunity to arise from proper words, put into Scripture and the
prayers of the Church opposite words and seeds, to produce their fruit
in due time.

––

[110] Cf. Montaigne, *Essays* II, chap. 12 (Ariew and Grene trans., p. 70): "Chrysippus said
that what Plato and Aristotle wrote on logic must have been written as a game and for
practice, and he could not believe they had said anything serious on so frivolous a
subject."

In the same way, he includes charity in morals to produce fruits against concupiscence.

———

When wickedness has reason on its side, it becomes   S458/L537 proud and displays reason in all its luster.

———

When austerity or stern choice has not succeeded in achieving the true good and we have to go back to following nature, it becomes proud at this reversal.

———

He who knows the will of his master will be beaten with   S458/L538 more blows, because of the power given him by his knowl-edge.[111] *He who is righteous, let him be righteous still,*[112] because of the power given him by justice.

From him who has received most, the greatest reckoning will be de-manded, because of the power given him by this help.

There is a universal and essential difference between acts   S458/L539 of will and all other acts.

———

The will is one of the principal organs of belief, not that it creates be-lief, but because things are true or false according to the aspect from which we observe them. The will, which prefers one aspect to another, turns the mind away from considering the qualities of the one it does not care to see. And thus the mind, moving as one with the will, keeps looking at the aspect it likes, and so judges by what it sees.

———

All the good maxims are in the world: we only fail to apply   S458/L540 them.

For example, no one doubts that he should risk his life to defend the public good, and many do so, but not for religion.

———

There must be inequality among men. This is true, but once this is granted, the door is opened not only to the greatest control, but also to the greatest tyranny.

---

[111] Cf. Luke 12:47.

[112] *Qui justus est, justificetur adhuc.* Revelations 22:11.

It is necessary to relax the mind a little, but this opens the door to the greatest excesses.

Let us specify the limits. There are no boundaries in things: laws attempt to place some there, and the mind cannot suffer it.

<Nature diversifies and imitates. Artifice imitates and diversifies. S459/L541

Chance gives rise to thoughts, and chance removes them: no art for keeping or acquiring them. S459/L542

———

A thought has escaped, I wanted to write it down: I write instead that it has escaped me.>

All the land of Judaea, and all those of Jerusalem, and were baptized of him.[113] Because of all the conditions of men who came there. S460/L544

———

Stones **can** be children of Abraham.[114]

———

All that is in the world is concupiscence of the flesh, or concupiscence of the eyes, or pride of life.[115] *The desire for sensations, the desire for knowledge, the desire to dominate.*[116] Wretched is the cursed land consumed rather than watered by these three rivers of fire! Happy are those who, on these rivers, are not immersed or carried away, but unalterably stable on these rivers; not standing, but sitting on a low and secure position, from which they do not rise before the light; but, having rested there in peace, stretch out their hands to him who will raise them up and hold them upright and firm in the porches of holy Jerusalem, where pride can no longer assail them nor cast them down! And yet they weep, not at the sight of all those perishable things swept away by the torrents, but at the memory of their beloved country, the heavenly Jerusalem, which they constantly remember during their prolonged exile. S460/L545

———

---

[113] *Omnis Judaea regio, et Jerosolmymi universi, et baptizabantur.* Mark 1:5.

[114] Cf. Matthew 3:9.

[115] I John 2:16.

[116] *Libido sentiendi, libido sciendi, libido dominandi.*

The chosen will not know their virtues, nor the outcast   S460/L546
the greatness of their crimes: *Lord, when have we seen you*
hungry, thirsty,[117] etc.

———

Jesus Christ did not want the testimony of devils nor of   S460/L547
those who were not called, but of God and John the Baptist.

———

If people changed their ways, God would heal and pardon   S460/L548
them. *Lest they should be converted and that I may heal*
them, Isaiah.[118] *And their sins should be forgiven them,* Mark 3.[119]

Jesus Christ never condemned without hearing.   S460/L549
To Judas: *Friend, what have you come to do?*[120] The same
to the one who had no wedding garment.[121]

Pray that you do not enter into temptation.[122] It is   S461/L550
dangerous to be tempted. And those who are tempted are so
because they do not pray.

———

And when you are converted, strengthen your brothers. But first, *Jesus*
turned, and looked upon Peter.[123]

———

Saint Peter asks permission to strike Malchus and strikes before
hearing the answer. And Jesus Christ replies afterward.[124]

———

The word, **Galilee**, pronounced by the crowd of Jews as if by chance,
when they accused Jesus Christ before Pilate, gave Pilate a reason for
sending Jesus Christ to Herod. In this way was accomplished the
mystery, that he was to be judged by both Jews and Gentiles. Apparent
chance was the cause of the mystery being accomplished.[125]

———

---

[117] Matthew 25:37.

[118] *Ne convertantur et sanem eos.* Isaiah 6:10.

[119] *Et dimittantur eis peccata.* Mark 4:12.

[120] *Amice, ad guid venisti?* Matthew 26:50.

[121] Matthew 22:12.

[122] Luke 22:40, 46.

[123] *Et tu conversus confirma fratres tuos.* . . . *conversus Jesus respexit Petrum.* Luke 22:32, 61.

[124] Luke 22:48–51.

[125] Luke 23:5–7.

The imagination enlarges small objects to the point of   S461/L551
filling our souls with a fantastic exaggeration, and with bold
insolence it diminishes large ones to its own measure, as when speaking
of God.

———

He lit the earth with his lamp.[126] The weather and my   S461/L552
mood have little connection. I have my foggy and fine
weather inside me. Whether my affairs go well or badly has little to do
with it. I sometimes struggle of my own accord against luck: the glory of
mastering it makes me do it cheerfully, whereas I sometimes act dis-
gusted in the midst of good fortune.

Write against those who delve too deeply in the sciences.   S462/L553
Descartes.

Power is the ruler of the world, and not opinion. But it is   S463/L554
opinion that makes use of power.

It is power that makes opinion. An indolent life is beautiful in our
opinion. Why? Because whoever wants to dance on a rope will be
alone. And I can gather together a more powerful group of people who
will say that it is not beautiful.

There are some who speak well but do not write well. It is   S464/L555
because the place and audience warm them up and elicit
from their minds more than they can manage without that warmth.

Languages are ciphers in which letters are not changed   S465/L557
into letters, but words into words. So an unknown language
can be deciphered.

———

Diversity is so abundant that all vocal tones, ways of   S465/L558
walking, coughing, blowing one's nose, sneezing [are differ-
ent]. We distinguish grapes from fruits, and between them Muscat
grapes, then those from Condrieux, then [those grown] by Desargues,
and then the particular graft. Is this all? Has a vine ever produced two
bunches the same? And has a bunch two grapes the same, etc.?

I have never judged the same thing exactly in the same way. I cannot
judge my work while doing it: I must act like painters and stand back,
but not too far. How far, then? Guess.

———

[126] *Lustravit lampade terras*, Homer, *Odyssey*, xviii.

S466/L559
Miscellanea
Language

Those who construct antitheses by forcing words are like those who construct false windows for symmetry.

Their rule is not to speak properly, but to construct proper figures of speech.

The sepulcher of Jesus Christ   S467/L560

Jesus Christ was dead, but seen, on the cross. He was dead and hidden in the sepulcher.

Jesus Christ was buried only by the saints.

Jesus Christ performed no miracle at the sepulcher.

Only the saints entered it.

It is there that Jesus Christ takes a new life, not on the cross.

It is the ultimate mystery of the Passion and the Redemption.

<Jesus Christ teaches while living, dead, buried, resurrected.>

Jesus Christ had nowhere to rest on earth except at the sepulcher.

His enemies only ceased to torment him at the sepulcher.

They say that eclipses portend misfortune, because   S468/L561
misfortunes are common. So that, as misfortune happens so often, they often predict it; whereas if they said that eclipses portended good fortune, they would often be wrong. They assign good fortune only to rare conjunctions of the heavens. Thus they seldom fail in prediction.

There are only two kinds of men: the ones righteous, who   S469/L562
believe themselves sinners; the others sinners, who believe themselves righteous.

Heretics   S470/L563

Ezekiel.

All the heathen spoke ill of Israel, and so did the prophet. But the Israelites were far from justified in saying to him, "You speak like the heathen," since his greatest strength was that the heathen spoke like him.

The true and only virtue, then, is to hate ourselves—for   S471/L564
we are worthy of hate because of our concupiscence—and to seek to love a being truly worthy of love. But as we cannot love what is outside us, we must love a being within us who is not ourselves. And this is true for each and every man. Now, only the universal being is like that. The kingdom of God is within us. The universal good is within us, is both ourselves and not us.

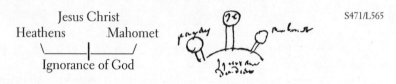

```
          Jesus Christ                                      S471/L565
Heathens            Mahomet
    _____|_____/
       Ignorance of God
```

All things turn out well for the chosen.[127]   S472/L566
Even the obscurities of Scripture, for they honor them because of what is divinely clear. And everything turns out badly for the
others, even what is clear; for they blaspheme against them, because of
the obscurities they do not understand.

We must not judge what the Pope is by some words of the   S473/L567
Fathers (as the Greeks said at a council, *Important Rules*),
but by the acts of the Church and the Fathers, and by the canons.

———

Unity and plurality: *Two or three / in one*.[128] It is an error to exclude
one of the two, as the papists do who exclude plurality, or the
Huguenots who exclude unity.

———

It is not possible to have a reasonable belief against   S473/L568
miracles.

———

The Pope is leader. Who else is known of all? Who else is   S473/L569
recognized by all, having power to insinuate himself into the
whole body, because he holds the primary branch, which insinuates
itself everywhere?

How easy was it to have this degenerate into tyranny! That is why
Jesus Christ has laid down for them this precept: *But you shall not be
so.*[129]

Jesus Christ prefigured by Joseph.   S474/L570
The beloved of his father, sent by his father to see his
brothers, etc., innocent, sold by his brothers for twenty pieces of silver,
and thereby becoming their lord, their savior, the savior of strangers and
the savior of the world; which had not been but for their plot to destroy
him, their sale and their rejection of him.

———

[127] Romans 8:28.

[128] *Duo aut tres / in unum.* Matthew 18:20.

[129] *Vos autem non sic.* Luke 22:26.

In prison, Joseph innocent between two criminals; Jesus Christ on the cross between two thieves. Joseph foretells the salvation of one and death of the other from the same indications. Jesus Christ saves the chosen and condemns the outcast for the same crimes. Joseph only foretells; Jesus Christ acts. Joseph asks of the person who will be saved to remember him when he comes into his glory; and the person Jesus Christ saves asks him to be remembered when he comes into his kingdom.

———

There is heresy in always interpreting *omnes* as all and   S474/L571
heresy in not interpreting it sometimes as all. "Drink all of
this":[130] the Huguenots are heretics in interpreting it as all. "For all have sinned":[131] the Huguenots are heretics by excluding the children of the faithful. We must, then, follow the Fathers and tradition in order to know when to do which, since there is heresy to be feared on both sides.

Miscellanea.   S475/L572
A manner of speaking.
I wanted to apply myself to that.

The Synagogue did not perish, because it was a figure.   S476/L573
But, because it was only a figure, it fell into servitude. The
figure lasted until the truth came, so that the Church should be always visible, either in the image that promised it or in its effect.

A miracle, we say, would strengthen my faith. We say this   S477/L574
when we do not see one. Reasons, seen from afar, appear to
limit our view, but when we come closer, we begin to see beyond: nothing stops the fecundity of our mind. There is no rule, we say, that does not have an exception, no truth so general that it does not have an aspect in which it fails. It suffices that it is not absolutely universal to give us a pretext for applying the exception to the present subject and for saying: this is not always true, so there are cases where it is not so. It only remains to show that this is one of them. And that is why we are very unskilled or unlucky, if we do not find some such case.

Extravagances of the Apocalyptics, Preadamites, Mil-   S478/L575
lenarians, etc.[132]

---

[130] *Bibite ex hoc omnes.* Matthew 26:27.

[131] *In quo omnes peccaverunt.* Romans 5:12.

[132] For Apocalyptics, see fragment S250. Preadamites believed (following Isaac de La Peyrère) that there were men who lived before Adam; Millenarians believed in the second coming of Christ to rule on Earth for a thousand years before the Final Judgment, based on an interpretation of Revelations 20.

Whoever would base extravagant opinions on Scripture will, for example, base them on this:

It is said that ***this generation shall not pass until all these things are fulfilled***.[133] To this I will say that after that generation will come another generation, and always another in succession.

———

In II Chronicles,[134] Solomon and the King are spoken of as if they were two different persons: I say that they were two.

Two contrary reasons. We must begin with that; other-   S479/L576
wise we understand nothing and everything is heretical. And
we must even add at the end of each truth that we are remembering the opposite truth.

If we should do nothing except for what is certain, we   S480/L577
should do nothing for religion, for it is not certain. But how
many things we do that are uncertain: sea voyages, battles! I say then we should do nothing at all, for nothing is certain, and there is more certainty in religion than that we will see the day tomorrow.

For it is not certain that we will see tomorrow, and it is certainly possible that we will not see it. We cannot say as much about religion. It is not certain that it is true, but who will dare say that it is certainly possible that it is not? Now when we work for tomorrow and what is uncertain, we are acting reasonably.

———

For we should work for what is uncertain, according to the rule of probability that was demonstrated.

———

Saint Augustine saw that we work for what is uncertain: at sea, in battle, etc., but he did not see the rule of probability proving that we should do so. Montaigne saw that we are shocked by a lame mind, and that habit can do everything, but he did not see the reason for this effect.

———

All these people saw the effects, but they did not see the causes. They are, in comparison with those who discovered the causes, like those who only have eyes with respect to those who have minds: for effects are like sensible things, and causes are visible only to the mind. And although these effects are seen by the mind, this mind is, in comparison with

---

[133] Matthew 24:34.
[134] II Chronicles 1:14.

the mind that sees the causes, as the bodily senses are with respect to the mind.

Eloquence is a painting of thought. And thus those who add more to what they have painted produce a picture instead of a portrait. S481/L578

A carriage upset or overturned, according to the intention. S482/L579

To spread or pour, according to the intention.

The advocacy of M. le Maitre[135] for the person forced to become a Franciscan.

Symmetry, S482/L580
in what we see at a glance,
based on the fact that there is no reason to do otherwise.
And based also on the figure of man.
Which is why we want symmetry only in width, not in height or depth.

Scaramouche,[136] who only thinks of only one thing. S483/L581

The doctor[137] who speaks for a quarter of an hour after having said everything. So full is he of the desire to talk.

Changing the figure, because of our weakness. S484/L582

To predict / The role I play, to your displeasure. S485/L583
The Cardinal did not want to be predicted.

"My mind is full of anxiety." "I am full of anxiety" is better.

Eloquence, which persuades by sweetness, not by authority, as a tyrant, not as a king. S485/L584

---

[135] Antoine le Maitre was a noted lawyer whose *Plaidoyers et Harangues* was published in 1657.

[136] A character in the *commedia dell'arte*.

[137] Another character of the *commedia dell'arte*, the pedant (not necessarily a medical doctor).

There is a certain model of attractiveness and beauty   S486/L585
consisting in a certain relation between our nature, weak or
strong as it is, and the thing pleasing to us.

———

Everything based on this model is agreeable to us: be it house, song,
discourse, verse, prose, woman, birds, rivers, trees, rooms, clothes, etc.

———

Everything not based on this model displeases those with good taste.

———

And since there is an exact relation between a song and a house
based on this good model, because they are like this single model,
though each in its own way, there is similarly an exact relation between
things based on a bad model. Not that the bad model is unique, for
there are countless of them; but because each bad sonnet, for example,
whatever false model it is based on, is exactly like a woman dressed
according to that model.

———

Nothing makes us understand better how absurd a false sonnet is
than to consider nature and the model and then to imagine a woman or
a house based on that model.

Poetic beauty   S486/L586

Just as we speak of poetic beauty, we should also speak of
mathematical beauty and medical beauty. But we do not, and the reason
why is that we know well what is the object of mathematics, and that it
consists in proofs, and what is the object of medicine, and that it consists
in healing. But we do not know in what consists attractiveness, which is
the object of poetry. We do not know the natural model we should imitate, and lacking this knowledge we have invented some bizarre terms:
"golden age," "wonder of our times," "fatal," etc. And we call this jargon
poetic beauty.

But whoever would imagine a woman on this model, which consists of
saying trivial things with big words, will see a pretty young lady loaded
with mirrors and chains, which will make him laugh, because we know
more about the nature of a woman's attractiveness than that of verse.
But those who do not know such things would admire her in this getup,
and there are many villages where she would be taken for the queen.
That is why we call sonnets based on this model "village queens."

No one passes in the world as skilled in verse unless he   S486/L587
displays the trademark of a poet, mathematician, etc. But
universal people want no trademark and draw little distinction between
the professions of poet and embroiderer.

Universal people are not called poets or mathematicians, etc. But
they are all of these things and judges of all of them. No one can guess
what they are. They will talk about whatever was being talked about
when they entered. We do not perceive in them one quality rather than
another, unless it becomes necessary for them to make use of one. But
then we remember it. For it is equally characteristic that we do not say
that they are good speakers, when it is not a question of language, and
that we say that they are good speakers, when this is in question.

It is therefore false praise when we say of someone, as he enters, that
he is a very able poet. And it is a bad sign when he is not called upon
when it is a matter of judging some verses.

Faith is a gift of God; do not believe that we have said it is   S487/L588
a gift of reasoning. Other religions do not say this about their
faith; they have offered only reasoning to arrive at it, and yet it does not
lead there.

The devil troubled the zeal of the Jews before Jesus Christ   S488/L589
because he would have been advantageous to them, but not
afterward.

———

The Jewish people, mocked by the Gentiles; the Christian people,
persecuted.

Adam, the figure of him who was to come.[138] The six days   S489/L590
to make the one, the six ages to make the other. The six days
Moses represents for the creation of Adam are only the image of the six
ages for creating Jesus Christ and the Church. If Adam had not sinned
and Jesus Christ had not come, there would have been only one
covenant, only one age of men, and the Creation would have been represented as completed at a single time.

If they were being led by terror, without guidance, it would   S490/L591
seem like wicked domination.[139] Augustine, *Epistle* 48 or 49.

Fourth Volume: *Against Falsehood.* To Consentius.[140]

---

[138] *Adam forma futuri.* Romans 5:14. See fragments S11/L392 and S315/L283.

[139] *Nisi terrerentur et non docerentur, improba quasi dominatio videretur.* The quotation is
from letter 93 to Vincent (letter 48 in the Louvain edition used by Pascal).

[140] *Contra Mendacium* ad Consentium.

[34. Miscellaneous Thoughts 2]

General conduct of the world toward the Church. S491/L594
God wanting to blind and to enlighten.
Since the event proved the divinity of these prophecies, the rest
should be believed. And thus we see the order of the world in this way.

The miracles of the Creation and the Flood being forgotten, God
sent the law and the miracles of Moses, the prophets who foretold particular things. And to prepare a lasting miracle, he prepared prophecies
and their fulfillment. But, as the prophecies could be suspected, he
wanted to put them above suspicion, etc.

If we do not know ourselves to be full of pride, ambition, S491/L595
concupiscence, weakness, wretchedness, and injustice, we
are indeed blind. And if, knowing this, we do not desire deliverance,
what can we say of a man . . . ?
What then can we have but esteem for a religion that knows man's
defects so well, and but desire for the truth of a religion that promises
remedies so desirable?
If the Jews had all been converted by Jesus Christ, we S492/L592
would only have questionable witnesses remaining. And if
they had been exterminated, we would have had none at all.
The Jews reject him, but not all: the holy ones accept him S493/L593
and not the carnal ones. And far from telling against his
glory, it is its crowning feature. Their reason for it, and the only one found
in all their writings, in the *Talmud* and the Rabbis, is only that Jesus
Christ did not subdue the nations by force of arms, *Your sword, O most
mighty:*[141] is this not all they have to say? Jesus Christ was slain, they say;
he surrendered; he did not subdue the heathen with his might; he did
not give us their spoils; he gives us no riches: is this not all they have to
say? This is what makes me love him. I would not want the person they
imagine. It is evident that only their vice has prevented them from accepting him. And because of this rejection they are unimpeachable witnesses, and, moreover, in this way they are fulfilling the prophecies.
<As a result of this people not accepting him, this miracle here
occurred:

------

[141] *Gladium tuum, potentissime.* Psalms 44:4.

The prophecies are the only lasting miracles that could be brought about, but they are liable to be denied.>

<Those who are unhappy in finding themselves without   S493/L596 faith show us that God does not enlighten them. But the others show us there is a God who blinds them.>

The self is hateful. You, Miton, cover it up; thus you do   S494/L597 not take it away. You are, therefore, still hateful.

"Not at all. For in behaving obligingly toward everyone, as we do, we provide no more cause for hating us."

That is true, if we only hated in the self the unpleasantness that comes from it.

But if I hate it because it is unjust and makes itself the center of everything, I will always hate it.

In a word, the self has two qualities: it is unjust in itself, in that it makes itself the center of everything; it is irritating to others, in that it would subjugate them, for each self is the enemy and would like to be the tyrant of all others. You take away the irritation, but not the injustice.

And thus you do not make it pleasing to those who hate its injustice. You make it pleasing only to the unjust who no longer find it their enemy. And thus you remain unjust and can please only the unjust.

What spoils us in comparing what once happened in the   S495/L598 Church with what we see there now is that we usually regard Saint Athanasius, Saint Theresa, and the others as crowned with glory and [. . .][142] considered as gods before our time. Now that time has cleared things up, it does so appear. But at the time when he was being persecuted, this great saint was a man called Athanasius and Saint Theresa a mad woman. *Elias was a man like us,* subject to the same passions as we are, said Saint Peter,[143] to disabuse Christians of the false idea that makes us reject the example of the saints as disproportionate to our state. They were saints, we say; they are not like us. What actually happened then? Saint Athanasius was a man called Athanasius, accused of several crimes, condemned by such and such a council for such and such a crime. All the bishops agreed, and finally the Pope. What did they say to those dissenting? That they were disturbing the peace, causing a schism, etc.

Zeal, illumination. Four kinds of persons: zeal without knowledge, knowledge without zeal, neither knowledge nor zeal, both zeal and knowledge.

---

[142] Undecipherable word.

[143] Actually, James 5:17.

The first three condemn him; the last acquit him and are excommunicated by the Church, and yet save the Church.

But is it probable that probability brings certainty? S496/L599

Difference between tranquility and certainty of conscience. Nothing brings certainty but truth. Nothing brings tranquility but the sincere search for truth.

The corruption of reason is shown by the number of S497/L600
different and extravagant customs. Truth had to come so that man should no longer live for himself.

The casuists submit decisions to corrupt reason and the S498/L601
choice of decisions to corrupt will, so that everything corrupt in man's nature takes part in his conduct.

You want the Church to judge neither the internal, S499/L923
because that belongs to God alone, nor the external, because God is concerned only with the internal. And thus, taking from it all choice of men, you keep within the Church the most dissolute, those who dishonor it so greatly that the Jewish synagogues and philosophical sects would have banished them as unworthy and have abhorred them as impious.

Anyone who wants can be ordained a priest, as under S500/L602
Jeroboam.[144]

It is a terrible thing that the discipline of the present-day Church is represented as so excellent that wanting to change it is made into a crime. Formerly it was infallibly excellent, and we find that it could be changed without sinning. And now, such as it is, we cannot wish it changed?

Indeed, the custom of not ordaining priests without such great circumspection that hardly any were worthy has been allowed to change. And are we not allowed to complain about the custom that produces so many unworthy ones?

———

Abraham took nothing for himself, but only for his S500/L603
servants. So, the righteous man takes nothing for himself from the world or its applause, but only for his passions, which he uses as a master, saying to one, *Go* and [to another] *Come. Your desire shall lie below you.*[145] The passions thus subdued become virtues: avarice,

---

[144] 1 Kings 12:31.

[145] *Sub te erit appetitus tuus.* Genesis 4:7.

jealousy, anger, even God attributes them to himself; and these are virtues as much as kindness, pity, constancy, which are also passions. We must use them as slaves, leaving them their nourishment, but preventing the soul from taking any. For, when the passions are masters, they become vices, and then they give their food to the soul, and the soul nourishes itself upon it and is poisoned.

The Church, the Pope   S501/L604
Unity / plurality

Considering the Church as a unity, the Pope, who is its head, is like the whole. Considering it as a plurality, the Pope is only a part of it. The Fathers considered it sometimes one way, sometimes the other, and so they spoke of the Pope in different ways.

Saint Cyprian, *Priest of God*.[146]

But in establishing one of these truths, they did not exclude the other.

Plurality not reduced to unity is confusion. Unity that does not depend on plurality is tyranny.

———

There is scarcely anywhere else than France where it is permissible to say that the council is above the Pope.

Man is full of needs. He likes only those who can satisfy   S502/L605
them all. He is a good mathematician, you will say, but I have
little to do with mathematics: he would take me for a proposition. He is a good soldier: he would take me for a place under siege. I need, then, an honorable man who can adapt himself generally to all my needs.

———

A true friend is something so valuable, even for the   S502/L606
greatest noblemen, that they should do all they can to have
one, so that he can speak well of them and support them even in their absence. But they should choose well! For, if they expend all their efforts on fools, it will be no use, however well these may speak of them; and even then, these will not speak well of them if they find themselves on the weaker side, because they have no authority, and thus they will speak ill of them to curry the favor of those around them.

<See the discourses of the Jansenist in [*Provincial Letters*]   S503/L610
2, 4, and 5: this is elevated and serious.>

———

---

[146] *Sacerdos Dei*. Epistle 63.

<I equally dislike the fool and the overblown person.> You would not make a friend of either.

———

We only consult the ear because we are lacking in heart.

———

The rule is integrity.   S503/L611

———

A poet and not an honorable man.[147]
Beauties of omission, of judgment.

Figures.   S504/L607
Savior, father, sacrificer, offering, food, king, wise, law-
giver, afflicted, poor, needing to create a people he should lead and feed, and bring into his land.

Jesus Christ. Offices.   S504/L608
He alone had to produce a great people, elect, holy, and chosen; lead, nourish, and bring it into the place of tranquility and holiness; make it holy to God, make it the temple of God, reconcile it with God and save it from the wrath of God; free it from the bondage of sin that visibly reigns in man; give laws to this people, engrave these laws on their hearts; offer himself to God for them and sacrifice himself for them; be a victim without blemish, and himself the sacrificer, having to offer himself, his body, and his blood, and yet offer bread and wine to God.
When he comes into the world.[148]

———

Stone upon stone.[149]

———

What preceded and what followed. All the Jews surviving and all wanderers.

———

They have pierced.[150] Zechariah 12:10.   S504/L609
Prophecies.

---

[147] After this sentence, the original text has the following deleted text, which is not found in copy B (L611): <After my eighth Letter, I thought I had replied sufficiently.>

[148] *Ingrediens mundum.* Hebrews 10:5.

[149] Mark 13:2.

[150] *Transfixerunt.*

That a deliverer should come who would crush the demon's head and deliver his people from their sins, *from all their iniquities*.[151] That there should be a New Testament, which would be eternal; that there should be another priesthood *after the order of Melchisedek*,[152] and this one should be eternal; that the Christ should be glorious, mighty, strong, and yet so wretched that he would not be recognized; that he would not be taken for what he is, but rejected and slain; that his people who denied him would no longer be his people; that the idolaters would receive him and take refuge in him; that he would leave Zion to reign in the center of idolatry; that nevertheless the Jews would continue forever; that he should be of Judah, even when there would no longer be a king there.

It is indubitable that the question of the mortality or   S505/L612
immortality of the soul must make all the difference in
ethics. And yet philosophers have managed their ethics independently of this!

They deliberate to pass an hour.

Plato, to dispose toward Christianity.
                    Greatness, wretchedness   S506/L613
The more enlightened we are, the more greatness and
lowliness we discover in man.
The common sort of men.
Those who are more educated.
Philosophers.
They surprise the common sort of men.
Christians. They surprise the philosophers.
Who will be surprised then to see that religion only allows us deep knowledge of what we already recognize in proportion to our enlightenment?
                        Figurative   S507/L614
God made use of the Jews' concupiscence so that they be
of use to Jesus Christ <who brought the remedy for concupiscence.>
                        Figurative   S508/L615
Nothing is so like charity as greed, and nothing is so un-
like. Thus the Jews, full of possessions to flatter their greed, were very

------

[151] *Ex omnibus iniquitatibus.* Psalms 130:8.
[152] Psalms 110:4.

like Christians and very unlike them. And by this means they had the two qualities they needed to have: to be very like the Messiah, so as to prefigure him, and very unlike, so as not to be suspect witnesses.

Concupiscence has become natural to us and constitutes   S509/L616
our second nature. Thus there are two natures in us: the one good, the other bad. Where is God? Where you are not. And *the kingdom of God is within you.*[153] Rabbis.

Whoever does not hate in himself his self-love and this   S510/L617
instinct that leads him to make himself God is indeed blinded. Who does not see that there is nothing so contrary to justice and truth? For it is false that we deserve this, and it is unfair and impossible to achieve it, since everyone demands the same thing. It is, therefore, a manifest injustice in which we are born, which we cannot get rid of, and which we must get rid of.

Yet no religion has indicated that this was a sin, nor that we were born with it, nor that we were obliged to resist it, nor has thought of giving us remedies for it.

If God exists, we must love only him and not transitory   S511/L618
creatures. The argument of the impious in *Wisdom* is based solely on the nonexistence of God. "That granted," they say, "*let us take delight in creatures.*"[154]

That is the worst case. But if there were a God to love, they would not have reached this conclusion, but quite the opposite one. And the conclusion of the wise is this: "God exists; let us therefore not take delight in creatures."

———

Therefore everything that prompts us to become attached to creatures is bad, since it prevents us from serving God, if we know him, or from seeking him, if we do not. Now we are full of concupiscence; therefore we are full of evil; therefore we ought to hate ourselves, and everything that prompts us to any other attachment than to God alone.

All their principles are true, those of the skeptics, stoics,   S512/L619
atheists, etc. But their conclusions are false, because the opposite principles are also true.

Man is obviously made to think. It is his whole dignity and   S513/L620
merit, and his whole duty is to think properly. Now, the order of thought is to begin with self and its author and its end.

———

[153] Luke 17:21.
[154] Wisdom of Solomon 2:6.

Now, what does the world think about? Never about this! But about dancing, playing the lute, singing, making verses, tilting at the ring, etc., about fighting, becoming king, without thinking of what it is to be king or to be man.

Internal war in man between reason and the passions.   S514/L621

If there were only reason without passions.

If there were only passions without reason.

But having both, he cannot be without war, being unable to have peace with one without war with the other.

Thus he is always divided and contrary to himself.

Boredom   S515/L622

Nothing is so intolerable for man as to be in complete tranquility, without passions, without dealings, without diversion, without effort. He then feels his nothingness, isolation, insufficiency, dependence, weakness, emptiness. Immediately there arises from the depth of his soul boredom, gloom, sadness, chagrin, resentment, despair.

If it is a supernatural blindness to live without seeking   S516/L623
what we are, it is a terrible one to live badly believing in God.

Prophecies   S517/L624

That Jesus Christ will sit on the right hand, while God will subdue his enemies.[155]

Therefore he will not subdue them himself.

Injustice   S518/L625

That presumption should be joined to wretchedness is an extreme injustice.

Search for the true good   S519/L626

The common sort of men places the good in fortune and external goods, or at least in diversion.

Philosophers have shown the vanity of all this and have placed it where they could.

Vanity is so anchored in the human heart that a soldier, a   S520/L627
camp servant, a cook, a dockhand brags and wants to have his admirers, and even philosophers want them; and those who write in opposition want to have the glory of having written well; and those who read them want the glory of having read them; and I writing this have perhaps this desire, and perhaps those who will read it . . .

On the desire for being esteemed by those with whom   S521/L628
we are.

---

[155] Psalms 110:1–2.

Pride takes such natural hold of us in the midst of our miseries, errors, etc., that we even lose our lives gladly, provided people talk about it.

Vanity: gaming, hunting, visits, theater, false perpetuity of name.

This duality of man is so evident that some have thought   S522/L629
we had two souls.

A single subject seemed to them incapable of such sudden variations as these: from inordinate presumption to an appalling weakness of heart.[156]

Man's nature is: wholly nature. *Every animal.*[157]   S523/L630
There is nothing that cannot be made natural. There is nothing natural that cannot be lost.

It is good to be tired and weary from the useless search   S524/L631
after the true good, so that we may stretch out our arms to the Redeemer.

Man's sensibility for trifles and his insensibility for the   S525/L632
greatest things: signs of a strange reversal.

Despite the sight of all our miseries pressing upon us and   S526/L633
taking us by the throat, we have an instinct we cannot suppress that lifts us up.

The most important thing in all of life is the choice of   S527/L634
vocation: chance decides it. Custom makes men masons, soldiers, roofers. He is an excellent roofer, someone says. And, speaking of soldiers: They are quite crazy, someone says. But others, on the contrary: There is nothing great but war, the rest are rascals. As we hear these vocations praised in our childhood and all others disdained, we make our choice. For we naturally love virtue and hate folly. These very words move us; we only fail in applying them. So great is the force of custom that, where nature has created only men, we create all conditions of men.

For some places are full of masons, others soldiers, etc. No doubt nature is not so uniform. It is custom, therefore, that does this, for it con-

---

[156] See Montaigne, *Essays* II, chap. 1: "This supple variation and contradiction evident in us has made some imagine that we have two souls . . . for such sudden diversity cannot well be reconciled with a simple subject" (Frame trans., p. 242; Screech trans., p. 376).

[157] *Omne animal.* Allusion to Ecclesiasticus 13:15 (Every animal loves its like) or to Genesis 7:14 (every animal after its kind).

strains nature. But sometimes nature gains the upper hand and keeps man to his instinct, in spite of all customs, good or bad.

[35. Miscellaneous Thoughts 3]

We like to see the error, the passion of Cléobuline,[158]   S528/L635
because she is unaware of it. She would be displeasing if she were not deceived.

___

Prince is pleasing to a king, because it diminishes his rank.   S528/L636
To extinguish the torch of sedition: too lavish.   S529/L637

___

The restlessness of his mind (génie): two bold words too many.

___

When we are well, we wonder how we could manage if   S529/L638
we were ill. But when we are ill, we take medicine cheerfully: the illness settles it; we no longer have the passions and desires for the diversions and outings our health provided us, but which are incompatible with the demands of illness. Nature then provides passions and desires suitable to the present condition. It is only the fears that we, and not nature, give ourselves that trouble us, because they join to the condition in which we are, the passions of the state in which we are not.

___

Since nature makes us constantly unhappy in every   S529/L639
condition, our desires depict for us a happy condition, because they join to the condition in which we are, the pleasures of the condition in which we are not. And if we attained these pleasures, we would not be happy even then, because we would have other desires suitable to this new condition.

We must particularize this general proposition.

___

Those who continue to have good hope and are delighted   S529/L640
with good luck when something goes wrong are suspected of being very pleased with the failure if they are not distressed equally by the bad luck; and they are thrilled to find these excuses for hope to show that they are concerned, and to conceal, with the joy they pretend to feel, the one they have at seeing the failure.

---

[158] The queen of Corinth, in Madeleine de Scudery's novel, *Le Grand Cyrus*.

———

Our nature consists in motion; complete rest is death.   S529/L641

———

Miton sees very well that nature is corrupt and that men   S529/L642
are averse to integrity. But he does not know why they cannot
fly higher.

———

Noble deeds are most estimable when hidden. When I   S529/L643
see some of these in history (as on page 184),[159] they please
me greatly; but after all they were not completely hidden, since they
were known. And although people have done what they could to hide
them, the little by which they have become known spoils everything.
For what is best in them is wanting to have them hidden.

———

Can it be anything but the acquiescence of the world that   S529/L644
makes you find things probable? Will you have us believe
that it is truth and that, if dueling were not the fashion, you would find
fighting probable, looking at the thing in itself?

Justice is what is established. And thus all our established   S530/L645
laws will necessarily be held to be just without examination,
since they are established.

Feeling   S531/L646

Memory, joy, are feelings. And even geometrical propositions become feelings, for reason produces natural feelings and natural
feelings are eradicated by reason.

Gentleman   S532/L647

We should be able to say of him not: he is a mathematician, or a preacher, or eloquent; but that he is an honorable man. That
universal quality alone pleases me. It is a bad sign when, seeing a person, we remember his book. I would prefer no quality be perceptible
until it arises and there is occasion to use it, "**Nothing in excess**,"[160] for
fear of one quality prevailing and labeling the person. Let no one think
him a good speaker unless speaking well is in question. But then we
should think him so.

---

[159] Montaigne, *Essays* I, chap. 41: p. 184 of the 1652 edition.
[160] *Ne quid nimis.*

Miracle   S533/L648

The people concluded this by themselves, but if you must
give its reason . . .

———

It is annoying to be the exception to the rule. We must even be strict,
and opposed to exceptions. But yet, since it is certain there are exceptions to the rule, we must judge them severely, though justly.

Montaigne   S534/L649

What is good in Montaigne can only have been acquired
with difficulty. What is bad in him, I mean apart from morals, could
have been corrected in a moment, if someone had told him that he
made too much of a fuss and spoke too much about himself.

Have you never seen people who, in order to complain of   S535/L650
the lack of regard you have for them, display before you
examples of great men who think well of them? I would reply: "Show
me the merit by which you have charmed these persons and I, too, will
think well of you."

Memory is necessary for all the operations of reason.   S536/L651

When a natural discourse depicts a passion or an effect,   S536/L652
we find within ourselves the truth of what we hear, which we
did not know to be there, such that we are inclined to love the person who
made us feel it, for he has not shown us his own wealth, but ours. And
thus this kindness makes him pleasing to us, in addition to the fact that
the community of intellect we necessarily share moves our heart to love
him.

Probability   S537/L653

Anyone can add to it; no one can take it away.

You never accuse me of falsity about Escobar, because he   S538/L654
is so common.

Discourses about humility are a source for pride to the   S539/L655
proud and humility to the humble. In the same way, discourses about skepticism are a source for assertion to the assertive. Few
speak humbly of humility, chastely of chastity, doubtingly of skepticism.
We are but falsehood, duplicity, contradiction, and we both conceal
and disguise ourselves from ourselves.

When writing down my thought, it sometimes escapes   S540/L656
me, but this makes me remember my weakness, which I am
constantly forgetting. This is as instructive to me as my forgotten
thought, for I care only to know my nothingness.

Feeling sorry for the unfortunate does not go against   S541/L657
concupiscence. On the contrary, we are quite happy to provide such evidence of friendship and acquire a reputation for kindness
without giving anything.

Conversation   S542/L658

Big words about religion: "I deny it."

Conversation

Skepticism is useful to religion.

Must we kill to prevent there being any wicked people?   S543/L659
This is to make two wicked ones instead of one, "*Overcome evil with good*,"[161] Saint Augustine.

Spongia solis[162]   S544/L660

When we see the same effect always occurring, we infer
from this a natural necessity, like: there will be a day tomorrow, etc. But
nature often deceives us, and does not obey its own rules.

The mind naturally believes and the will naturally loves.   S544/L661
As a result, lacking true objects, they must attach themselves
to false ones.

There will always be grace in the world, and nature also,   S544/L662
so that grace is in some way natural. And thus there will always be Pelagians,[163] and always Catholics, and always strife.

Because the first birth creates the former and the grace of rebirth the
latter.

Nature always begins the same things over again: years,   S544/L663
days, hours; spaces too; and numbers follow one another
from beginning to end. Thus is created a kind of infinity and eternity.
Not that anything in all this is infinite and eternal, but these finite beings
are infinitely multiplied. Thus, it seems to me, only number, which
multiplies them, is infinite.

Man is properly *every animal*.[164]   S545/L664

---

[161] *Vince in bono malum*. Romans 12:2. The quotation comes from Sermon 302 of Saint
Augustine.

[162] Literally "sponge of the sun," name given to a phosphorescent rock discovered in
1604, which became luminescent when exposed to sunlight.

[163] Pelagians are disciples of Pelagius, an English theologian excommunicated in 417 due
to pressure exerted by Saint Augustine. Augustine objected to Pelagius' denial of original
sin and to his claim that salvation does not depend wholly on grace, but also requires an
act of free will on the part of the agent.

[164] *Omne animal*, allusion to Ecclesiasticus 13:15 or to Genesis 7:14. See fragment
S523/L630.

The empire based on opinion and imagination reigns for   S546/L665
some time, and this empire is sweet and voluntary. The one
based on force reigns forever. Thus opinion is like the queen of the
world, but force is its tyrant.

Anyone condemned by Escobar will be well condemned!   S547/L666

Eloquence   S547/L667

It requires something of the pleasant and the real, but the
pleasant must itself be taken from the true.

Each person is everything to himself, for once dead every-   S547/L668
thing is dead for him. As a result, each person believes he is
everything to everybody. We must not judge nature according to ourselves, but according to it.

In every dialogue and discourse, we must be able to say to   S548/L669
those who take offense, "What are you complaining about?"

Witty narrator, bad character.   S549/L670

Do you want people to think well of you? Do not speak   S550/L671
well of yourself.

Not only do we look at things from different sides, but   S551/L672
with different eyes. We are far from finding them alike.

He no longer loves the person he loved ten years ago. I   S552/L673
quite believe it: she is no longer the same, nor is he. He was
young and so was she; she is now quite different. He would perhaps still
love her as she was then.

We do not keep ourselves virtuous by our own strength,   S553/L674
but by the counterbalancing of two opposed vices, just as we
remain upright between two contrary gusts. Remove one of the vices,
we fall into the other.

Style   S554/L675

When we see a natural style, we are surprised and delighted, for we expected to see an author and find a man. Instead, those
with good taste, and who, seeing a book, expect to find a man, are quite
surprised to find an author. ***You have spoken more as a poet than as a
man.***[165] Those people honor nature well who show it that it can talk
about everything, even theology.

The world must be truly blind if it believes you.   S555/L676

The Pope hates and fears scholars who have not taken a   S556/L677
vow to obey him.

---

[165] *Plus poetice quam humane locutus es.* Petronius, 90.

Man is neither angel nor beast, and unfortunately S557/L678
whoever wants to act the angel acts the beast.[166]

Prou[167] S558/L679

Those who love the Church complain about the corruption of morals; but at least the laws remain. But these people corrupt the laws. The model is damaged.

Montaigne S559/L680

Montaigne's faults are great. Lewd words: this is worthless, despite Mademoiselle de Gournay.[168]

Credulous: **people without eyes**. Ignorant: **squaring the circle, a greater world**. His views on voluntary homicide,[169] on death. He inspires indifference about salvation, **without fear and without repentance**. As his book was not written to encourage piety, he was not obliged to do so; but we are always obliged not to discourage it. We can excuse his rather free and licentious views on some circumstance of life — 730, 731 — but we cannot excuse his thoroughly heathen views on death. For we would have to renounce all piety if we did not at least want to die as a Christian. Now, throughout the whole of his book he only thinks of dying in a cowardly and weak manner.

I do not admire the excess of a virtue like valor, unless I S560/L681
see at the same time an excess of the opposite virtue, as with Epaminondas,[170] who possessed extreme valor and extreme kindness. For otherwise it is not rising but falling. We do not show greatness by being at one extreme, but by touching both at the same time and filling everything in between.

But perhaps it is only a sudden movement of the soul from one extreme to the other, and it is never in fact but at one point, as in the case of a fire ember. So be it, but at least this indicates the agility of the soul, if it does not indicate its range.

---

[166] Cf. Montaigne, *Essays* III, chap. 13: "They want to get out of themselves and escape from their humanity. This is madness: instead of changing into angels, they change to beasts; instead of raising themselves, they lower themselves" (Frame trans., p. 856; Screech trans., p. 1268).

[167] That is, Prov., which is shorthand for *Provincial Letters*.

[168] Marie Jars De Gournay was Montaigne's literary executrix and the author of a preface to the *Essays*.

[169] Meaning suicide. See Montaigne, *Essays* II, chap. 3: "The most voluntary death is the fairest." (Frame trans., p. 252.)

[170] See Montaigne, *Essays* III, chap. 1, end.

Infinite motion   S561/L682

Infinite motion, the point that fills everything, motion at
rest, infinite without quantity, indivisible and infinite.

Order   S562/L683

Why should I choose to divide my ethics into four rather
than six? Why should I set up virtue as four, rather than as two, as one?
Why as **abstain and sustain**[171] rather than *follow nature*, or, **conduct
your private affairs without injustice**, like Plato, or something else?

But, you will say, there everything is captured in a word. Yes, but it is
useless if you do not explain it. And when you come to explain it, as
soon as you open up this precept that contains all the others, they
emerge in that original confusion you wanted to avoid. So, when they
are all enclosed in one, they are hidden and useless there, as in a box,
and never appear except in their natural confusion. Nature has established them all without enclosing one inside the other.

Nature has placed all its truths each in itself. Our art   S563/L684
encloses some inside others, but this is not natural. Each
holds its own place.

Glory   S564/L685

Animals do not admire each other. A horse does not admire its companion. Not that there is not some rivalry between them in
a race, but it is without consequence, for, in the stable, the heavier and
less powerfully built horse does not give up its oats to the other, as men
want others to do for them. Their virtue is self-sufficient.

When it is said that heat is merely the motion of certain   S565/L686
globules and light the **conatus recedendi**[172] we feel, it surprises us. What! Is pleasure nothing more than a dance of [animal]
spirits? We had such a different idea of it! And these feelings seem so far
removed from the others that we say are the ones with which we are
comparing them! The feeling of fire, this warmth that affects us in a
wholly different way from touch, the reception of sound and light, all
this seems mysterious to us, and yet it is as crude as being hit by a stone.
It is true that, in their smallness, the spirits entering the pores touch
other nerves, but it is still nerves that are being touched.

I had spent a long time in the study of abstract sciences,   S566/L687
and I was disheartened by what little exchange of ideas can

---

[171] *Abstine et sustine.* Stoic maxim.

[172] The *conatus recedendi* is the effort of bodies moving in a circle to recede from their
centers of motion (see Descartes, *Principles of Philosophy* III, art. 54; he makes use of the
term in III, art. 59).

be had in them. When I began the study of man, I saw that these abstract sciences were not proper to man, and that I was straying farther from my own condition by trying to penetrate them than others were by not knowing them. I forgave the others their little knowledge. But I thought at least I should find many companions in the study of man, since it is the true study proper to man.[173] I was mistaken: even fewer people study it than geometry. It is only because we do not know how to study this that we seek other studies. But is it not the case that this is still not the knowledge man should have, and that it is better for him not to know himself in order to be happy?

What is the self?   S567/L688

A man goes to the window to see the passersby; if I pass by, can I say he went there to see me? No, for he is not thinking of me in particular. But does someone who loves another because of her beauty really love her? No, because the smallpox, which will destroy beauty without destroying the person, will cause him to love her no more.

And if someone loves me for my judgment, for my memory, does he love me, myself? No, because I can lose these qualities without losing myself. Where, then, is this self, if it is neither in the body nor in the soul? And how to love the body or the soul, except for its qualities that do not constitute the self, since they are perishable? For would we love the substance of a person's soul in the abstract, whatever qualities might be in it? This would be impossible and wrong. Therefore we never love a person, but only some qualities.

Let us, then, stop mocking those who are honored for their appointments and offices! For we love no person but for their borrowed qualities.

It is not in Montaigne, but in myself, that I find every-   S568/L689 thing I see in him.

Let God not impute to us our sins;[174] that is to say, all the   S569/L690 consequences and results of our sins, which are dreadful, even in our smallest faults, if we want to pursue them without mercy.

Skepticism   S570/L691

Skepticism is the truth. For, after all, men before Jesus Christ did not know where they stood, nor if they were great or small. And those who said one or the other knew nothing about it, and guessed without reason and by chance, and indeed they always erred by excluding the one or the other.

---

[173] Cf. Pierre Charron, *Wisdom*, Preface: "The true science and true study of man is man."

[174] Cf. Psalms 32:2.

What you seek without knowing, religion will announce to you.[175]

Montalte[176]   S571/L692

Lax opinions please men so much that it is strange that theirs displease. It is because they have exceeded all bounds. Moreover, many people see the truth and cannot attain it, but few do not know that the purity of religion is contrary to our corruptions. Absurd to say that an eternal reward is offered to Escobardian morals.

The easiest conditions to live in according to the world   S572/L693 are the most difficult according to God. On the other hand, nothing is as difficult, according to the world, as the religious life; nothing is easier than living this way, according to God. Nothing is easier than having high office and great wealth, according to the world. Nothing is more difficult than living this way, according to God, and without acquiring an interest and a taste for it.

Order   S573/L694

I could well have taken this discourse in an order like this, to show the vanity of all sorts of conditions: to show the vanity of ordinary lives, and then the vanity of philosophical lives, skeptic or stoic. But the order would not have been kept. I know a bit about it, and how few people understand it. No human science can keep it. Saint Thomas did not keep it. Mathematics keeps it, but it is useless in its depths.

Original sin is folly in the eyes of men, but it is given as   S574/L695 such. You must not, therefore, reproach me for the lack of reason in this doctrine, since I give it as being without reason. But this folly is wiser than all the wisdom of men, *is wiser than men.*[177] For without it, what will we say man is? His whole state depends on this imperceptible point. And how could he perceive it through his reason, since it is something contrary to his reason, and his reason, far from discovering it by its own ways, draws away when presented with it?

Let no one say I have said nothing new: the arrangement   S575/L696 of the material is new. When we play handball, we both play with the same ball, but one of us places it better.

I would just as soon be told I have used old words. As if the same thoughts did not form a different discourse by being arranged differently, just as the same words form different thoughts by their being arranged differently!

---

[175] *Quod ergo ignorantes, quaeritis, religio annuntiat vobis.* Cf. Acts 17:23.

[176] Louis de Montalte was Pascal's pseudonym in the *Provincial Letters.*

[177] *Sapientius est hominibus.* I Corinthians 1:25

People who lead disordered lives tell those who lead   S576/L697
ordered ones that they are the ones deviating from nature,
and believe themselves to be following it: as people on a ship think
those on the shore are moving away. The language is the same in all
cases. We need a fixed point in order to judge it. The harbor decides for
those who are on a ship. But where will we find a harbor in morals?

Nature copies itself   S577/L698

Nature copies itself: a seed cast on good ground produces
fruit; a principle cast into a good mind produces fruit.

Numbers copy space, though they are of such a different nature.

Everything is made and directed by the same master: root, branches,
fruits, principles, consequences.

When everything moves equally, nothing appears to be   S577/L699
moving, as on a ship. When everyone tends toward debauch-
ery, none appears to do so: whoever stops draws attention to the excess of
others, like a fixed point.

Generals[178]   S578/L700

It is not enough for them to introduce such behavior into
our temples, **to bring their customs into the temples**.[179] Not only do
they want to be tolerated in the Church, but, as they become the most
powerful, they want to drive out those who are not theirs . . .

Mohatra,[180] **one does not have to be a theologian to be astonished
by it.**

Who could have told your generals that the time was so near when
they would offer such customs to the universal Church, and call the rejection of these disorders an act of war? **Such great plagues they called
peace**.[181]

When we want to correct another usefully and show him   S579/L701
he is wrong, we must notice from what side he takes up the
matter, for from that side it is usually true; and we must admit that truth
to him, but show him the side from which it is false. This will satisfy
him, for he will see that he was not wrong and merely failed to see all
sides. Now, we are not offended at not seeing everything, but we do not
like to be wrong. Perhaps this comes from the fact that man by nature

---

[178] The head of the Jesuit order was called the General of the Jesuits.

[179] *Templis inducere mores.*

[180] According to Pascal's 8th *Provincial Letter*, "Mohatra is the name of a contract by
which someone purchases fabric at a high price on credit, in order to resell it at once to
the same person for cash at a lower price."

[181] *Tot et tanta mala pacem.* Wisdom of Solomon 14:22.

cannot see everything, and that by nature he cannot be wrong from the side he takes up, since our sense perceptions are always true.

Movements of grace, hardness of heart, external cir-   S580/L702
cumstances.

Grace   S581/L703

Romans 3:27: boasting (*gloire*) excluded. *By what law?
That of works? No, but by faith.* Then faith is not within our power like the works of the law, and it is given to us in another way.

Venice[182]   S582/L704

What advantage will you derive from it, unless it be from
the needs of princes and horror of the people . . . ? If they had asked you and implored the assistance of Christian princes in obtaining it, you might have justified this attempt. But for fifty years all princes have tried uselessly to get it and it took such an urgent need to obtain it . . . !

The great and the small are liable to the same accidents,   S583/L705
the same annoyances, the same passions. But the one is at
the top of the wheel, and the other near the center, and thus less disturbed by the same movements.[183]

Binding and loosening[184]   S584/L706

God has not wanted to grant absolution without the
Church: since it has a role in the offense, he wants it to have a role in the pardon. He associates it with this power, as do kings their parliaments. But if it absolves or binds without God, it is no longer the Church. The same with parliament: for while the king may have granted a pardon to a person, it must be ratified; but if parliament ratifies without the king, or refuses to ratify on the king's order, it is no longer the king's parliament, but a rebellious body.

They cannot have perpetuity and they seek universality.   S585/L707
And for this they make the whole Church corrupt, so that
they can be saints.

---

[182] The Jesuits were banished from Venice in 1606 and reestablished there in 1657.

[183] Cf. Montaigne, *Essays* II, chap. 12: "The souls of Emperors and of cobblers are cast in the same mold. . . . They are pushed and pulled in their movements by the same mechanism that we are in our own. The same reason that makes us tangle with a neighbor, between princes, starts a war; the same reason that makes us whip a lackey, when it happens in a king, makes him ruin a province. <Their wishes are as frivolous as ours, but they can do more.> Like appetites agitate a mite and an elephant" (Ariew and Grene trans., p. 38).

[184] Cf. Matthew 16:19.

Popes
S586/L708

Kings dispose of their empire, but the Popes cannot dispose of theirs.

S587/L709
We know ourselves so little that many people think they
are about to die when they are quite well, and many think
they are quite well when they are near death, being unaware of the approaching fever or the abscess ready to form.

Language
S588/L710

We should not turn the mind to something else, except
for relaxation when the time is right: relaxation when it is necessary, and not otherwise. For anyone who relaxes at the wrong time wearies, and he who wearies at the wrong time relaxes and gives up everything. So much does our perverse concupiscence delight in doing the opposite of what people want to get from us without giving us pleasure, the coin for which we will do whatever people want.

Power
S589/L711

Why do we follow the majority? Is it because they have
more reason? No, but more power.

Why do we follow the ancient laws and opinions? Is it because they are sounder? No, but they are unique and remove from us the root of diversity.

S590/L712
Someone told me one day that he felt great joy and
confidence after leaving confession. Another told me that he
remained in fear. I thought about this that the two together would make up a good man, and that each was lacking by not having the feelings of the other. The same often happens in other things.

S591/L713
It is not absolution alone that remits sins by the sacrament of penance, but contrition, which is not true if it does
not seek the sacrament.

Thus it is not the nuptial blessing that takes away sin in procreation, but the desire to produce children for God, which is genuine only in marriage.

And as a contrite person without the sacrament is better disposed to receive absolution than an impenitent one with the sacrament, so the daughters of Lot, for example, who wanted only to have children, were purer without marriage than married people with no desire for children.

P. P. Pope
S592/L714

There is some contradiction, for on the one hand they say
that tradition must be followed and that they would not dare to disavow it, and on the other they say what they like. We will always believe the former, since it would also be contrary to them not to believe it.

Principal talent that rules all the others.   S593/L715

Fear death outside of danger, and not when in danger, for   S594/L716
one must be a man.

Rivers are roads that move and that carry us wherever we   S595/L717
want to go.

The five propositions were equivocal; they are no longer so.   S596/L718

I have reserved 7,000 for me.[185] I love these worshipers who   S597/L719
are unknown to the world and to the very prophets.

Universal   S598/L720

Ethics / and language / are special, but universal sciences.

Probability   S598/L721

The ardor of the saints in seeking the truth was useless if
the probable is sure.

The fear of the saints who always followed the surest course.
Saint Teresa, who always followed her confessor.

It is in vain that the Church established the words   S599/L967
anathema, heresies, etc.: they are used against it.

Probable   S600/L722

Let us see whether we seek God sincerely, by comparing
the things we care about.

It is probable that this food (*viande*) will not poison me.

It is probable that I shall not lose my suit by not prosecuting it.

Two infinites. Mean.   S601/L723

When we read too quickly or too slowly, we understand
nothing.

Do you dare trifle with the king's edicts, as when you say   S602/L722
that going into a field and waiting for someone is not dueling?

Probable   S603/L722

Even if it were true that serious authors and reasons were
sufficient, I say that they are neither serious nor reasonable.

Why! A husband can take advantage of his wife according to Molina!
Is the reason he gives reasonable? And is Lessius' contrary reason reasonable as well?

That the Church has truly prohibited dueling, but not   S604/L723
going out for a walk.

And also usury, but not . . .

---

[185] Cf. 1 Kings 19:18.

And simony, but not . . .
And revenge, but not . . .
And sodomites, but not . . .
And *as soon as possible*,[186] but not . . .

What a man's virtue is able to do must not be measured by   S605/L724
his efforts, but by his ordinary behavior.

Sinners without penitence.   S606/L725
Just people without charity.
A God without power over the will of men, predestination without
mystery.

P. P. Pope   S607/L726

God does not perform miracles in the ordinary conduct of
his Church. It would be a strange miracle if infallibility resided in one
man. But for it to reside in a multitude appears so natural, since God's
conduct is hidden under nature, as in all his other works.

They make a rule of exception. Have the ancients given   S608/L727
absolution before penance? Do this in the spirit of an exception. But from this exception you make a rule without exceptions, so
that you do not even want the rule to be exceptional.

Miracles   S609/L728

Saint Thomas, vol. 3, bk. 8, chap. 20.

All the false beauties we disparage in Cicero have their   S610/L728
admirers, and in great number.

Casuists   S611/L729

Considerable alms, reasonable penance: although we
cannot define what is just, we can easily see what is not. It is absurd of
the casuists to think that they can interpret it as they do.

———

People become accustomed to speak and to think badly.

———

Their great numbers, far from indicating their perfection, indicate
the contrary.

———

The humility of one is the pride of many.

---

[186] *Quam primum*: the obligation to confess one's sin.

[III. The Final Miscellaneous Folders (July 1658–July 1662)]

[36. Miscellaneous Thoughts 4]

CC. *You being a man make yourself God.*[1] S612/L730

––––

CC. *Is it not written: you are Gods . . . and the Scripture cannot be broken.*[2]

––––

CC. *This sickness is not unto death [but unto life].*[3]
But it is unto death.

––––

Lazarus sleeps. Then he said: Lazarus is dead.[4]
These people are lacking in heart. S613/L731

––––

We should not make friends of them.

––––

Poet, and not honorable man. S613/L732

The Church has always been attacked by contrary errors. S614/L733
But perhaps never before at the same time, as it is now. And
if it suffers more because of the multiplicity of errors, it derives this advantage: that they destroy each other.

––––

It complains of both, but much more of the Calvinists, because of
the schism.

––––

It is certain that many on the two contrary sides are mistaken. They
must be disabused.

––––

---

[1] *Homo existens te Deum facis.* John 10:33.

[2] *Scriptum est: Dii estis . . . et non potest solvi Scriptura.* John 10:34–35.

[3] *Haec infirmitas non est ad mortem.* John 11:4.

[4] *Lazarus dormit. Et deinde manifeste dixit: Lazarus mortuus est.* John 11:11 and 14.

Faith embraces many seemingly contradictory truths. *Time to laugh, time to weep,*[5] etc. *Answer, answer not,*[6] etc.

The source of this is the union of two natures in Jesus Christ.

———

And also the two worlds, the creation of a new heaven and a new earth, a new life, a new death. All things doubled, and the same names remaining.

———

And finally the two men who are among the righteous, for they are the two worlds, both a member and an image of Jesus Christ. And thus all the names are suitable for them: righteous sinners, dead living, living dead, chosen outcast, etc.

———

There are then a great number of truths, both of faith and morality, that seem incompatible and all subsist together in a wonderful order.

———

The source of all heresies is the exclusion of some of these truths.

———

And the source of all the objections made by the heretics against us is the ignorance of some of our truths.

———

And it usually happens that, unable to conceive the connection of two opposing truths and believing that the acceptance of one entails the exclusion of the other, they adhere to the one, exclude the other, and think of us as doing the opposite. Now exclusion is the cause of their heresy; and ignorance that we hold the other truth causes their objections.

———

First example: Jesus Christ is God and man. The Arians, unable to connect these things, which they believe incompatible, say that he is man; in this they are Catholics. But they deny that he is God; in this they are heretics. They claim that we deny his humanity; in this they are ignorant.

———

———

[5] Ecclesiastes 3:4.

[6] *Responde. Ne respondeas*; Proverbs 26:4–5.

Second example: On the subject of the Holy Sacrament. We believe that when the substance of the bread is changed and transubstantiated into that of our Lord's body, Jesus Christ is really present in it; that is one of the truths. Another is that this sacrament is also a figure of the cross and glory, and a commemoration of the two. That is the Catholic faith, which encompasses these two seemingly opposed truths.

Today's heresy, not conceiving that this sacrament contains both the presence of Jesus Christ and a figure of him, and that it is a sacrifice and a commemoration of a sacrifice, believes for this reason that one of these truths cannot be admitted without the other's being rejected.

They fasten on this point alone, that this sacrament is figurative; and in this they are not heretics. They think that we exclude this truth; as a result they raise so many objections about passages of the Fathers asserting it. Finally, they deny the presence; and in this they are heretics.

———

Third example: Indulgences.

———

That is why the shortest way to prevent heresies is to teach all truths. And the surest way to refute them is to proclaim them all.

For what will the heretics say?

In order to know whether an opinion is that of a Father . . .

> How it happens that we believe so many   S615/L734
> liars, who say that they have
> seen miracles, and do not
> believe any of those who say
> that they have secrets to
> make men immortal or to
> make them young again.

Having considered how it happens that we give such great credence to so many impostors who say they have remedies, often to the extent of putting our lives into their hands, it has seemed to me that the true cause is that some are true. For it would not be possible that there should be so many false ones and that so much faith should be placed in them, if none were true. If there had never been any remedy for any ill, and all ills had been incurable, it is impossible that men should have imagined that they could have been given any, and still more so that so many others should have given credence to those who boasted of having some; in the same way that, if a man boasted of preventing death, no one would believe him, because there is no instance of this. But since there have been a number of remedies found to be true and even known by the greatest of men, men's belief is induced by this. And, since this is known to be possible, we have therefore concluded that it is. For people commonly reason thus: a thing is possible, therefore it is; because the thing cannot be denied generally, given that particular effects are true, the people, who cannot distinguish which among these particular effects are true, believe them all. In the same way, what makes us believe so many false effects of the moon is that some are true, like ocean tides.

It is the same with prophecies, miracles, divination by dreams, magic spells, etc. For if there had been nothing true in all of this, we would never have believed any of it; and thus, instead of concluding that there are no true miracles because there are so many false ones, we must, on the contrary, say that there certainly are true miracles, since there are so many false ones, and that there are false ones only because some are true. We must reason in the same way about religion, for it would not be possible that men should have imagined so many false religions, if there had not been a true one. The objection to this is that savages have a religion. But we answer that it is because they have heard about it, as can be seen by the Flood, circumcision, the cross of Saint Andrew, etc.[7]

Having considered how it happens that there are so many   S616/L735
false miracles, false revelations, magic spells, etc., it has
seemed to me that the true cause is that some are true. For it would not be possible that there should be so many false miracles if none were true, nor so many false revelations if none were true, nor so many false religions if there were not a true one. For if there had never been any of this, it is almost impossible that men should have imagined it, and still more impossible that so many others should have believed it. But as very great things have been true, and as a result believed by great men, they made such an impression that nearly everybody has become capable of believing the false as well. And thus, instead of concluding that there are no true miracles, since there are so many false ones, we must, on the contrary, say that there are true miracles, since there are so many false ones; and that there are false ones only because there are true ones, and that, in the same way, there are false religions because there is a true one.

Objection to this: savages have a religion. But this is because they have heard about the true one, as can be seen by the cross of Saint Andrew, the Flood, circumcision, etc.

---

[7] Cf. Montaigne, *Essays* II, chap. 12: "For nations have been found there having, so far as we know, no news of us, where circumcision was approved; [. . .] where our crosses were in use in different ways: here sepulchers were honored with them; there they were used, and in particular that of Saint Andrew, [. . .] their territory changed and their natural condition worsened; that of old they had been submerged by the inundation of the waters of heaven; that only a few families were saved" (Ariew and Grene trans., pp. 134–35).

This comes from the fact that the human mind, finding itself inclined to that side by the truth, becomes susceptible in this way to all the falsehoods of this . . .

When we are accustomed to use bad reasons to prove   S617/L736
natural effects, we are not willing to accept good reasons
when they are discovered. The example given was about the circulation of the blood, to account for why the vein swells below the ligature.

———

We are ordinarily persuaded better by the reasons we   S617/L737
have discovered ourselves than by those that came into the
mind of others.

———

Liancourt's story of the pike and the frog:[8] they always act   S617/L738
in this way, and never otherwise, nor in any other way entailing a mind.

———

Truth is so obscure in these times, and falsehood so well   S617/L739
established, that, unless we loved the truth, we could not
know it.

———

The weak-minded are people who know the truth, but   S617/L740
who affirm it only as far as it is consistent with their own interest. But beyond that they renounce it.

———

The arithmetical machine produces effects that come   S617/L741
closer to thought than all the actions of animals. But it does
nothing that would allow us to attribute will to it, as to the animals.

Even if people happen to have no interest in what they are   S617/L742
saying, we must not absolutely conclude from this that they
are not lying. For there are some people who lie merely for the sake of lying.

———

---

[8] In an attempt to argue against the Cartesian account of animals as machines, the duc de Liancourt must have told a story, taken out of Izaac Walton's The Compleat Angler (1653), of a frog that blinded a pike.

There is pleasure in being on a ship battered by a storm,   S617/L743
when we are sure that it will not founder; the persecutions
buffeting the Church are of this nature.

When we do not know the truth of a thing, it is good that   S618/L744
there should be a common error man's mind can settle on,
as, for example, the moon, to which we attribute the change of seasons,
the progress of diseases, etc. For the principal illness of man is restless
curiosity about things he cannot know. And it is not as bad for him to be
in error as to be curious to no purpose.

_____

The manner in which Epictetus, Montaigne, and   S618/L745
Salomon de Tultie[9] wrote is the commonest, the most sug-
gestive, the most remembered, and the most often quoted, because it
consists entirely of thoughts born out of ordinary conversations; as,
when we speak of the commonly received error that the moon is the
cause of everything, we never fail to say that Salomon de Tultie says
that, when we do not know the truth of a thing, it is good that there
should be a common error, etc., which is the thought on the other side.

On the fact that neither Josephus, nor Tacitus,   S619/L746
nor other historians,
have spoken of Jesus Christ

So far is this from telling against, that on the contrary it tells for it.
For it is certain that Jesus Christ existed and that his religion made a
great stir and that these people were not unaware of it, and so it is obvious
that they purposely concealed it, or that they did speak of it and their
account has been suppressed or changed.

On the fact that the Christian   S620/L747
religion is not unique

So far is this from being a reason for believing it is not the true religion that, on the contrary, it is what makes us see it to be so.

Objection: those who hope for salvation are happy in this   S621/L748
respect, but they have as counterweight the fear of hell.
Reply: who has most reason to fear hell: someone who does not know
there is a hell, and who is certain of damnation if there is; or someone
who certainly believes there is a hell and hopes to be saved if there is?

_____

[9] Anagram of Louis de Montalte, Pascal's pseudonym in the *Provincial Letters*.

How disordered is the judgment by which everyone   S622/L749
places himself above the rest of the world and prefers his own
good and continued happiness and life to that of the rest of the world!

———

Cromwell was about to ravage all Christendom, the royal   S622/L750
family was lost, and his own established forever, save for a little
grain of sand getting into his bladder. Even Rome was about to tremble
under him. But this small piece of gravel having gotten there, he died,
his family was debased, all is peaceful, and the king restored.

———

Those who are accustomed to judge by feeling do not   S622/L751
understand matters involving reasoning. For they want first
to penetrate at a glance and are not used to looking for principles. And
others, on the contrary, who are accustomed to reason from principles,
do not at all understand matters involving feeling, looking for principles
and being unable to see at a glance.

———

Two kinds of people make everything the same, like   S622/L752
holidays and working days, Christians and priests, all sins
among themselves, etc. And hence some conclude that what is bad for
priests is also bad for Christians, and others that what is not bad for
Christians is permissible for priests.

When Augustus learned that among the children less   S623/L753
than two years old put to death by Herod was Herrod's own
son, he said that it was better to be Herod's pig than his son. Macrobius,
Saturnalia, ii. 4.

First step: to be blamed for doing badly, and praised for   S624/L754
doing well.

Second step: to be neither praised nor blamed.

Everyone fashions a God after himself.[10]   S625/L755

———

Disgust.

Thought   S626/L756

All the dignity of man consists in thought. But what is this
thought? That it is foolish?

———

[10] *Unusquisque sibi Deum fingit.* Wisdom of Solomon 15:8, 16.

Thought, then, is a wonderful and incomparable thing by its very nature. It must have strange defects to be contemptible. But it does have such defects, so that nothing is more ridiculous. How great it is in its nature, how vile it is in its defects!

Ebbing away   S626/L757

It is a horrible thing to feel all that we possess ebbing away.

Clarity / Obscurity   S627/L758

There would be too much obscurity if truth had no visible signs. One such wonderful sign is to have always resided in a visible Church and congregation. There would be too great clarity if there were only one opinion in this Church. The one that has always been there is the true one. For the true one has always been there, and nothing false has always been there.

Thought constitutes man's greatness.   S628/L759

Objection. Plainly Scripture is full of things not dictated   S629/L760
by the Holy Spirit.

Answer. Therefore they do not harm the faith.

Objection. But the Church has decided that everything is by the Holy Spirit.

Answer. I answer two things: that the Church has never decided this, and if the Church should so decide, it could be maintained.

———

There are many unsound minds.   S629/L761

———

Dionysius has charity;[11] he was in the right place.   S629/L762

———

Do you think that the prophecies cited in the Gospel are   S629/L763
told to make you believe? No, it is to move you away from believing.

All great diversions are dangerous to the Christian life.   S630/L764
But among all those the world has invented, none is more to be feared than the theatre. It is such a natural and delicate representation of the passions that it excites and engenders them in our hearts, especially that of love, principally when it is represented as very chaste

---

[11] Dionysius the Areopagite, Athenian converted to Christianity by Saint Paul, thought to be the first Bishop of Paris and the author of mystical works now attributed to pseudo-Dionysius, such as *The Divine Names* and *Mystical Theology*.

and virtuous; for the more innocent it seems to innocent souls, the more liable they are to be touched by it. Its violence pleases our self-love, which immediately forms a desire to produce the same effects we see so well represented. And, at the same time, our conscience is conditioned by the propriety of the feelings we perceive there, which remove the fear from pure souls, who imagine their purity cannot be hurt by a love that seems so reasonable.

So, we depart from the theatre with our hearts so filled with all the beauty and tenderness of love, our souls and minds so persuaded of its innocence, that we are quite ready to receive its first impressions, or rather to seek an opportunity for awakening them in someone else's heart, so that we may receive the same pleasures and sacrifices we have seen so well depicted in the theatre.[12]

If lightning struck low-lying places, etc.   S631/L765

Poets, and those who know how to reason only about things of this kind, would lack proofs.

There are many people who listen to a sermon in the   S631/L766
same way as they listen to vespers.

Since dukes, kings, and magistrates are real and neces-   S632/L767
sary (because power rules everything), they exist everywhere
and always. But because only fancy makes this or that person such a one, this is not consistent, but subject to variation, etc.

Reason commands us far more imperiously than does a   S633/L768
master; for in disobeying the one we are wretched, and in disobeying the other we are foolish.

<*You stand in the ways, and see, and ask for the old paths,*   S634/L769
and walk in there. But they say: We will not walk in there,
[. . .] but we will go after our own devices.[13] *They said to the nations:*
Come with us. Let us follow the opinions of the new authors. Natural
reason will be our guide. We shall also be like other nations who all follow
their natural light. The philosophers have . . . >

All religions and sects in the world have had natural reason for a guide. Christians alone have been constrained to take their rules from outside themselves, and to acquaint themselves with those Jesus Christ bequeathed to the ancients to be transmitted to the faithful. This

---

[12] This fragment consists of Pascal's minor emendations of Maxim 81 of Mme. de Sablé's *Maxims.*

[13] *State super vias et interrogate de semitis antiquis et ambulate in eis. Et dixerunt: Non ambulabimus, [. . .] sed post cogitationem nostram ibimus.* Jeremiah 6:16 and 18:12.

constraint wearies these good Fathers; like other people, they want the freedom to follow their own imaginations. In vain we cry to them, as the prophets once said to the Jews: *Go to the midst of the Church; acquaint yourselves with the precepts that the men of old left to it, and follow those paths. They have answered* like the Jews: *We will not walk in there; but we will follow the thoughts of our hearts; and they have said: We will be like the other nations.*[14]

[37. Miscellaneous Thoughts 5]

The example of Alexander's chastity has not made as   S635/L770
many people continent as the example of his drunkenness
has made intemperate. It is not shameful to be less virtuous than he, and it seems excusable to be no more vicious. We do not quite believe that we are sharing in the vices of the ordinary sorts of men when we see ourselves sharing those of great men. And yet we do not notice that they are ordinary sorts in this respect: we take after them in the same way they take after the people, for, however exalted they may be, they are still joined at some point to the lowest of men. They are not suspended in the air, quite detached from our society. No, no, if they are greater than we, it is because their heads are higher, but their feet are as low as ours; they are all at the same level, and rest on the same earth, and by that extremity they are as lowly as we are, as the smallest of us, as children, as beasts.

Continual eloquence is boring.   S636/L771

———

Princes and kings sometimes play; they are not always on their thrones. They would get bored there. Grandeur needs to be put aside to be appreciated. Continuity in anything is distasteful. Cold is agreeable, that we may get warm.

———

Nature acts by progress, *back and forth.*[15] It goes and returns, then advances farther, then regresses twice as much, then moves more forward than ever, $\gtrless$

etc.

———

---

[14] I Kings 8:18–20.

[15] *Itus et reditus.*

Ocean tides behave like this; the sun seems to advance like this:

———

You are awkward: "Please excuse me." Without that   S636/L772
apology, I would not have noticed there was any offense.

"Respectfully speaking":[16] there is nothing wrong but their apology.

The contest alone pleases us, not the victory.   S637/L773

We like to see animals fighting, not the victor tearing into
the vanquished. What did we want to see if not the final victory? And, as
soon as it comes, we have had enough. It is the same with gaming, the
same with the pursuit of truth. We like to see the clash of opinions in
disputes, but not at all to contemplate truth when it is found. To point it
out with pleasure, we must see it emerging from the dispute. The same
in passions: there is pleasure in seeing the collision of two opposites, but
when is one of them achieves mastery, it becomes mere brutality. We
never seek things themselves, but the pursuit of things. Likewise in
theatre, happy scenes lacking anxiety are worthless, as are those containing extreme hopeless misery, brutal love affairs, and bitter cruelty.

> Against those who, trusting in   S638/L774
> God's mercy, remain indifferent, without
> performing good works

Since the two sources of our sins are pride and sloth, God has revealed to us two of his attributes to cure them: his mercy and justice.
The characteristic of justice is to lower pride, however holy the works
may be: *and do not enter into judgment*,[17] etc.; and the characteristic of
mercy is to combat sloth by inviting good works, according to that passage: **God's mercy invites repentance**,[18] and this other one of the
Ninevites: **Let us do penance to see if by chance he will have pity on
us**.[19] And thus mercy, far from authorizing slackness, is on the contrary
the quality formally attacking it. So, instead of saying: if there were no
mercy in God we should have to make every kind of effort toward

---

[16] "Respectfully speaking"—that is, *révérence parler*—is used in ordinary language when
one is saying something one fears may be hurtful.

[17] *et non intres in judicium.* Psalms 143:2.

[18] Romans 2:4.

[19] Jonas 3:9.

virtue, we must say, on the contrary, that it is because there is mercy in God that we must make every kind of effort.

> Against those who misuse passages of   S639/L775
> Scripture and who pride themselves in finding one
> that seems to favor their error

The chapter for Vespers, for Passion Sunday, the *Prayer for the King*.

> Explanation of these words: *Whoever is not*   S640/L775
> *with me is against me.* And of these others:
> *Whoever is not against you is for you.*[20]

A person who says: "I am neither for nor against." We ought to reply to him . . .

The history of the Church must properly be called the   S641/L776
history of truth.

One of the anthems for Christmas Vesper: *Unto the*   S642/L777
upright there arises light in the darkness.[21]

Men are never taught to be honorable men and are   S643/L778
taught everything else. And they never pride themselves so
much on anything as on being honorable men. They only pride themselves on knowing the one thing they have not been taught.

———

Children who become frightened by the face they have   S643/L779
darkened are just children.[22] But how will someone so weak
in childhood become really strong at a greater age? We only change our
fancies. Everything made perfect by progress perishes also by progress.
What has been weak can never become absolutely strong. We say in
vain: he has grown, he has changed; he is also the same.

Preface to the first part   S644L780

Talk about those who have dealt with knowledge of self;
Charron's depressing and bothersome divisions; Montaigne's confusion: that he truly felt the lack of proper method, which he avoided by
jumping from subject to subject; that he sought to look good.

His foolish project to depict himself! And this not in passing and
against his maxims, since anyone can make mistakes, but through his
maxims themselves, by a prime and principal intention. For to say foolish things by accident and through weakness is a common illness, but to
say them intentionally is intolerable. And to say things such as these . . .

---

[20] Matthew 12:30 and Mark 9.

[21] *Exortum est in tenebris lumen rectis corde.* Cf. Psalms 112:4.

[22] See fragment S168/L136.

Preface to the second part   S644/L781

Talk about those who have dealt with this matter.

I admire the boldness with which these persons set about to speak of God. In addressing their argument to the impious, their first chapter is to prove divinity from the works of nature. I should not be astonished at their enterprise if they were addressing their arguments to the faithful; for it is certain [that those] with living faith in their hearts see at once that all existence is nothing other than the work of the God they adore. But for those in whom this light is extinguished and in whom we are trying to rekindle it, these people destitute of faith and grace, who, seeking with all their light whatever they see in nature that can lead them to this knowledge, find only obscurity and darkness; to tell them that they have only to look at the smallest things surrounding them to see God openly, to give them as the only proof of this great and important matter the course of the moon and planets, and to claim to have completed the proof with such an argument, is to give them ground for believing that the proofs of our religion are indeed weak. And I see by reason and experience that nothing is more calculated to arouse their contempt. This is not how Scripture, which has a better knowledge of the things that are of God, speaks of this. It says, on the contrary, that God is a hidden God, and that, since the corruption of nature, he has left people in a blindness from which they cannot escape except through Jesus Christ, without whom all communion with God is cut off: *No man knows the Father, save the Son, and those to whom the Son chooses to reveal him.*[23]

This is what Scripture indicates to us, when it says in so many places that those who seek God will find him. That light is not spoken of like the midday sun. We do not say that those who seek the midday sun, or water in the sea, will find it. And hence the evidence of God must not be of this kind in nature. So it tells us elsewhere: *Truly, you are a God who hides himself.*[24]

How many things have telescopes revealed to us that did   S645/L782
not exist for our past philosophers! We sincerely represented Holy Scripture on the great number of stars by saying, "There are only 1,022 of them;[25] we know it."

---

[23] *Nemo novit Patrem, nisi Filius, et cui voluerit Filius revelare.* Matthew 11:27.

[24] *Vere tu es Deus absconditus.* Isaiah 45:15.

[25] In the star catalog of his *Almagest*, Ptolemy listed 1,022 stars.

"There is grass on the earth; we see it. From the moon we would not see it. And on this grass are filaments, and in these filaments small animals; but after that, nothing more?" O presumptuous man!

"Mixtures are composed of elements; and the elements not?" O presumptuous man! Here is a delicate point. We must not say that there is something we do not see. We must then talk like others, but not think like them.

———

When we try to pursue virtues to their extremes, vices   S645/L783 appear from everywhere, insinuating themselves imperceptibly, in their imperceptible paths from the direction of the infinitely little. And vices appear in a multitude from the direction of the infinitely great. As a result, we lose ourselves in the vices and no longer see the virtues.

We take issue with perfection itself.

———

Words differently arranged have different meanings. And   S645/L784 meanings differently arranged produce different effects.

———

Do not fear, little flock.[26] *With fear and trembling.*[27]   S645/L785
Why then? Do not fear, provided you fear.[28]
Do not fear, provided you fear; but if you do not fear, then fear.

———

Whoever receives me does not receive me, but receives the one who sent me.[29]

———

No man knows, [. . .] not the Son.[30]

———

If there is ever a time when we should profess two   S645/L786 contrary truths, it is when we are accused of omitting one.
The Jesuits and Jansenists, therefore, are wrong to conceal them, but the Jansenists more so, for the Jesuits have been better at professing both.

---

[26] *Ne timeas pusillus grex.* Luke 12:32.

[27] *Timore et tremore.* Philippians 2:12.

[28] *Quid ergo? Ne timeas modo timeas.*

[29] *Qui me recipit, non me recipit, sed eum qui me misit.* Mark 9:37.

[30] *Nemo scit, neque Filius.* Mark 13:32.

M. de Condren: There is no comparison, he says,   S645/L787
between the union of saints and that of the Holy Trinity.[31]
Jesus Christ says the contrary.[32]

The dignity of man consisted, in his innocence, in using   S645/L788
and having dominion over creatures, but today in separating
himself from them and submitting to them.

Meanings.   S645/L789
The same meaning changes according to the words ex-
pressing it.
Meanings receive their dignity from words instead of giving it to
them. We must search for examples.

I believe that Joshua[33] was the first of God's people to have   S645/L790
this name, as Jesus Christ was the last of God's people.

A *bright cloud* **overshadowed** *them.*[34]   S645/L785

Saint Jehan [John the Baptist] was to turn the hearts of the fathers to
the children, and Jesus Christ to plant division.
Without contradiction.

Effects *in general* and *in particular.*[35] The semi-Pelagians   S645/L791
err in saying about things *in general* what is true only *in
particular*, and the Calvinists in saying *in particular* what is true *in
general* (it seems to me).

---

[31] Charles de Condren (1588–1641) was the successor to Pierre de Bérulle as the head of
the Oratorians. The passage criticized by Pascal occurs in his *Lettres et discours* (1642),
letter 17.

[32] John 17:21–23.

[33] Joshua is a variant of Jesus, or Savior.

[34] *Nubes lucida* **obumbravit**. Matthew 17:5.

[35] *In communi* and *in particulari*. For this scholastic distinction, see Thomas Aquinas,
Summa Theologiae I, quest. 23, art. 5.

[38. Miscellaneous Thoughts 6]

I contend that if all men knew what they said of each   S646/L792
other, there would not be four friends in the world. This is evident from the quarrels brought about by occasional, indiscreet remarks.

———

Hence I reject all other religions.   S646/L793

———

In this way I find an answer to all objections.

———

It is right that so pure a God should disclose himself only to those
whose hearts are purified.

———

Hence this religion is attractive to me, and I find it already sufficiently justified by so divine a morality. But I find more in it than that: I
find it convincing that, as far back as man can remember, a people
more ancient than any other people has existed. Men have been constantly told that they are universally corrupt, but that a Redeemer will
come. It is not just one man saying this, but innumerable men, and a
whole people, prophesying expressly for 4,000 years. Their books scattered for 400 years. Finally, the Jews without idols and king.
A whole people foretelling him before his coming. A whole people
worshiping him after his coming.
The more I examine this, the more truths I find: both what has preceded and what came after; both this synagogue that preceded him and
this synagogue, <this number of Jews,> wretches without prophets who
came after him and who, being enemies, are for us admirable witnesses
of the truth of these prophecies, in which their wretchedness and blindness are foretold.
The darkness of the Jews, frightful and foretold: *And you shall grope
at midday.*[36] *A book men delivered to one who is learned, and he said, I
cannot read.*[37]

———

The scepter still being in the hands of the first foreign usurper.[38]

———

The rumor of Jesus Christ's coming.

---

[36] *Eris palpans in meridie.* Deuteronomy 28:29.

[37] *Dabitur liber scienti literas, et dicet: Non possum legere.* Isaiah 29:11.

[38] This is a reference to Herod; see fragment S369.

I find this sequence, this religion, wholly divine in its authority, in its duration, in its perpetuity, in its morality, in its conduct, in its doctrine, in its effects. So, I stretch out my arms to my Savior, who, having been foretold for 4,000 years, came to suffer and to die for me on earth, at the time and in all the circumstances foretold. And by his grace, I await death in peace, in the hope of being eternally united to him; and yet I live with joy, whether in the blessings it pleases him to bestow upon me, or in the afflictions he sends for my good and has taught me to endure by his example.

It is amusing to consider that there are people in the world who, having renounced all the laws of God and nature, made laws for themselves that they strictly obey, as, for example, Mahomet's soldiers, thieves, heretics, etc. And so with logicians. S647/L794

It seems that their license must be without any limits or barriers, since they have broken through so many just and holy ones.

Sneezing absorbs all the functions of the soul, as does sexual intercourse. But we do not draw from this the same conclusions against man's greatness, because it is done against his will. And although we bring it about, it is nevertheless done against our will: not for the sake of the act itself, but for another end. And thus it is not a sign of man's weakness and of his subjection to that act. S648/L795

———

It is not shameful for man to yield to pain, but it is shameful for him to yield to pleasure. This is not because pain comes to us from outside, and that we ourselves seek pleasure; for we may seek pain, and yield to it on purpose, without this kind of abasement. How does it happens, then, that reason thinks it glorious to succumb to the effect of pain and shameful to yield to that of pleasure? It is because it is not pain that tempts and attracts us. It is we ourselves who choose it voluntarily and want it to prevail over us, so that we are masters of the situation; and in this, man yields to himself. But in pleasure it is man who yields to pleasure. Now mastery and control alone bring glory, and subjection alone brings shame.

God S649/L796
created everything for himself,
provided the power of pain and blessing for himself.

———

You can apply this to God or to yourself.

———

If to God, the Gospel is the rule.

———

If to yourself, you would be taking the place of God.

———

As God is surrounded by persons full of charity who ask of him the blessings of charity that are in his power, so . . .

———

Know yourself, then, and recognize that you are only a king of concupiscence, and take the paths of concupiscence.

King and tyrant. S650/L797

———

I, too, will have thoughts in the back of my head.

———

I will take care on every journey.

———

Greatness of establishment, respect for establishment.

———

The pleasure of the great is the ability to make people happy.

———

The characteristic of riches is to be given liberally.

———

The characteristic of everything must be sought. The characteristic of power is to protect.

———

When force attacks dissimulation, when a private soldier takes the square cap of a chief magistrate and lets it fly out of the window.

———

Martial's *Epigrams* S650/L798

Men like to be malicious, not against the half-blind or the wretched, but against the fortunate and proud. Otherwise we go wrong. For concupiscence is the source of all our movements, and humanity . . .

———

We must please those who have humane and tender feelings.

———

That epigram about the two half-blind people is worthless, for it does not console them and only enhances the author's reputation.

What is only for the sake of the author is worthless.

He will curtail pretentious ornaments.[39]

———

[39] *Ambitiosa recident ornamenta.* Horace, *Ars poetica*, 447.

[39. Miscellaneous Thoughts 7]

Genesis 17:7. *I will establish my covenant between me and*   S651/L799
you [. . .] for an everlasting covenant, to be a God unto you.[40]
You shall therefore keep my covenant.[41]

Scripture has provided passages to console every condition   S652/L800
and to inhibit every condition.

Nature seems to have done the same thing by her two infinites, natural and moral: for we will always have the higher and the lower, the more able and the less able, the more exalted and the more wretched, in order to humble our pride and exalt our abasement.

Fascination.   S653/L801
They have slept their sleep.[42]
The fashion of this world.[43]

———

The Eucharist
You *will eat bread.*[44] **Our** *daily bread.*[45]

———

The enemies of the Lord shall lick the dust.[46] Sinners lick the dust; that is to say, love earthly pleasures.

The *Old Testament* contained the figures of the joy to come, and the *New* contains the means of attaining it.

The figures were of joy, the means of penitence; and yet the paschal lamb was eaten *with bitter herbs, cum amaritudinibus.*[47]

While I alone escape.[48] Before the death of Jesus Christ, he was almost the sole martyr.

———

Time heals pains and quarrels, because we change: we   S653/L802
are no longer the same persons; neither the offender nor the
offended are themselves any more. It is like a people we have angered

---

[40] *Statuam pactum meum inter me et te foedere sempiterno, us sim Deus tuus.*

[41] *Et tu ergo custodies pactum meum.* Genesis 17:7–9.

[42] *Somnum suum.* Psalms 75:5.

[43] *Figura hujus mundi.* I Corinthians 7:31.

[44] *Comedes panem tuum.* Deuteronomy 8:9.

[45] *Panem nostrum.* Luke 11:3.

[46] *Inimici Dei terram lingent*; Psalms 71:9.

[47] Exodus 12:8.

[48] *Singularis sum ego donec transeam*; Psalms 140:10.

but meet again after two generations: they are still French, but not the same ones.

――――

If we dreamed the same thing every night, it would affect   S653/L803
us as much as the objects we see every day. And if an artisan
were sure to dream every night for twelve hours that he was a king, I believe he would be almost as happy as a king who dreamed every night
for twelve hours that he was an artisan.

If we dreamed every night that we were pursued by enemies and
harassed by these painful phantoms, or that we spent every day in different occupations, as when traveling, we would suffer almost as much as
if it were real, and would dread going to sleep, as we dread waking up
when we are afraid in fact to encounter such mishaps. And, indeed, this
would cause pretty much the same discomforts as reality.

But since dreams are all different, and even each is varied, what we
see in them affects us much less than what we see when we are awake,
because of the continuity, which is not, however, so continuous and
even as not to change too, though less abruptly, even if rarely, as when
we travel; and then we say: it seems to me I am dreaming. For life is a
dream, a little less unstable.

――――

Will it be said that men knew of original sin because they   S653/L804
have stated that justice has abandoned the earth? *No one is
happy before death*:[49] is this to say that they realized that eternal and essential happiness begins upon death?

――――

By knowing each person's dominant passion, we can be   S653/L805
sure of pleasing him. And yet each has his fancies contrary to
his own good, in the very idea he has of the good. This is something
bizarre that puts us off the scale.

――――

We are not satisfied with the life we have in ourselves and   S653/L806
in our own being: we want to live an imaginary life in the
minds of others, and for this purpose we endeavor to make an impression. We labor constantly to embellish and preserve this imaginary
being, and neglect the real one. And if we are calm, or generous, or
faithful, we are eager to make it known, so as to attach these virtues to

――

[49] *Nemo ante obitum beatus est*; Ovid, *Metamorphoses*, iii.

our other being, and would rather separate them from ourselves to unite them with the other. We would willingly be cowards to acquire the reputation for being brave. This is a great sign of our own being's nothingness, of not being satisfied with the one without the other, and of renouncing the one for the other! For whoever would not die to save his honor would be infamous.

John 8 S654/L807

Many believed him. Then Jesus said: If you continue . . . then you are my disciples **indeed . . . and the truth shall make you free**.

They answered him: We are Abraham's seed, and were never in bondage to any man.[50]

There is a great difference between disciples and **true** disciples. We can recognize them by telling them that the truth will make them free. For if they answer that they are free and that it is in their power to come out of the devil's bondage, they are indeed disciples, but not true disciples.

There are three ways to believe: reason, custom, inspira-   S655/L808
tion. The Christian religion, which alone has reason, does
not admit as its true children those who believe without inspiration. It is not that it excludes reason and custom, on the contrary; but we must open our minds to proofs, confirm them through custom, but offer ourselves in humbleness to inspirations, which alone can produce a true and salutary effect: Lest Christ's cross be made of no effect.[51]

It is incomprehensible that God should exist, and   S656/L809
incomprehensible that he should not; that the soul should be
joined to the body, that we should have no soul; that the world should be created, that it should not, etc.; that original sin should be, that it should not.

What will become of men who despise small things and do   S657/L810
not believe in the greater?[52]

The world's two oldest books are Moses[53] and Job, the one   S658/L811
Jewish, the other heathen, both looking upon Jesus Christ as
their common center and object: Moses by relating God's promises to

---

[50] Multi crediderunt in eum. Dicebat ergo Jesus: "Si manseritis . . . **vere** mei discipuli eritis, **et veritas liberabit vos**." Responderunt: "Semen Abrahae sumus, et nemini servimus unquam." John 8:30–33.

[51] Ne evacuetur crux Christi. I Corinthians 1:17.

[52] Quid fiet hominibus qui minima contemnunt, majora non credunt?

[53] That is, the Pentateuch.

Abraham, Jacob, etc., and his prophecies; and *Job, who will grant me, etc., for I know that my Redeemer lives,* etc.[54]

The style of the gospel is admirable in so many ways, and   S658/L812
among others, in producing no invectives against the
butchers and enemies of Jesus Christ. For there are none in any of the
historians against Judas, Pilate, or any of the Jews.

If this moderation of the writers of the Gospels had been assumed,
together with many other traits of so beautiful a character, and they had
only assumed it to attract notice, even if they had not dared to draw attention to it themselves, they would not have failed to secure friends to
make such remarks for their benefit. But as they acted thus without pretense and from wholly disinterested motives, they did not point it out to
anyone; and I believe that many such facts have not been noticed until
now, which is evidence of how neutrally the thing has been done.

We never do evil so completely and cheerfully as when   S658/L813
we do it out of conscience.

Just as we corrupt our minds, we corrupt our feelings also.   S658/L814

Our minds and feelings are improved by conversation; our minds
and feelings are corrupted by conversation. Thus good or bad society
improves or corrupts them. It is, then, important to know how to
choose in order to improve and not corrupt them. But we cannot
make this choice if we have not already improved and not corrupted
them. Thus a circle is formed, and they are fortunate who escape it.

Ordinary people have the ability of not thinking about   S659/L815
what they do not want to think about: "Do not think about
the passages concerning the Messiah," said the Jew to his son. Our
people often act in this way. Thus false religions are preserved, and even
the true one, with respect to many people.

But there are some who do not have this ability of preventing themselves from thinking, and who think all the more to the extent that they
are forbidden to do so. These people undo false religions, and even the
true one, if they do not find solid arguments.

---

[54] *Quis mihi det ut,* etc. *Scio enim quod redemptor meus vivit,* etc. Job 19:23–25.

I would soon have renounced pleasures, they say, if I had   S659/L816
faith. And I tell you: you would soon have faith, if you renounced pleasures. Now, it is for you to begin. If I could, I would give
you faith; I cannot do so, nor can I test the truth of what you say. But
you can well renounce pleasures and test whether what I say is true.

It is fine to say: we must admit that the Christian religion   S659/L817
has something astonishing in it. "This is because you were
born in it," they will say. Far from it: I stiffen myself against it for this
very reason, for fear this prejudice should lead me astray. But, although
I am born in it, I cannot help finding it astonishing.

The victory over death.   S660/L818
What shall it profit a man if he gains the whole world and
loses his own soul?
Whoever will save his soul shall lose it.[55]
I have come not to destroy the law, but to fulfill it.[56]
Lambs did not take away the sins of the world, but *I am the lamb that*
takes away the sins.
Moses did not give you the bread from heaven.
Moses did not lead you out of captivity, and did not make you *truly*
free.[57]

The prophecies of particular things are mingled with   S660/L819
those about the Messiah, so that the prophecies of the
Messiah should not be without proof and the particular prophecies
should not be without fruit.

There are two ways of persuading people of the truths of   S661/L820
our religion: one by the power of reason, the other by the authority of the person speaking.
We do not use the latter, but the former. We do not say: this must be
believed, because Scripture, which says it, is divine. But we say that it
must be believed for such and such a reason, which are weak arguments, since reason is completely malleable.

---

[55] Luke 9:24–25; Mark 8:35–36.
[56] Matthew 5:17.
[57] John 6:32–35 and 8:3.

[40. Miscellaneous Thoughts 8]

For we must not misunderstand ourselves: we are as much   S661/L821
automata as minds. And thus the instrument by which we
are persuaded is not solely demonstration. How few things are demonstrated! Proofs only convince the mind; custom provides our strongest
and most firmly believed proofs. It inclines the automaton, which drags
the mind unconsciously with it. Who has demonstrated that tomorrow
will dawn and that we shall die? And what is more believed? It is, then,
custom that persuades us, that makes so many Christians; it is custom
that makes Turks, heathens, professions, soldiers, etc. (There is faith received at baptism, which is more for Christians than for heathens.) Finally, we must have recourse to it once the mind has seen where the
truth lies, in order to quench our thirst and steep ourselves in this belief,
which constantly escapes us. For always to have proofs before us is too
much trouble. We must acquire an easier belief, which is that of habit,
which, without violence, art, or argument, makes us believe things and
inclines all our powers to this belief, so that our soul falls naturally into
it. It is not enough to believe only by power of conviction and when the
automaton is inclined to believe the contrary. Both parts of us must be
made to believe: the mind by reasons that need only to be seen once in
a lifetime; and the automaton by custom, and by not allowing it any inclination to the contrary.

Incline my heart, O Lord . . .[58]

———

Reason acts slowly, and with so many perspectives, on so many principles, which must be always present, that it constantly falls asleep or
wanders, when it fails to have all its principles present. Feeling does not
act in this way; it acts instantaneously, and is always ready to act. We
must then put our faith in feeling; otherwise it will always be vacillating.

<We should feel sorry for both, but we should feel sorry   S662/L432
for the former out of affection and the latter out of contempt.   [after L821]

———

We must belong to the religion they despise in order not to despise
them.

———

That is not good form.

———

———

[58] *Inclina cor meum, Deus.* Psalms 119:36

That shows there is nothing to be said to them, not out of contempt, but because they have no common sense. God must touch them.

———

People of that kind are academics, students, and that is the nastiest type of man I know.

———

You will convert me.

———

I do not accept this out of bigotry, but because of the way man's heart is made; not out of zealous devotion and detachment, but on purely human grounds and for motives of self-interest and self-love.

———

It is quite certain that there is no good without knowledge of God, that we are happy to the extent we get closer to him, and that ultimate happiness is to know him with certainty; that to the extent we get farther from him, the more wretched we are, and that ultimate wretchedness would be to be the certainty of the opposite.

———

To doubt then is to be unhappy, but there is an indispensable duty to seek in doubt. And thus anyone who doubts and does not seek is at once unhappy and wrong. If, in addition, he is cheerful and presumptuous, I can find no words to describe so extravagant a creature.>

———

Yet it is certain that man is so denatured that in his heart there is a seed of joy in this.

———

<Is it something to be said with joy? It is something that ought to be said then with sadness.

———

A fine reason to rejoice and proudly boast, the head raised, like this . . . : "Let us therefore rejoice, live without fear and anxiety, and wait for death, since it is all uncertain, and then we shall see what will happen to us." I do not see how this follows.>

———

Is it not enough that miracles should be performed in one place and that Providence should be manifest in one people?

———

It is good form not to be self-righteous (*avoir de complaisance*), and good piety to be righteous (*avoir complaisance*) to others.

———

<Is it courage for a dying man to go, in weakness and agony, and confront an omnipotent and eternal God?>

———

How happy I would be if I were in this state and someone took pity on my foolishness and had the kindness to save me from it in spite of myself!

———

<Not to be bothered by this and not to love, this points to so much weakness of mind and so much malice of will.

———

What subject for joy, to await nothing but helpless misery! What comfort, to have no hope of any comforter!>

———

But the very people who seem most opposed to the glory of religion will constitute a first argument that there is something supernatural in this. [They] will not be without their use for others in this respect. For such blindness is not a natural thing. And if their folly makes them so counter to their own good, the horror of such a deplorable example and a folly so worthy of compassion will serve to keep others from it. Are they so firm as to be insensitive to everything affecting them? Test them with the loss of their wealth and honor: What! It is a magic spell . . .

History of China   S663/L822

I only believe histories in which witnesses were to be slaughtered.

<Which is the more credible of the two, Moses or China?>

There is no question of seeing this broadly. I tell you there is something in this to blind and something to enlighten.

With this one word, I destroy all your arguments. "But China obscures the matter," you say. And I answer, "China obscures the matter, but there is clarity to be found. Look for it.

Thus everything you say works for one of the designs and does nothing against the other. So, this serves, and does no harm.

We must therefore see this in detail; we must put the documents on the table."

An heir finds the title deeds to his house. Will he say: S664/L823
"Perhaps they are false," and neglect to examine them?

The law required people to have what it did not give;   S665/L824
grace gives what it requires people to have.

Seems to refute.   S666/L825

God gives grace to the humble. But did he not give them
humility?[59]

And his own did not receive him.[60] *However many did not receive him,*
were they not his own?[61]

[41. Miscellaneous Thoughts 9]

Do all things according to the pattern shown to you on the   S667/L826
mount.[62]

The Jewish religion has therefore been formed on the pattern of
the Messiah's truth. And the Messiah's truth has been recognized by the
Jewish religion, which was the figure of it.

Among the Jews the truth was only figurative. In heaven it is revealed.
In the Church it is hidden and recognized by its relation to the figure.

———

The figure was fashioned from the truth, and the truth was recognized from the figure.

———

Saint Paul himself says that people will forbid marriage,   S667/L827
and he himself speaks of it to the Corinthians in a manner
that is a trap. For if a prophet had said one thing, and Saint Paul had
then said another, he would have been accused.

The bonds that bind the respect of men to one another   S668/L828
are generally bonds of necessity. For there must be different
degrees in this, all men wishing to dominate, and not all, but some,
being able to.

Let us, then, imagine that we see them in the process of formation.
They will doubtless fight until the stronger party overcomes the weaker,
and a dominant party is finally established. But once this is determined,
the masters, who do not want the continuation of strife, then decree that

---

[59] *Humilibus dat gratiam.* Peter 5:5. *An ideo non dedit humilitatem?* James 4:6.

[60] *Sui eum non receperunt;* John 1:11–12.

[61] *quotquot autem non receperunt. An non erant sui?*

[62] *Fac secundum exemplar quod tibi ostensum est in monte.* Exodus 25:40. See fragment
S279/L247.

the power in their hands shall pass down as it pleases them: some entrust it to election by the people, others to hereditary succession, etc.

And it is here where imagination begins to play its part. Until then, pure power did it. Now power is sustained by imagination in a certain party: in France, by gentlemen; in Switzerland, by the working class;[63] etc.

These bonds that bind the respect of men to such and such a person in particular are therefore the bonds of imagination.

———

Those great mental efforts, on which the soul sometimes   S668/L829
alights, are things on which it does not take hold. It only
leaps there, not as onto a throne, for always, but merely for an instant.

[42] Geometry/Intuition [1]

To mask nature and disguise it: no more king, pope,   S669/L509
bishop, but "august monarch," etc. Not Paris, but "the
capital of the realm."

———

There are places where we should call Paris, Paris, and others where we should call it the capital of the realm.

———

The greater one's mind, the more one finds original men.   S669/L510
Ordinary sorts of persons find no difference between men.

———

Different kinds of right thinking: some in a certain order   S669/L511
of things, and not in other orders, where they talk nonsense.

———

Some draw consequences well from a few principles, and this is rightness of thinking.

Others draw well the consequences of things involving many principles.

For example, the former understand well the effects of water, which involve few principles; but these consequences there are so subtle that only acute right thinking can get to them. And, in spite of that, these people might not be great geometers, because geometry comprises a great number of principles, and a mind may be of such a nature as to be

---

[63] See fragment S83/L50.

able to penetrate easily to the bottom of a few principles without in the least being able to penetrate those things involving many principles.

There are therefore two kinds of minds: the one, penetrating rapidly and deeply the consequences of principles, is the intuitive mind; the other, grasping a great number of principles without confusing them, is the geometric mind. The first has strength and rightness of mind, the second breadth of mind. Now, one can exist without the other; the mind can be strong and narrow, and also broad and weak.

[43] Geometry/Intuition [2]

Difference   S670/L512
between the geometric
and the intuitive mind

In the one, principles are obvious, but removed from ordinary use, so that we find it difficult to turn our head in that direction, for lack of habit. But if it was turned that way ever so little, we would see the principles fully and would need to have a wholly defective mind to reason wrongly about such principles so obvious that it is almost impossible for them to escape notice.

But with the intuitive mind, principles are in common use and before everybody's eyes. You have only to look, and no effort is necessary; it is only a question of good sight. But it must be good, because the principles are so subtle and numerous that it is almost impossible but that some escape notice. Now the omission of one principle leads to error. Thus you must have very clear sight to see all the principles, as well as an accurate mind to avoid reasoning falsely from known principles.

All geometers would then be intuitive if they had clear sight, for they do not reason wrongly from principles known to them. And intuitive minds would be geometric if they could bend their thinking to the principles of geometry to which they are unaccustomed.

The reason, then, that some intuitive minds are not geometric is that they simply cannot turn their attention to the principles of geometry. But the reason that geometers are not intuitive is that they do not see what is before them, and that, accustomed to the exact and plain principles of geometry, and not reasoning until they have clearly seen and handled their principles, they are lost in matters of intuition, where the principles do not allow such handling. The principles are scarcely seen; they are felt rather than seen; there is endless difficulty in making them felt by those who do not themselves apprehend them. These principles are so delicate and numerous that a very delicate and clear sense is needed to apprehend them, and to judge rightly and correctly according to this feeling, without most often being able to demonstrate them in order as in geometry; because the principles are not known to us in this way, and because it would be an endless task to undertake it. We must see the matter at once, at a glance, and not by a process of reasoning, at least up to a point. And thus it is rare for geometers to be intuitive and for intuitive people to be geometers, because geometers want to treat matters of intuition geometrically and make themselves ridiculous, wanting to begin by definitions and then by principles, which is not the way to proceed in this kind of reasoning. Not that the mind does not do this, but it does so tacitly, naturally, and without art, for its expression surpasses all men, and only a few can apprehend it.

Intuitive minds, on the contrary, being thus accustomed to judge at a single glance, when presented with propositions of which they understand nothing and the paths to which consist of such sterile definitions and principles, which they are not accustomed to see in such detail, are so surprised that they are repelled and disheartened.

But false minds are never either intuitive or geometrical.

Geometers who are only geometers, then, have rightness of mind, provided all things are explained to them by means of definitions and principles; otherwise they are wrong and insufferable, for they are only right when the principles are quite clear.

And intuitive minds that are only intuitive cannot have the patience to reach the first principles of speculative and imaginative things, which they have never seen in the world and which are altogether out of the common.

Geometry/Intuition S671/L513

True eloquence makes light of eloquence. True morality makes light of morality; that is to say, the morality of judgment makes light of the morality of the mind, which is without rules.

For it is to judgment that feeling belongs, as the sciences belong to intellect. Intuition is part of judgment, geometry is part of intellect.

To make light of philosophy is to philosophize truly.[64]

The nourishment of the body is little by little.　　　　　S671/L514
Much nourishment and little substance.

---

[64] See Montaigne, *Essays* II, chap. 12: "One of the ancients, who was reproached for professing philosophy, of which, however, in his own judgment, he did not take great stock, replied that this was really to philosophize." (Ariew and Grene trans., p. 73.)

[44] Authority

Authority   S672/L504

They hide themselves in the crowd and call numbers to their rescue.

Tumult.

So far from making it a rule to believe a thing because you   S672/L505
have heard it, you ought to believe nothing without putting
yourself into the position you would have been in if you had never
heard it.

It is your own assent to yourself, and the constant voice of your own reason, and not of others, that should make you believe.

Belief is so important.

A hundred contradictions might be true.

If antiquity were the rule of belief, the ancients would then be without rule.

If general consent, if men had perished?

False humanity, pride.

Punishment of those who sin: error.

Lift the curtain.

You try in vain: still you must either believe, or deny, or doubt.

Shall we then have no rule?

We judge that animals do well what they do. Is there no rule for judging men?

To deny, to believe, and to doubt well are to a man what the race is to a horse.

A common happening does not astonish, even though the   S673/L506
cause is unknown. An event such as has never been seen before
passes for a prodigy.[65]

583.[66] *There is one who will speak great foolishness with*   S674/L506
great effort (Terence).[67]

Who is unhappier than a man whom his fictions govern (Pliny).[68]

588. *It is by virtue of senatorial decrees and plebiscites that*   S675/L507
crimes are committed (Seneca).[69]

---

[65] *Quod crebro videt non miratur, etiamsi cur fiat nescit; quod ante non viderit, id si evenerit, ostentum esse censet.* Cicero, *De Divinatione*, ii. 22.

[66] The page numbers refer to the 1652 edition of Montaigne's *Essays*.

[67] *Nae iste magno conatu magnas nugas dixerit.* Terence, *Heauton Timorumenos*, III. v. 8.

[68] *Quasi quidquam infelicius sit homini cui sua figmenta dominantur.* Pliny, ii.

[69] *Ex senatus-consultis et plebiscitis scelera exercentur.* See fragment S94/L60.

Nothing can be said so absurd that it is not said by some philosopher (*De divinatione*).[70]

Committed to certain fixed and determinate opinions, to the point where they are reduced to defending even things of which they do not approve (Cicero).[71]

We suffer from an excess of literature as from an excess of anything (Seneca).[72]

588. What suits each one best is what is most natural to him.[73]

Nature gave them first these limits (Georgics)[74]

Wisdom does not demand much teaching.[75]

What is not shameful begins to become so when it is approved by the multitude.[76]

That is how I use it. You must do as you wish (Terence).[77]

It is rare that one sufficiently respects oneself.[78]   S676/L508

So many gods are busy around a single head.[79]   S677/L508

Nothing is more shameful than to affirm before knowing (Cicero).[80]   S678/L508

I am not ashamed, as they are, to admit that I do not know what I do not know.[81]   S679/L508

It is better not to begin.[82]

---

[70] *Nihil tam absurde dici potest quod non dicatur ab aliquo philosophorum.* Cicero, *De Divinatione*, ii. 58.

[71] *Quibusdam destinatis sententiis consecrati quae non probant coguntur defendere.* Cicero, *Disputationes Tusculanae*, ii. 2

[72] *Ut omnium rerum sic litterarum quoque intemperantia laboramus.* Seneca, *Epistles*, cvi.

[73] *Id maxime quemque decet, quod est cujusque suum maxime.* Cicero, *De officiis*, i. 31.

[74] *Hos natura modos primum dedit.* Virgil, *The Georgics*, ii.

[75] *Paucis opus est litteris ad bonam mentem.* Seneca, *Epistles*, cvi.

[76] *Si quando turpe non sit, tamen non est non turpe quum id a multitudine laudetur.* Cicero, *De finibus bonorum et malorum.*

[77] *Mihi sic usus est, tibi ut opus est facto, fac.* Terence, *Heauton Timorumenos*, I. i. 21.

[78] *Rarum est enim ut satis se quisque vereatur.* Quintillian, x. 7.

[79] *Tot circa unum caput tumultuantes deos.* Seneca the Elder, *Suasoriae*, i. 4.

[80] *Nihil turpius quam cognitioni assertionem praecurrere.* Cicero, *Academica*, i. 45.

[81] *Nec me pudet, ut istos, fateri nescire quid nesciam.* Cicero, *Disputationes Tusculanae*, i. 25.

[82] *Melius non incipient.* Seneca, *Epistles*, lxxii.

[IV. Developments from
July 1658 to July 1662]

[45] Discourse on the Machine

Infinity, nothingness.   S680/L418

___

Our soul is cast into the body, where it finds number, time, dimensions; it reasons about these things and calls them nature, necessity, and can believe nothing else.

___

Unity added to infinity does not increase infinity at all, any more than a foot added to an infinite length. The finite is annihilated in the presence of the infinite and becomes pure nothingness. So it is with our mind before God, with our justice before divine justice. Yet the disproportion between our justice and God's justice is not as great as that between unity and infinity.

___

God's justice must be as vast as his mercy. Now, his justice toward the damned is less vast and should be less shocking to us than his mercy toward the chosen.

___

We know that there is an infinite, but do not know its nature, just as we know it to be false that numbers are finite. It is therefore true that there is an infinite in number, but we do not know what it is. It is false that it is even, false that it is odd, for the addition of a unit does not change its nature. Yet it is a number, and every number is odd or even. (It is true that this is understood of every finite number.)

So, we may well know that there is a God without knowing what he is.

Is there no substantial truth, seeing that there are so many true things that are not truth itself?

___

We know then the existence and nature of the finite, because we also are finite and have extension.

We know the existence of the infinite and do not know its nature, because it has extension like us, but not limits like us.

But we do not know either the existence or the nature of God, because he has neither extension nor limits.

——

But by faith we know his existence. In glory we shall know his nature.

Now, I have already shown that we can know the existence of a thing without knowing its nature.

Let us now speak according to our natural lights.

If there is a God, he is infinitely incomprehensible, since, having neither parts nor limits, he bears no relation to us. We are therefore incapable of knowing either what he is or whether he is. This being so, who will dare undertake to resolve the question? Not we, who bear no relation to him.

Who then will blame Christians for not being able to give rational grounds for their belief, they who profess a religion for which they cannot give rational grounds?

They declare, in proclaiming it to the world, that it is a folly—*stultitiam*[1]—and then you complain that they do not prove it! If they proved it, they would not be keeping their word. It is by lacking proofs that they are not lacking sense. "Yes, but although this excuses those who offer their religion in this way and removes the blame of putting it forward without rational grounds, it does not excuse those who accept it."

Let us then examine this point and say: either God is or he is not. But to which side shall we incline? Reason can determine nothing here. There is an infinite chaos that separates us. At the extremity of this infinite distance, a game is being played in which heads or tails will turn up. How will you wager? You have no rational grounds for choosing either way or for rejecting either alternative.

Do not, then, blame as wrong those who have made a choice, for you know nothing of the matter! "No, but I will blame them for having made, not this choice, but a choice. For although the player who chooses heads is no more at fault than the other one, they are both in the wrong. The right thing is not to wager at all."

Yes; but you must wager. It is not optional. You are committed. Which will you choose, then? Let us see. Since you must choose, let us see what is the less profitable option. You have two things to lose, the true and the good; and two things to stake, your reason and your will, your knowledge and your beatitude; and your nature has two things to avoid, error and wretchedness. Since you must necessarily choose, your reason is no more offended by choosing one rather than the other. This settles one point. But your beatitude? Let us weigh the gain and the loss in calling heads that God exists. Let us assess the two cases. If you win,

---

[1] Paul, I Corinthians 1:18.

you win everything; if you lose, you lose nothing. Wager, then, without hesitation that he exists! "This is wonderful. Yes, I must wager. But perhaps I am wagering too much." Let us see: since there is an equal chance of winning and losing, if there were two lives to win for one, you could still wager. But if there were three lives to win, you would have to play (since you must necessarily play), and it would be foolish, when you are forced to play, not to risk your life to win three at a game in which there is an equal chance of losing and winning. But there is an eternity of life and happiness. This being so, if there were an infinity of chances, and only one in your favor, it would still be right to wager one life in order to win two; and, being obliged to play, you would be making the wrong choice if you refused to stake one life against three in a game in which, out of an infinity of chances, there is only one in your favor, if there were an infinite life of infinite happiness to be won. But here there is an infinite life of infinite happiness to be won, there is one chance of winning against a finite number of chances of losing, and what you are staking is finite. All bets are off wherever there is an infinity and wherever there is not an infinite number of chances of losing against the chance of winning. There is no time to hesitate; you must give everything. And thus, when you are forced to play, you must be renouncing reason to preserve life, instead of risking it for an infinite gain, which is as likely to happen as is a loss amounting to nothing.

It is no use saying that it is uncertain whether you will win, that it is certain you are taking a risk, and that the infinite distance between the **certainty** of what you are risking and the **uncertainty** of what you stand to gain makes the finite good you are certainly staking equal to the infinite good that is uncertain. It is not so. All players take a certain risk for an uncertain gain; and yet they take a certain finite risk for an uncertain finite gain without sinning against reason. It is not true that there is an infinite distance between the certain risk and the uncertain gain. Indeed, there is an infinity between the certainty of winning and the certainty of losing. But the uncertainty of winning is proportional to the certainty of the risk, in proportion to the chances of winning and losing. Hence, if there are as many chances on one side as on the other, you are playing for even odds, and then the certainty of what you are risking is equal to the uncertainty of what you may win—so far is it from being infinitely distant. Thus our proposition is infinitely powerful, when the stakes are finite in a game where the chances of winning and losing are even, and the infinite is to be won.

This is conclusive and if people are capable of any truth, this is it.

"I confess it, I admit it. But, still . . . Is there no means of seeing what is in the cards?" Yes, Scripture and the rest, etc. "Yes, but my hands are tied and my mouth is shut; I am forced to wager, and am not free. I have not been released and I am made in such a way that I cannot believe. What, then, would you have me do?" That is true. But at least realize that your inability to believe comes from your passions, since reason brings you to this and yet you cannot believe. Work, then, on convincing yourself, not by adding more proofs of God's existence, but by diminishing your passions. You would like to find faith and do not know the way? You would like to be cured of unbelief and ask for the remedies? Learn from those who were bound like you, and who now wager all they have. These are people who know the way you wish to follow, and who are cured of the illness of which you wish to be cured. Follow the way by which they began: they acted as if they believed, took holy water, had masses said, etc. This will make you believe naturally and mechanically.[2] "But this is what I am afraid of." And why? What do you have to lose? But to show you that this is the way, this diminishes the passions, which are your great obstacles, etc.

"Oh! This discourse moves me, charms me, etc." If this discourse pleases you and seems cogent, know that it is made by a man who has knelt, both before and after it, in prayer to that being, infinite and without parts, before whom he submits all he has, so that he might bring your being to submit all you have for your own good and for his glory, and that thus strength may be reconciled with this lowliness.

End of This Discourse

Now, what harm will come to you by taking this side? You will be faithful, honest, humble, grateful, generous, a sincere, true friend. Certainly you will not be taken by unhealthy pleasures, by glory and by luxury, but will you not have others?

I tell you that as a result you will gain in this life, and that, at each step you take on this road, you will see such a great certainty of gain and so much nothingness in what you risk, that you will at last recognize that you have wagered for something certain and infinite, for which you have given nothing.

We owe a great debt to those who point out faults. For   S680/L422
they mortify us. They teach us that we have been despised.
They do not prevent our being so in the future, for we have many other

---

[2] Pascal's word is *abêtira*—literally, will make you more like the beasts. Man is in part a beast or machine, and one needs to allow that part its proper function: that is, one needs to act dispassionately or mechanically.

faults for which we may be despised. They prepare for us the exercise of correction and freedom from a fault.

———

Custom is our nature. He who is accustomed to faith   S680/L419
believes it, can no longer fear hell, and cannot believe anything else. He who is accustomed to believe that the king is terrible, etc.
Who doubts, then, that our soul, being accustomed to see number,
space, and motion, believes that and nothing else?

———

Do you believe it to be impossible that God is infinite,   S680/L420
without parts? Yes. I wish, therefore, to show you <an image
of God and his immensity,> an infinite and indivisible thing: it is a
point moving everywhere with infinite speed.

For it is one in all places and completely whole in every location.

Let this effect of nature, which previously seemed impossible to you,
allow you to understand that there may be others you still do not know.
Do not draw the conclusion from your experiment that there remains
nothing for you to learn, but rather that there remains an infinity for you
to learn.

It is false that we are worthy of the love of others; it is   S680/L421
unfair that we should want it. If we were born reasonable and
indifferent, knowing ourselves and others, we would not give this inclination to our will. However, we are born with it. Therefore we are born
unfair. For all tends to self; this is contrary to all order. We must tend to
the general, and the tendency to self is the beginning of all disorder, in
war, politics, economy, and man's particular body.

The will is therefore depraved. If the members of natural and civil
communities tend toward the good of the body, the communities themselves ought to look to another, more general body of which they are
members. We should, therefore, tend to the general. We are, therefore,
born unfair and depraved.

No religion but our own has taught that man is born in sin. No sect
of philosophers has said this. Therefore none has told the truth.

No sect or religion has always existed on earth, save for the Christian
religion.

The Christian religion alone makes man altogether   S680/L426
lovable and **happy**. In polite society we cannot be both
lovable and happy.

It is the heart that experiences God, and not reason. Here,   S680/L424
then, is faith: God felt by the heart, not by reason.

unlike Aquinas

The heart has its reasons, which reason does not know. S680/L423
We know this in a thousand things.

I say that the heart loves the universal being naturally and itself naturally, according to its practice. And it hardens itself against one or the other as it chooses. You have rejected the one and kept the other. Is it through reason that you love yourself?

The single knowledge contrary to common sense and S680/L425
human nature is the only one to have existed always among
men.

[46] A Letter to Further the Search for God

... Let them at least learn what is the religion they attack, S681/L427
before they attack it. If this religion boasted of having a clear
view of God and of possessing it openly and unveiled, to say that we see
nothing in the world proving it so clearly would be to attack it. But this
religion says, on the contrary, that men are in darkness and estranged
from God, that he has hidden himself from their knowledge—this is
even the name he is given in the Scriptures: **The Hidden God**.[3] If indeed it strives equally to establish these two things: that God has established visible signs in the Church by which those who would sincerely
seek him can know him, and nevertheless so disguised them that he will
be perceived only by those who seek him with all their heart, then what
advantage can they derive when, in their carelessness, as they profess to
be searching for the truth, they cry out that nothing reveals it to them?
For that darkness in which they exist and with which they reproach the
Church merely establishes one of the things this religion affirms without
affecting the other, and, far from destroying its doctrine, establishes it.

To attack it, they would have to proclaim that they have spent all
their efforts searching everywhere, even in what the Church offers for
instruction, but without any satisfaction. If they spoke in this manner,
they would indeed be attacking one of these claims. But I hope to show
here that no reasonable person can speak in this way, and I even venture
to say that no one has ever done so. We know well enough how people
in this frame of mind behave. They think they have made great efforts to
learn when they have spent a few hours reading some book of Scripture
and questioned a priest on the truths of the faith. After that, they boast
that they have searched without success in books and among men. But
in truth I will tell them what I have often said: that this carelessness is

---

[3] *Deus absconditus.* Isaiah 45:15.

insufferable. We are not concerned here with the insignificant interest of some strangers, that we should treat the question in this manner. This is about ourselves, and our all.

The immortality of the soul is something so important to us, something that touches us so profoundly, that we must have lost all feeling to be indifferent to knowing the facts of the matter. All our actions and thoughts must take paths so different, according to whether there is hope for eternal blessings or not, that it is impossible to take one step with sense and judgment unless we regulate our path in light of this point, which ought to be our ultimate object.

Thus our prime interest and prime duty is to become enlightened on this subject, on which all our conduct depends. And that is why, with respect to those who are not convinced, I make a sharp distinction between the ones who labor with all their power to inform themselves and the ones who live without being troubled or thinking about it.

I can have nothing but compassion for those who sincerely lament their doubt, who regard it as the ultimate misfortune, and who, sparing no effort to escape from it, make this inquiry their principal and most serious occupation.

But as for those who spend their lives without thinking of this ultimate end of life and who, for this sole reason, that they do not find the light of conviction within themselves, fail to look elsewhere and to examine thoroughly whether this opinion is one of those people receive with credulous simplicity or one of those which, although obscure in themselves, nevertheless have a very solid and unshakable foundation, I consider them in a completely different manner.

This carelessness in a matter where they themselves, their eternity, their all, are at stake, irritates me more than it moves me. It astonishes and appalls me; to me it is monstrous. I do not say this out of a pious zeal for spiritual devotion. I expect, on the contrary, that we should have this feeling from a principle of human interest and from self-love. For that we only need to see what the least-enlightened persons see.

We do not need a greatly elevated soul to understand that there is no real and solid satisfaction here; that all our pleasures are only vanity; that our ills are infinite; and that finally death, which threatens us at every moment, must in a few years infallibly place us under the horrible necessity of being either annihilated or wretched eternally.

There is nothing more real than this, nothing more terrible. However brave we pretend to be, this is the end that awaits the finest life in the world. Let us reflect on this and then say whether it is not beyond doubt that the only good in this life lies in the hope of another; that we are happy only to the extent that we draw nearer to it; and that, as there will be no more unhappiness for those who have complete assurance of eternity, so there is no happiness for those who have no insight into it.

Surely, then, it is a great evil to be in such doubt. But it is at least an indispensable duty to seek when we are in this doubt. And thus someone who doubts and who does not seek is altogether quite unhappy and quite wrong. If he is calm and satisfied with this, let him profess to be so, and indeed let him boast of it and make this very condition the reason for his joy and his vanity; I have no words to describe so extravagant a creature.

Where do these feelings come from? What reason for joy can be found in the expectation of nothing but wretchedness without remedy? What reason for boasting is seeing oneself in impenetrable darkness? And how can the following reasoning occur to a reasonable man?

"I do not know who put me into the world, nor what the world is, nor what I myself am. I am in terrible ignorance of everything. I do not know what my body is, nor my senses, nor my soul and even this part of me that thinks what I say, that reflects on everything and on itself, and knows itself no more than the rest. I see those terrifying spaces of the universe that surround me, and I find myself tied to one corner of this vast expanse, without knowing why I am put in this place rather than in another, nor why the short time given me to live is assigned to me at this point rather than at another of the whole eternity that preceded me or the one that will follow me.

I see nothing but infinites on all sides, surrounding me like an atom and like a shadow that lasts only for an instant and returns no more.

All I know is that I must soon die, but what I know least is this very death I cannot escape.

As I do not know from where I come, so I do not know to where I am going, and I know only that, in leaving this world, I fall forever either into nothingness or into the hands of an angry God, without knowing to which of these two conditions I must forever be allotted. Such is my state, full of weakness and uncertainty. And from all this I conclude that I must spend all the days of my life without trying to inquire into what must happen to me. Perhaps I could find some illumination in my doubts, but I do not want to take the trouble nor take a step to seek it. And after treating with scorn those who have labored with this concern, I want to go without foresight and without fear to confront so great an event, and let myself be led carelessly to death, uncertain as to the eternity of my future condition."

Who would wish to have as friend a man who talks in this way? Who would choose him from among others to tell him of his affairs? Who would turn to him in adversity?

And indeed to what use in life could we put him?

In truth, it is glorious for religion to have as enemies such unreasonable men (whatever certainty they possess, it is a reason for despair rather than vanity). And their opposition to it is so little dangerous that it serves, on the contrary, to establish its truths. For the Christian faith works mainly to establish these two facts: the corruption of nature, and redemption by Jesus Christ. Now I contend that, if these men do not serve to prove the truth of the redemption by the holiness of their behavior, at least they serve admirably to show the corruption of nature by such unnatural sentiments.

Nothing is so important to man as his own state; nothing is so terrifying to him as eternity. And thus it is not natural that there should be men indifferent to the loss of their existence and to the peril of an eternity of wretchedness. They behave quite differently with regard to all other things: they fear even the slightest ones, foresee them, feel them. And this same man who spends so many days and nights in rage and despair at the loss of some office, or because of an imaginary insult to his honor, is the very one who knows, without anxiety and without emotion, that he will lose everything through death. It is a monstrous thing to see in the same heart and at the same time this sensitivity to the slightest things and this strange insensitivity to the greatest.

It is an incomprehensible enchantment and a supernatural slumber that points to an all-powerful force as its cause.

There must be a strange upheaval in the nature of man for him to glory in being in this state in which it seems incredible that a single individual should be. However, experience has shown me this in so great a number that it would be surprising if we did not know that most of those who take part in this are disingenuous and not, in fact, what they seem. They are people who have heard it said that worldly manners require them to display such extravagance. It is what they call shaking off the yoke, and what they are trying to imitate. But it would not be difficult to make them understand how mistaken they are to court esteem in this manner. This is not the way to acquire it; not even, I say, among those worldly people who judge things sensibly and who know that the only way to succeed is to appear honest, faithful, judicious, and capable of useful service to one's friends because by nature men love only what may be useful to them. Now, what advantage is it for us to hear someone say that he has now thrown off the yoke, that he does not believe there is a God who watches over our actions, that he considers himself the sole master of his conduct, and that he thinks he is accountable for it only to himself? Does he think that he has persuaded us in this way to have complete confidence in him from now on and to look to him for consolation, advice, and help in all of life's needs? Do they claim to have delighted us by telling us that they hold our soul to be only a little wind or smoke, and in addition by having told it to us in a proud and self-satisfied tone of voice? Is this something to be said light-heartedly? Is it not, on the contrary, something to be said sadly, as the saddest thing in the world?

If they thought about it seriously, they would see that this is so mis-guided, so contrary to good sense, so opposed to decency, and so remote in every respect from that good appearance they are seeking, that they would be more likely to reform than to corrupt those who might have an inclination to follow them. And, indeed, make them give an account of the feelings and reasons they have for doubting religion; they will say to you things so weak and so petty that they will persuade you of the contrary. This is what someone appropriately said to them one day: "If you continue to talk in this manner, you will really convert me." And he was right, for who would not be horrified to find himself sharing the same feelings with companions who are such contemptible persons!

Thus those who only feign these feelings would be very unhappy, if they constrained their nature to make themselves the most impertinent of men. If, at the bottom of their heart, they are troubled at not having more light, let them not disguise it; this admission will not be shameful. The only shame is in having none. Nothing reveals more an extreme weakness of mind than not to recognize the unhappiness of a man with-out God. Nothing more surely indicates an evil heart than not desiring the truth of the eternal promises. Nothing is more cowardly than to pre-tend to be brave before God. Let them then leave these impieties to those sufficiently ill bred to be really capable of them. Let them at least be honorable men, if they cannot be Christians. Finally, let them rec-ognize that there are two kinds of people who can be called reasonable: those who serve God with all their heart because they know him, and those who seek him with all their heart because they do not know him.

But as for those who live without knowing him and without seeking him, they judge themselves so little worthy of their own care that they are not worthy of the care of others; and it takes all the charity of the re-ligion they despise not to despise them to the point of abandoning them to their folly. But because this religion requires us always to regard them, as long as they are in this life, as being capable of the grace that can enlighten them, and to believe that they may, in a short time, be filled with more faith than we are, and that we, on the other hand, may fall into the blindness in which they are, we must do for them what we would want to be done for us if we were in their place, and call upon them to have pity on themselves and to take at least some steps in the attempt to find enlightenment. Let them spend on reading this some of the hours they otherwise spend so uselessly; whatever aversion they may bring to the task, they will perhaps gain something, and at least they will not be losing much. But as for those who approach the task with perfect sincerity and a real desire to find the truth, I hope they will be satisfied and convinced of the proofs of so divine a religion, which I have collected here, and in which I have followed more or less this order . . .

Before entering into the proofs of the Christian religion, I   S682/L428
find it necessary to point out how wrong are these men who
live indifferent to the search for the truth of something so important to them, that touches them so closely.

Of all their faults, this doubtless is the one that most convicts them of foolishness and blindness, and in which it is easiest to confound them with the first inklings of common sense and natural feelings. For it is indubitable that the duration of this life is but an instant; that the state of death is eternal, whatever its nature may be; and that thus all our actions and thoughts must take such different paths, according to the state of that eternity, that the only possible way of acting with sense and judgment is to regulate our course in light of that point, which must be our final objective.

There is nothing clearer than this, and so, according to the principles of reason, men's behavior is wholly unreasonable if they do not take another path. Let us, therefore, on this point judge those who live without thinking of the ultimate end of life, who let themselves be guided by their inclinations and their pleasures without reflection and without concern, as if they could annihilate eternity by turning their thought away from it, and think only of making themselves happy for the moment.

Yet this eternity exists, and death, which must begin it and which threatens them every hour, must in a short time inevitably put them under the horrible necessity of being annihilated or unhappy eternally, without their knowing which of these eternities has been prepared for them forever.

This is a doubt with a terrible consequence. They risk an eternity of wretchedness; and yet, as if the matter were not worth the trouble, they neglect to consider whether this is one of those opinions people receive too credulously, or one of those which, obscure in themselves, have a very solid, though hidden, foundation. Thus they do not know whether there is truth or falsity in the matter, nor whether there is strength or weakness in the proofs. They have the proofs before their eyes, but they refuse to look at them, and in that ignorance they choose to do everything necessary to fall into this misfortune—if it exists—to wait until death before testing the proofs, yet be very satisfied in this state, proclaim it, and indeed boast about it. Can we think seriously of the importance of this matter without being horrified at so extravagant a behavior?

To rest thus in ignorance is a monstrous thing, and they who spend their lives in it must be made to feel its extravagance and stupidity by having it represented to them, so that they are confounded by the sight of their folly. For here is how men reason when they choose to live in such ignorance of what they are and without seeking enlightenment. "I know not," they say . . .

"This is what I see and what troubles me. I look in all   S682/L429
directions and see only darkness everywhere. Nature offers
me nothing that is not a matter of doubt and concern. If I saw nothing in it that revealed a divinity, I would come to a negative conclusion; if I saw everywhere the signs of a creator, I would settle down peacefully in faith. But, seeing too much to deny and too little to reassure me, I am in a pitiful state, in which I have wished a hundred times that if a God maintains nature, it should proclaim him unequivocally, and that if the signs it gives are deceptive, it should suppress them altogether; nature should say all or nothing, that I might see which side I ought to take. Instead, in my present state, not knowing what I am and what I must do, I know neither my condition nor my duty. My whole heart longs to know where the true good is in order to follow it. Nothing would be too costly for eternity.

I envy those of the faith whom I see living with such unconcern and who make such a poor use of a gift that, it seems to me, I would use so differently."

No other has recognized that man is the most excellent   S683/L430
creature. Some who have well understood the reality of his
excellence, have taken for cowardice and ingratitude the low opinions men naturally have of themselves; and others who have well understood how real is this lowliness, have treated with haughty ridicule those feelings of greatness that are equally natural to man.

"Lift your eyes to God," say the first. "Look at him whom you resemble and who has created you to worship him. You can make yourselves similar to him. Wisdom will make you his equal, if you want to follow him." — "Hold your heads high, free men," says Epictetus. — And the others say, "Lower your eyes toward the earth, puny worm that you are, and look at the beasts whose companion you are." What then will man become? Will he be equal to God or to the beasts? What a terrifying distance! What then shall we be? Who does not see from all this that man has gone astray, that he has fallen from his place, that he anxiously seeks it, that he can no longer find it again? And who then will direct him there? The greatest men have failed.

We cannot conceive Adam's glorious state, or the nature   S683/L431
of his sin, or the transmission of it to us. These are things that
took place under a state of nature altogether different from our own,
and that surpass our present understanding.

All of this would be useless for us to know in order to escape. All that
is important for us to know is that we are wretched, corrupt, separated
from God, but redeemed by Jesus Christ. And we have wonderful
proofs of this on earth.

Thus the two proofs of corruption and redemption are drawn from
the ungodly, who live in indifference to religion, and from the Jews,
who are its irreconcilable enemies.

<Self love, and because it is something of sufficient   S684/L432
interest to move us that we should be certain that, after all
the ills of life, an inevitable death, which threatens us at every moment,
must infallibly in a few years . . . in the horrible necessity . . . >

The three conditions.

We must not say that this is a mark of reason.

It is all a man could do if he was sure of the falsity of this news. Even
so, he should not be delighted about it, but dejected.

Nothing else matters, and we neglect only this!

Our imagination so enlarges the present by our thinking about it
continually, and so reduces eternity by our failing to think about it, that
we turn eternity into nothingness and nothingness into eternity. And all
this is so strongly rooted in us that all our reason cannot defend us from
it and that . . .

I would ask them if it is not true that they confirm in themselves the
foundation of the faith they attack, which is that man's nature lies in
corruption.

Then Jesus Christ comes to tell men that they have no   S685/L433
other enemies but themselves; that it is their passions separating them from God; that he comes to destroy these and give them his
grace, so as to make of them all one Holy Church.

That he comes to bring back the heathen and Jews to this Church,
that he comes to destroy the idols of the former and the superstition of the
latter. To this all men are opposed, not only through the natural opposition of concupiscence; but, above all, the kings of the earth join together
to destroy this religion at birth, as it had been foretold. (Prophecy: *Why do
the heathen rage . . . the kings of the earth . . . against the Lord.*)[4]

---

[4] *Quare fremuerunt gentes . . . reges terrae . . . adversus Christum.* Psalms 2:1–2.

All that is great on earth is united: scholars, sages, kings. Some write, others condemn, others kill. And notwithstanding all these oppositions, the simple, powerless people resist all these powers and subdue even these kings, scholars, sages, and remove idolatry from all the earth. And all this is done by the power that had foretold it.

Imagine a number of men in chains, all condemned to   S686/L434
death, where some are slaughtered each day in the sight of
the others, and those who remain see their own condition in that of their fellows and, looking at each other with grief and without hope, wait for their turn!

The Creation and the Flood having taken place, and God   S687/L435
no longer having to destroy the world, nor to create it anew,
nor to give such great signs of himself, he began to establish a people on the earth, purposely formed, who were to last until the Messiah would fashion a people through his spirit.

[47] Preface to the Second Part

Antiquity of the Jews   S688/L436

What a difference there is between one book and another!
I am not surprised that the Greeks composed the *Iliad*, nor the Egyptians and the Chinese their histories.

We have only to see how this arose. These historians of fables are not contemporary with the things they write about. Homer composes a story, which he gives as such and it is received as such; for nobody doubted that Troy and Agamemnon existed any more than the golden apple. He did not think he was composing a history as well, but only an amusement. He is the only writer of his time; the beauty of the work has made it last; everyone learns it and talks of it; it is necessary to know it; each one knows it by heart. Four hundred years later, the witnesses to these things are no longer alive; no one knows from his own knowledge whether it is a fable or history; one has only learned it from his ancestors; this can pass for truth.

Every history that is not contemporary is suspect. Thus the books of the Sibyls and of Trismegistus and many others who have enjoyed credit in the world are false and found to be false in the course of time. It is not so with contemporary authors.

There is a great difference between a book that an individual composes and gives to the people and a book that itself creates a people. We cannot doubt that the book is as old as the people.

Without feelings, we are not wretched. A ruined house is not wretched. Only man is wretched. *I am the man who sees.*[5]   S689/L437

That if God's mercy is so great that he instructs us beneficially, even when he hides himself, what enlightenment should we not expect when he reveals himself?   S690/L438

Recognize, then, the truth of religion in the very obscurity of religion, in the little illumination we have of it, in our indifference to understand it.   S690/L439

The eternal being exists always if he exists once.   S690/L440

All the objections of this or that side only go against themselves, and not against religion. Everything the ungodly ones say.   S690/L441

Thus the whole universe teaches man either that he is corrupt or that he is redeemed. Everything teaches him his greatness or his wretchedness. God's abandonment can be seen in the heathen, God's protection in the Jews.   S690/L442

All err the more dangerously as they each follow a truth. Their mistake is not in following a falsehood, but in not following another truth.   S690/L443

It is therefore true that everything teaches man his condition, but he must properly understand this. For it is not true that everything reveals God, and it is not true that everything conceals God. But it is at the same time true that he hides himself from those who tempt him, and that he reveals himself to those who seek him, because men are all at once unworthy and capable of God: unworthy through their corruption, capable through their original nature.   S690/L444

What shall we conclude from all our obscurities, then, if not our unworthiness?   S690/L445

If there were no obscurity, man would not feel his corruption; if there were no illumination, man would not hope for a remedy. Thus it is not simply right, but useful for us, that God should be partly hidden and partly revealed, since it is equally dangerous for man to know God without knowing his own wretchedness and to know his own wretchedness without knowing God.   S690/L446

---

[5] *Ego vir videns.* Lamentations 3:1.

The conversion of the heathen was solely reserved for the S690/L447
grace of the Messiah. The Jews had fought them so long
without success! Everything Solomon and the prophets said about it was
useless. Sages, such as Plato and Socrates, were unable to persuade them.

If nothing had ever appeared of God, this eternal priva- S690/L448
tion would have been ambiguous, and might have equally related to the absence of all divinity or to men's unworthiness to know
him. But the fact that he appears occasionally, and not always, removes
the ambiguity. If he appears once, he exists always. And thus we cannot
but conclude that there is a God and that men are unworthy of him.

They blaspheme against what they do not know. The S690/L449
Christian religion consists in two points. It is equally important for men to know them, and it is dangerous to be ignorant of them.

And it is equally merciful of God to have given indications of both.

And yet they take occasion to conclude against one of these points,
from what should have led them to conclude for the other.

Sages who have said there is only one God have been persecuted;
the Jews were hated; Christians even more so.

They have seen by the light of nature that if there is a true religion on
earth, the course of all things must tend to it as to its center.

(The whole course of things must have as object the establishment
and greatness of religion. Men must have within them feelings coincid-
ing with what religion teaches us. And, finally, religion must be the object and center to which all things tend in such a way that anyone
knowing its principles would be able to explain the whole nature of
man in particular, and the whole course of the world in general.)[6]

And on this basis they take occasion to blaspheme against the Christian religion, because they understand it badly. They imagine that it
consists simply in worshiping a God considered to be great, powerful,
and eternal; this is properly deism, which is almost as remote from the
Christian religion as atheism, its complete opposite. And in this way
they conclude that this religion is not true, because they do not see that
all things concur in establishing this point: that God does not manifest
himself to men with all the evidence he could supply.

But let them conclude what they want against deism; they will conclude nothing against the Christian religion, which properly consists in
the mystery of the Redeemer, who, uniting in himself the two natures,
human and divine, has saved men from the corruption of sin in order to
reconcile them with God in his divine person.

---

[6] The passage in parentheses is a marginal addition.

It therefore teaches men both these two truths: that there is a God of whom men are capable, and that there is a corruption in their nature that makes them unworthy of him. It is equally important for men to know both these points, and it is equally dangerous for man to know God without knowing his own wretchedness, and to know his own wretchedness without knowing the Redeemer who can cure him of it. Knowledge of only one of these points gives rise either to the arrogance of philosophers, who have known God and not their own wretchedness, or to the despair of atheists, who know their own wretchedness without a Redeemer.

And so, since it is equally necessary for man to know these two points, is it also equally merciful of God to let us know them. The Christian religion does this; indeed, it consists in this.

Let us examine the order of the world about this, and see whether all things do not tend to establish these two main points of our religion!

(Jesus Christ is object of everything and the center to which everything tends. Whoever knows him knows the reason for everything.)[7]

Those who go astray do so only for lack of seeing one of these two things: we can therefore easily know God without our wretchedness and our wretchedness without God. But we cannot know Jesus Christ without knowing together both God and our wretchedness.

And that is why I will not undertake here to prove by natural reasons either the existence of God, or the Trinity, or the immortality of the soul, or anything of that kind; not only because I would not feel myself sufficiently capable of finding in nature arguments to convince hardened atheists, but also because such knowledge without Jesus Christ is useless and barren. If a man were convinced that proportions between numbers were immaterial truths, eternal and dependent on a first truth in which they subsist, called God, I would not consider him as having made much progress toward his salvation.

The God of Christians does not consist in a God who is merely the author of geometrical truths and of the order of the elements; that is the part given by the heathens and Epicureans. He does not consist simply in a God who exercises his Providence over the life and property of men, so as to grant those who worship him a happy span of years. That is the portion given by the Jews. But the God of Abraham, the God of Isaac, the God of Jacob, the God of Christians is a God of love and consolation; he is a God who fills the soul and heart of those whom he

---

[7] The parenthetical phrases are set off in the text, possibly because they were intended to be in the margin.

possesses; he is a God who makes them inwardly aware of their wretchedness and his infinite mercy; who unites himself to the depths of their soul; who fills their soul with humility, joy, confidence, love; who makes them incapable of any other end but himself.

All who seek God outside Jesus Christ, and who go no further than nature, either find no enlightenment to satisfy them or come to fashion for themselves a means of knowing God and serving him without a mediator. In this way they fall into either atheism or deism, two things that the Christian religion abhors almost equally.

Without Jesus Christ, the world would not exist, for it would either have to be destroyed or be a kind of hell.

If the world existed to teach man about God, his divinity would shine through every part of it in an indisputable manner. But since it only exists through Jesus Christ, and for Jesus Christ, and to teach men both their corruption and redemption, everything in it bursts out with the proofs of these two truths.

What appears there indicates neither a total absence nor a manifest presence of divinity, but the presence of a God who hides himself. Everything bears this mark.

Will the only one who knows nature know it only to be wretched?

Will the only one to know it be the only one to be unhappy?

He must not see nothing at all; he must also not see so much that he believes he possesses God, but he must see enough to know that he has lost him. For to know of loss, one must see and not see; and that is precisely the state of nature.

Whatever side he takes, I will not leave him at rest.

The true religion must teach greatness and wretchedness,   S690/L450
lead to self-esteem and self-contempt, to love and to hate.

[48] The State of the Jews [1]

Advantages of the Jewish people   S691/L451

In this inquiry, the Jewish people immediately attract my attention by the quantity of wonderful and singular things apparent in them.

I first see that they are a people wholly composed of brothers. And whereas all others are made up of an infinite set of families, this people, though so strangely abundant, has all arisen from one man alone;[8] and,

---

[8] Abraham.

being thus all one flesh, and members one of another, they constitute a powerful state of a single family. This is unique.

This family, or people, is the oldest known to man: a fact, it seems to me, that inspires a peculiar veneration for it, especially in view of our present inquiry; since, if God had revealed himself to men throughout time, it is to these we must have recourse in order to know the tradition.

This people is not only remarkable by its antiquity, but is also singular in its duration, which has extended continuously from its origin to the present. For, whereas the peoples of Greece and Italy, of Sparta, Athens, and Rome, and others who came so much later, have long since perished, these still remain, despite the efforts of so many powerful kings who have a hundred times tried to destroy them, as their historians testify and as can easily be judged from the natural order of things over so long a space of years. Nevertheless they have always been preserved (and this preservation has been foretold); and extending from the earliest times to the latest, their history comprehends in its duration that of all our histories.

The law that governs this people is at once the most ancient law in the world, the most perfect, and the only one that has always been observed without interruption in any state. This is what Josephus admirably proves in *Against Apion*, and Philo the Jew in various places; they show that it is so ancient that the very name of law was only known by antiquity more than a thousand years later; so that Homer, who wrote the history of so many states, never used the term. And it is easy to ascertain its perfection simply by reading it; for we see it has provided for everything with such wisdom, equity, and judgment that the oldest Greek and Roman legislators, having some hint of it, borrowed from it their principal laws; this emerges from what they call the Twelve Tables, and from the other proofs Josephus gives.

But this law is at the same time the most severe and rigorous of all in respect to religious worship, requiring this people to keep to their duty, imposing a thousand peculiar and painful observances on pain of death. Thus it is truly astonishing that the law has been constantly preserved during so many centuries by a rebellious and impatient people such as this, while all other states have from time to time changed their laws, although these were entirely lenient.

The book containing this first of all laws is itself the most ancient book in the world, those of Homer, Hesiod, and others being 600 or 700 years later.

[49] The State of the Jews [2]

Sincerity of the Jews   S692/L452

They carry with love and devotion this book in which
Moses declares that they have been ungrateful toward God all their lives;
that he knows they will be still more so after his death; but that he calls
heaven and earth to witness against them; that he has enough times . . .

He declares that God, at last, growing angry with them, will scatter
them among all the peoples of the earth; that as they have angered him
by worshiping gods who were not their gods, so he will provoke them by
calling on a people who are not his people; that he wants all his words
to be preserved forever, and his book to be placed in the ark of the
covenant to serve forever as a witness against them.[9]

Isaiah: Isaiah says the same thing, 30.8.

[50] The State of the Jews [3]

To show that the true Jews   S693/L453
and the true Christians
have but one and the same religion.

The religion of the Jews seemed to consist essentially in Abraham's
fatherhood, circumcision, sacrifices, ceremonies, the Ark, the temple,
Jerusalem, and finally in the law and covenant with Moses.

I say that it consisted in none of those things, but only in the love of
God, and that God disapproved of all the other things.

That God did not make any exception for (*accepter*) Abraham's
posterity.

That the Jews will be punished by God in the same way as strangers,
if they have offended him.

Deuteronomy 8:19[–20]: *If you forget God and follow other gods, I
predict that you shall surely perish in the same way as the nations God
destroyed before you.*

_____

That strangers will be received by God in the same way as the Jews, if
they love him.

Isaiah 56:3[–7]: *Let not the stranger say, "The Lord will not receive
me." The strangers join themselves to the Lord to serve and love him. I will
bring them to my holy mountain and accept their sacrifices. For my house
is a house of prayer.*

_____

[9] Deuteronomy 31:32.

That the true Jews considered their merit to come only from God, and not from Abraham.

Isaiah 63:16: *You are truly our Father, though Abraham is ignorant of us, and Israel does not acknowledge us. You are our Father and our Redeemer.*

Moses himself told them that God would not regard persons.

Deuteronomy 10:17: *God said: "I regard neither persons nor sacrifices."*

The Sabbath was only a sign (Exodus 31:13), and in memory of the exodus from Egypt (Deuteronomy 5:19). Therefore it is no longer necessary, since Egypt must be forgotten.

Circumcision was only a sign (Genesis 17:11).

And as a result, it came to pass that, being in the desert, they were not circumcised, because they could not be confused with other peoples; and after Jesus Christ came, it was no longer necessary.

That circumcision of the heart is commanded.

Deuteronomy 10:16; Jeremiah 4:4: *Circumcise the foreskin of your heart*; take away the superfluities of your heart, and no longer harden yourselves. *For your God is a mighty God, strong and terrible, who does not regard persons.*

That God said he would do it one day.

Deuteronomy 30:6: *God will circumcise your heart and that of your seed, that you may love him with all your heart.*

That the uncircumcised in heart shall be judged.

Jeremiah 9:26: For God will judge the uncircumcised peoples, and all the people of Israel, *because they are uncircumcised in heart.*

That the external is useless without the internal.

Joel 2:13: *Rend your heart*,[10] etc. Isaiah 58:3–4, etc.

The love of God is commanded through all of Deuteronomy.

Deuteronomy 30:19[–20]: *I call heaven and earth to record that I have set before you life and death, so that you should choose life, and love God, and obey him. For God is your life.*

That the Jews, for lack of that love, will be rejected for their offenses, and the heathen chosen in their place:

Hosea 1:10.

Deuteronomy 32:20[–21]. *I will hide my face from them at the sight of their later offenses. For it is a wicked and faithless nation. They have provoked me to anger with things that are not God's, and I will move them to jealousy with a people that is not my people and with a nation without knowledge or intelligence.*

---

[10] *Scindite corda vestra.*

Isaiah 65:1.

That temporal goods are false, and that the true good is to be united to God:

Psalm 143:15.

That their feasts are displeasing to God:

Amos 5:21.

That the sacrifices of the Jews are displeasing to God:

Isaiah 66:1–3.

1. 11.

Jeremiah 6:20.

David, *Have mercy.*[11]

   He has looked for.[12]

Even on the part of the good:

Psalms 49:8, 9, 10, 11, 12, 13, and 14.

That he has established them only for their hardness:

Micah, admirably, 6.

I Kings 15:22.

Hosea 6:6.

That the sacrifices of the heathen will be received by God, and that God will no longer take pleasure in the sacrifices of the Jews:

Malachi 1:11.

That God will make a new covenant through the Messiah, and the old covenant will be rejected:

Jeremiah 31:31.

Statutes that were not good.[13] Ezekiel.

That the old things will be forgotten:

Isaiah 43:18, 19.

65:17, 10

That the Ark will no longer be remembered:

Jeremiah 3:15–16

That the temple will be rejected:

Jeremiah 7:12, 13, 14.

That the sacrifices will be rejected and other pure sacrifices established:

Malachi 1:11.

------

[11] *Miserere.* Psalms 9:14.

[12] *Expectavi.* Isaiah 5:7.

[13] *Mandata non bona.* Ezekiel 20:25.

That the order of Aaron's priesthood will be reproved, and that of Melchizedek introduced by the Messiah: *Dixit Dominus*.[14]

That this priesthood will be eternal:

Ibid.

That Jerusalem will be reproved and Rome admitted:

Dixit Dominus.

That the name of the Jews will be cast out and a new name given: Isaiah 65:15.

That this last name will be better than that of the Jews and eternal: Isaiah 56:5.

That the Jews will be without prophets:

Amos.

Without king, without prince, without sacrifice, without idol.

That the Jews nevertheless will always remain as a people: Jeremiah 31:36

[51] The State of the Jews [4]

I see the Christian religion, founded on a previous reli-   S694/L454
gion, and this is what I find as a fact.

I am not speaking here of the miracles of Moses, Jesus Christ, and the Apostles, because they do not at first appear convincing, and here I only want to put into evidence all those foundations of the Christian religion that are beyond doubt and cannot be called into doubt by any person whatsoever.

It is certain that in several places of the world, we see a peculiar people, separated from all other peoples of the world, called the Jewish people.

_____

I therefore see religion mongers in several parts of the world and at all times. But they have neither a morality that can please me nor proofs that can convince me. Thus I would have equally rejected the religion of Mahomet, of China, of the ancient Romans, and of the Egyptians, for the sole reason that, since none of them bears greater marks of truth than any other, nor anything that would necessarily determine me, reason cannot incline toward one rather than the other.

But, when I consider this changeable and strange variety of customs and beliefs at different times, I find in one corner of the world a peculiar people, separated from all other peoples on earth, who are the most

_____

[14] Psalms 110.

ancient of all and whose histories precede by several centuries the most ancient histories we have.

I find then this great and numerous people, arisen from a single man, worshiping one God, and being guided by a law they claim to have obtained from his hand. They maintain they are the only people in the world to whom God has revealed his mysteries; that all men are corrupt and in disgrace with God; that they are all abandoned to their senses and their own minds; and that the unusual errors and continual changes of religions and customs among men arise from this, whereas they remain unshakable in their conduct, but that God will not leave other nations forever in this darkness; that a Savior will come for all; that they are in the world to announce him to men; that they are expressly made to be forerunners and heralds of this great advent and to call all peoples to unite with them in the expectation of this Savior.

The encounter with this people astonishes me and seems to me worthy of attention.

I consider this law they boast of having obtained from God, and I find it admirable. It is the first of all laws and of such a kind that, even before the word "law" was in use among the Greeks, they had received it and observed it without interruption for nearly a thousand years. Thus I find it strange that the first law of the world happens also to be the most perfect, so that the greatest legislators have borrowed their laws from it, as is apparent from the law of the Twelve Tables in Athens, subsequently adopted by the Romans; and as it would be easy to show, if Josephus and others had not sufficiently treated this matter.

<Prophecies   S695/L455
The promise that David will always have successors.
Jeremiah [13. 13].>

[52] The State of the Jews [5]

This is fact: S696/L456
While all philosophers separate into different sects, there are some people, in a corner of the world, who are the most ancient in the world, and who declare that the whole world is in error; that God has revealed the truth to them; that it will always be on the earth. In fact, all other sects come to an end; this one still endures. And for 4,000 years, they declare that they hold from their ancestors that man has fallen from communication with God, into complete estrangement from God; but that he has promised to redeem them, that this doctrine will always be on earth, that their law has a double meaning.

That for 1,600 years, they have had people they believed to be prophets foretelling both the time and the manner.

That 400 years later, they were scattered everywhere, because Jesus Christ had to be announced everywhere.

That Jesus Christ came in the manner and at the time foretold.

That since then the Jews have been scattered abroad under a curse and nevertheless subsisting.

Hypothesis that the apostles were impostors.   S696/L457

The time clearly, the manner obscurely.

———

Five proofs of the figurative [meanings of the Scriptures].

———

2000 $\left\{ \begin{array}{l} 1600 - \text{prophets.} \\ 400 - \text{scattered.} \end{array} \right.$

[53. Around Corruption]

Oppositions   S697/L458
Infinite wisdom and folly of religion

Zephaniah 3:9: *I will give my words to the people, so that*   S697/L459
all may serve me with a single consent.

Ezekiel 37:25: *My servant David will be their prince eternally.*

Exodus 4:22: *Israel is my first-born son.*

Jeremiah 7:4: *Do not trust in the lying words of those who say: "The temple of the Lord, the temple of the Lord, the temple of the Lord, are [these]."*

These are the effects of the sins of the peoples and of the   S698/L973
Jesuits. The great have wished to be flattered; the Jesuits have wished to be loved by the great.

They have all been worthy to be abandoned to the spirit of lying, the ones to deceive, the others to be deceived. They have been greedy, ambitious, lustful. *They shall heap to themselves teachers.*[15]

Worthy disciples of such teachers. *They are worthy.*[16]

They have sought flatterers and have found them.

———

[15] *Coacervabunt tibi magistros.* 2 Timothy 4:3.

[16] *Digni sunt.* Romans 1:32.

The God of the Christians is a God who makes the soul   S699/L460
feel that he is its unique good, that all its rest is in him, that it
will have joy only in loving him; and who at the same time makes it
abhor the obstacles holding it back and preventing it from loving God
with all its strength. Self-love and concupiscence, which hinder it, are
unbearable to it. This God makes the soul feel that it has this under-
lying self-love that is destroying it, and that he alone can cure.

The world exists for the exercise of mercy and judgment,   S700/L461
not as if the men in it came from the hands of God, but as if
they were as the enemies of God, to whom he grants by his grace
enough light to return, if they want to seek and follow him; but also for
punishing them, if they refuse to seek or follow him.

The prophets foretold, and were not foretold. Then the   S701/L462
saints were foretold, but did not foretell. Jesus Christ both
foretold and was foretold.

It is an astonishing fact that no canonical writer has ever   S702/L463
made use of nature to prove God. All of them strive to make
him believed. David, Solomon, and others never said: "There is no
void, therefore there is a God." They must have been cleverer than the
cleverest people who came after them, all of whom made use of this
argument.

This is very noteworthy.

I will not allow him to rest in either one or the other, so   S703/L464
that being without a resting place and without rest . . .

———

These children are astonished to see their comrades   S703/L465
respected.

———

If it is a sign of weakness to prove God by nature, do not   S703/L466
scorn Scripture for it. If it is a sign of strength to have known
these oppositions, respect Scripture for it.

Order   S704/L467

After corruption, say: it is right that all those who are in
that state should know it, both those who are content and those who are
not content with it. But it is not right that all should see Redemption.

There is nothing on earth that does not show either man's   S705/L468
wretchedness or God's mercy, man's weakness without God
or man's power with God.

God has used the blindness of this people for the good of   S706/L469
the chosen.

Man's greatest lowliness is the pursuit of glory. But this is   S707/L470
also the greatest mark of his excellence; for whatever possessions he may have on earth, whatever health or essential commodity, he is
not satisfied if he does not have men's esteem. He values human reason so
highly that, whatever advantages he may have on earth, he is not content
if he does not also enjoy an advantageous place in human reason. This is
the finest position in the world. Nothing can deflect him from that desire,
and this is the most indelible quality of the human heart.

And those who most despise men, and make them the equals of
beasts, still want to be admired and believed by them, and contradict
themselves by their own feelings; for their nature, which is stronger than
anything, convinces them more strongly of man's greatness than reason
convinces them of their lowliness.

For myself, I confess that, as soon as the Christian religion   S708/L471
reveals the principle that human nature is corrupt and fallen
from God, it opens one's eyes to see everywhere the mark of this truth:
for nature is such that it points everywhere to a lost God, both within
and outside man.

And a corrupt nature.

Greatness   S709/L472

Religion is such a great thing that it is right that those who
would not take the trouble to seek it, if it is obscure, should be deprived
of it. What, then, is there to complain about, if it is such that it can be
found by seeking?

Comprehension of the words "good" and "evil."   S710/L473

The creation of the world beginning to be distant, God   S711/L474
provided a single contemporary historian[17] and entrusted a
whole people with custody of this book, so that this history would be the
most authentic in the world and all men might learn from it something
so necessary to know that could not be known any other way.

The veil drawn over these books for the Jews is there also   S711/L475
for bad Christians and for all who do not hate themselves.

But how well disposed are we to understand them and to know Jesus
Christ when we truly hate ourselves!

I do not say that *mem* is mystical.[18]   S711/L476

Pride counterbalances and carries away all miseries. Here   S712/L477
is a strange monster, and a very visible aberration! Here he is,

---

[17] That is, Moses.

[18] See fragment S303.

fallen from his place and anxiously seeking it: that is what all men do. Let us see who will have found it.

Without examining every particular occupation, it is enough to comprehend them under [the heading of] diversion. S713/L478

For philosophers, 280 supreme goods.[19] S714/L479

In all religions, we must be sincere: true heathens, true Jews, true Christians. S715/L480

Against the *History of China* S716/L481

The histories of Mexico, the five suns, of which the last is only 800 years old.[20]

Difference between a book accepted by a people and one that creates a people.

Proofs S717/L482

1. The Christian religion, by its establishment: by establishing itself so strongly, so gently, being so contrary to nature.
2. The sanctity, loftiness, and humility of a Christian soul.
3. The miracles of Holy Scripture.
4. Jesus Christ in particular.
5. The apostles in particular.
6. Moses and the prophets in particular.
7. The Jewish people.
8. The prophecies.
9. Perpetuity. No religion has perpetuity.
10. The doctrine that accounts for everything.
11. The sanctity of this law.
12. By the course of the world.

Without a doubt, after considering what life is and what this religion is, we must not reject the inclination to follow the latter, if it comes into our heart. And it is certain that there is no ground for mocking those who follow it.

---

[19] See fragment S27.

[20] See Montaigne, *Essays* III, chap. 6 (Frame trans., p. 698).

[54] Prophecies [1]

215. In Egypt.   S718/L483

Talmud (*Pugio Fidei*, p. 659). *It is a tradition among us that, when the Messiah comes, the house of God, destined for the dispensation of his word, will be full of filth and impurity, and that the wisdom of the scribes will be corrupt and rotten. Those afraid to sin will be rejected by the people and treated as madmen and fools.*

Isaiah 49:

Listen to me, inhabitants of the isles and you people from afar: the Lord has called me by my name from the womb of my mother. He has hidden me in the shadow of his hand, made my words like a sharp sword, and said to me: "You are my servant in whom I will be glorified." Then I said: "Lord, have I labored in vain? Have I spent my strength for nothing? Yet surely my judgment is with You, O Lord, and my work with You." And now, says the Lord, who formed me from the womb to be his servant, to bring Jacob and Israel again to him: "You shall be glorious in my sight and I shall be your strength. It is a light thing that you should convert the tribes of Jacob; I have raised you up for a light to the gentiles, that you may be my salvation to the ends of the earth." Thus says the Lord to him who has humbled his soul, to him whom man despises, to him whom the gentiles abhor, to a servant of rulers: "Princes and kings shall worship you, because the Lord who has chosen you is faithful."

Again the Lord says to me: "I have heard you in the days of salvation and of mercy, and I have given you as a covenant for the people, to cause you to inherit the desolate nations, that you may say to the prisoners: 'Go forth,' and to those in darkness: 'Show yourselves, and possess these abundant and fertile lands.' They shall not hunger nor thirst, neither shall the heat nor sun smite them; for he who has mercy on them shall lead them; even by the springs of waters shall he guide them, and level the mountains before them. Behold, the peoples shall come from all parts, from the east and from the west, from the north and from the south. Let the heavens give glory to God! Let the earth be joyful, for it has pleased the Lord to comfort his people, and he will have mercy upon the poor who hope in him!"

Yet Zion dared to say: "The Lord has forsaken me, and has forgotten me." Can a woman forget her child, that she should not have compassion on the son of her womb? She may forget, yet will not I forget you, O Zion. I will bear you always between my hands, and your walls are continually before me. They who shall build you have come, and your destroyers shall go forth away from you. Lift up your eyes all round and behold all these who gather themselves together and come to you. As I live, says the Lord, you shall surely clothe yourself with them all, as with an ornament. Your waste and your desolate places, and the land of your destruction, shall even now be too narrow from the great number of your inhabitants, and the children you shall have after your barrenness shall say again: "The place is too strait: give us a place that we may dwell." Then shall you say in your heart: "Who has begotten me this abundance of children, seeing I have lost my children, and am desolate, a captive, and removing to and fro? And who brought up these? Behold, I was left alone; these, where had they been?" And the Lord shall say to you: "Behold, I will lift up my hand to the gentiles, and set up my standard to the people; and they shall bring your sons in their arms and in their bosoms. And kings shall be your nursing fathers, and queens your nursing mothers. They shall bow down to you with their face toward the earth, and lick up the dust of your feet; and you shall know that I am the Lord; for they who wait for me shall not be ashamed. For who shall take the prey from the strong and mighty? But even if they should be taken, nothing shall hinder me from saving your children and from destroying your enemies. And all flesh shall know that I am the Lord, your Savior, and the mighty Redeemer of Jacob.

Isaiah 50:

Thus says the Lord: "What is the bill of this divorce, with which I have put away the Synagogue? And why have I delivered it into the hand of your enemies? Is it not for its iniquities and transgressions that I have put it away?

For I came, and no man received me. I called and there was none to hear. Is my arm shortened, that I cannot redeem?

Therefore I will show the tokens of my anger: I will clothe the heavens with darkness, and make sackcloth their covering.

The Lord has given me the tongue of the learned that I should know how to speak a word in season to him who is weary. He has opened my ear, and I have listened to him as to a master.

The Lord has revealed his will to me, and I was not rebellious.

I gave my body to the blows and my cheeks to outrages. I did not hide my face from shame and spitting. But the Lord has helped me; therefore I have not been confounded.

He who justifies me is near; who will contend with me? Who will be my adversary, and accuse me of sin, God himself being my protector?

All men shall pass away and be consumed by time. Let those who fear God hearken to the voice of his servant! Let him who languishes in darkness put his trust in the Lord! But as for you, you do but kindle the wrath of God upon you; you walk in the light of your fire and in the sparks you have kindled. This you shall have from my hand; you shall lie down in sorrow.

[Isaiah 51:]

Hearken to me, you who follow after righteousness, you who seek the Lord. Look at the rock from which you have been hewn, and to the hole of the pit from which you have been drawn. Look to Abraham, your father, and to Sarah, who bore you. For I called him alone, when childless, and increased him. Behold, I have comforted Zion, and heaped upon it blessings and consolations.

Hearken to me, my people, and give your ear to me, for a law shall proceed from me and a judgment, which shall be for a light for the gentiles.

Amos 8

The prophet, having enumerated the sins of Israel, said that God had sworn to take vengeance on them.

He says this:

And it shall come to pass in that day, says the Lord, that I will cause the sun to go down at noon, and I will darken the earth in the clear day; and I will turn your feasts into mourning, and all your songs into lamentation.

You shall all have sorrow and suffering, and I will make this nation mourn as for an only son, and the end thereof as a bitter day. Behold, the days come, says the Lord, that I will send a famine in the land; not a famine of bread, nor a thirst for water, but of hearing the words of the Lord. And they shall wander from sea to sea, and from the north even to the east; they shall run to and fro to seek the word of the Lord, and shall not find it.

In that day shall the fair virgins and young men faint for thirst. They who have followed the idols of Samaria, and sworn by the god of Dan, and followed the manner of Beersheba, shall fall, and never rise up again.

Amos 3:3

Of all the families of the earth, I have known only you for my people.

Daniel 12:7

Having described the whole extent of the Messiah's reign, he says:

All these things shall be finished, when the scattering of the people of Israel shall be accomplished.

Haggai 2:4

You who, comparing this second house with the glory of the first, despise it, be strong, says the Lord, be strong, O Zerubbabel, and O Jesus, the high priest, be strong, all you people of the land, and work! For I am with you, says the Lord of hosts; according to the promise I made you when you came out of Egypt, so my spirit remains among you. Do not fear. For thus says the Lord of hosts: "In a little while I will shake the heavens, and the earth, and the sea, and the dry land (a way of speaking to indicate a great and an extraordinary change); *and I will shake all nations. And then the desire of all the gentiles shall come, and I will fill this house with glory, says the Lord.*

The silver is mine, and the gold is mine, says the Lord (that is to say, it is not thus that I wish to be honored; as it is said elsewhere: *All the beasts of the field are mine, what advantage is it to me that they are offered to me in sacrifice?). The glory of this latter house shall be greater than of the former, says the Lord of hosts; and in this place will I establish my house, says the Lord."*

[Deuteronomy 18, 16]

According to all that you desired in Horeb in the day of the assembly, saying, "Let us not hear again the voice of the Lord, neither let us see this fire any more, that we may not die." And the Lord said to me: "Their prayer is just. I will raise them a prophet like you from among their brothers, and will put my words in his mouth; and he shall speak to them all that I shall command him. And it shall come to pass that whoever will not hearken to the words he will speak in my name, I will require it of him.

Genesis 49

Judah, you are the one your brothers shall praise, and you shall conquer your enemies; your father's children shall bow down before you. Judah is a lion's whelp: from the prey, my son, you are raised, and are couched as a lion, and as a lioness that shall be aroused.

The scepter shall not depart from Judah, nor a lawgiver from between his feet, until Shiloh has come; and to him shall the gathering of the people be, to obey him.

[55] Prophecies [2]

Predictions of particular things   S719/L484

They were strangers in Egypt, without any possession of their own, either in that country or elsewhere. <There was not the least appearance, either of the royalty that existed so long afterward, or of that supreme council of seventy judges they called the **Sanhedrin**, which was instituted by Moses and lasted to the time of Jesus Christ. All these things were as far removed from their present state as they could be,> when Jacob, dying, and blessing his twelve children, declared to them that they would be owners of a great land, and foretold in particular to the family of Judah that the kings who would one day rule them would be of his race; and that all his brothers would be their subjects, <and that even the Messiah, who was to be the expectation of nations, would

be born from him; and that the kingship would not be taken from Judah, nor the ruler and lawgiver of his descendants, until the expected Messiah arrived into his family.>

This same Jacob, disposing of this future land as though he were its ruler, gave a portion to Joseph more than to the others. **"I give to you,"** **he said, "one part more than to your brothers".** And blessing his two children, Ephraim and Manasseh, whom Joseph had presented to him—the elder, Manasseh, on his right, and the young Ephraim on his left—he crossed his arms and, placing his right hand on the head of Ephraim and his left on Manasseh, he blessed them in this manner. And, upon Joseph's representing to him that he was giving preference to the younger, he answered with admirable resolution: "I know it well, my son; I know it well. But Ephraim will increase more than Manasseh." This has been indeed so true in the result that, being alone almost as fruitful as the two entire lines composing a whole kingdom, they were usually called by the name of Ephraim alone.

This same Joseph, when dying, bade his children carry his bones with them when they should go into that land to which they would come only 200 years later.

Moses, who wrote all these things so long before they happened, him-self assigned to each family portions of that land before they entered it, as though he had been its ruler, <and he foretold to them exactly all that was to happen to them in the land they were to enter after his death: the victories God would give them, their ingratitude toward God, the pun-ishments they would receive for it, and the rest of their adventures.>

He gave them judges to make the division. He prescribed the entire form of political government they should observe, the cities of refuge they should build, etc.

[56] Prophecies [3]

Daniel 2   S720/L485

All your soothsayers and wise men cannot show you the
secret you have demanded. (This dream must have caused him much anguish.)[21]

But there is a God in heaven who can do so, and who has revealed to you *in your dream what shall be in the latter days. And it is not by my own* *wisdom that I have knowledge of this secret, but by the revelation of this* *same God, who has revealed it to me to make it manifest in your presence.*

---

[21] The parenthetical passages are Pascal's marginal notes.

Your dream was then of this kind: you saw a great image, high and terrible, which stood before you. His head was of gold, his breast and arms of silver, his belly and his thighs of brass, his legs of iron, his feet part of iron and part of earth (clay). You saw it thus until a stone was cut out without hands, which smote the image upon his feet, which were of iron and of clay, and broke them into pieces.

Then were the iron, the clay, the brass, the silver, and the gold broken to pieces together, and the wind carried them away. But this stone that smote the image became a great mountain, and filled the whole earth. This is the dream, and now I will give you its interpretation.

You who are the greatest of kings, and to whom God has given a power so vast that you are renowned among all peoples, are the head of gold you have seen.

But after you shall arise another kingdom inferior to you, and another third kingdom of brass, which shall bear rule over all the earth.

But the fourth kingdom shall be strong as iron, and even as iron breaks in pieces and pierces all things, so shall this empire break in pieces and bruise all.

And whereas you saw the feet and toes, part of clay and part of iron, the kingdom shall be divided; but there shall be in it part of the strength of iron and part of the weakness of clay.

But as iron cannot be firmly mixed with clay, so they who are represented by the iron and the clay shall not cleave one to another, though united by marriage.

Now, in the days of these kings, shall God set up a kingdom that shall never be destroyed, nor ever be delivered to other people. It shall break in pieces and consume all these kingdoms, and it shall stand forever, according as you saw that the stone was cut out of the mountain without hands, and that it fell from the mountain, and broke in pieces the iron, the clay, the silver, and the gold.

God has made known to you what shall come to pass hereafter. This dream is certain, and the interpretation of it sure.

Then Nebuchadnezzar fell upon his face toward the earth, etc.

Daniel 8:8

Daniel having seen the fight of the ram and the goat, who vanquished him and ruled over the earth, whose principal horn being broken, four others came up toward the four winds of heaven, and out of one of them came forth a little horn, which waxed toward the south, and toward the east, and toward the land of Israel; and it rose up against the host of heaven, and cast down some of the stars, and stamped upon them; and at last he overthrew the prince, and by him the perpetual sacrifice was taken away and the sanctuary was cast down.

This is what Daniel saw. He sought the meaning of it, *and a voice cried in this manner, "Gabriel, make this man understand the vision."* And Gabriel said:

"The ram you saw is the king of the Medes and Persians, and the goat is the king of Greece, and the great horn between his eyes is the first king of this monarchy. Now, that being broken, whereas four stood up for it, four kingdoms shall stand up out of the nation, but not in his power.

And in the latter time of their kingdom, when iniquities have come fully, there shall arise a king, insolent and strong, but not by his own power, to whom all things shall succeed after his own will. And he shall destroy the holy people, and succeeding in his undertaking with a false and crafty spirit, he shall destroy many, and at the end will rise up against the prince of princes. But he shall perish miserably, and nevertheless by a violent hand."

Daniel 9:20

While I was praying with all my heart, and confessing my sin and the sin of all my people, and prostrating myself before my God, even Gabriel, whom I had seen in the vision at the beginning, came to me and touched me about the time of the evening oblation, and he informed me and said: "Daniel, I have now come forth to give you the knowledge of things. At the beginning of your supplications, I came to show what you did desire, for you are greatly beloved. Therefore understand the matter, and consider the vision. Seventy weeks are determined for your people, and for your holy city, to finish the transgression, and to make an end of sins, and to abolish iniquity, and to bring in everlasting righteousness, to accomplish the vision and the prophecies, and to anoint the most holy.

(After which this people shall be your people no more, nor this city the holy city.

The times of wrath shall have passed, and the years of grace shall come forever.)

Know therefore, and understand, that, from the going forth of the commandment to restore and to build Jerusalem, until the Messiah Prince, shall be seven weeks, and three score and two weeks. (The Hebrews were accustomed to divide numbers, and to place the small first. Thus seven and sixty-two make sixty-nine of this seventy. There will then remain the seventieth: that is to say, the seven last years of which he will speak next.) *The street shall be built again, and the wall, even in troubled times. And after three score and two weeks* (which have followed the first seven), *the Christ shall be slain* (Christ will then be slain after the sixty-nine weeks—that is, in the last week) *and a people shall come with their prince, who shall destroy the city and the sanctuary, and overwhelm all. And the end of that war shall accomplish the desolation.*

Now, one week (which is the seventieth that remains) *shall confirm the covenant with many, and in the midst of the week* (that is to say, the last three and a half years), *he shall cause the sacrifice and the oblation to cease, and for the overspreading of abominations he shall make it desolate, even until the consummation, and that determined shall be poured upon the desolate.*"

Daniel 11

The angel said to Daniel:

There shall stand up yet (after Cyrus, under whom this is written) *three kings in Persia* (Cambyses, Smerdis, Darius); *and the fourth who shall then come* (Xerxes) *shall be far richer and stronger, and shall stir up all his people against the Greeks.*

But a mighty king shall stand up (Alexander) *who shall rule with great dominion, and do according to his desire. And when he shall stand up, his kingdom shall be broken, and shall be divided into four parts toward the four winds of heaven* (as he had said above: 7:6; 8:8), *but not his posterity. And his successors shall not equal his power, for his kingdom shall be plucked up, even for others besides these* (his four principal successors).

And one of his successors, who shall rule toward the south (Egypt: Ptolemy, son of Lagos), *shall be strong. But another* (Seleucus, King of Syria) *shall be strong above him, and his dominion shall be a great dominion* (Appian says that he was the most powerful of Alexander's successors).

And in the end of years they shall join themselves together, and the king's daughter of the south (Berenice, daughter of Ptolemy Philadelphus, son of the other Ptolemy) *shall come to the king of the north* (to Antiochus Deus, King of Syria and of Asia, son of Seleucus Lagidas) *to make peace between these princes.*

But neither she nor her seed shall have a long authority. For she and they who brought her, and her children, and her friends, shall be delivered to death (Berenice and her son were killed by Seleucus Callinicus).

But out of a branch of her roots shall one stand up (Ptolemy Evergetes was the issue of the same father as Berenice) *who shall come with a mighty army into the land of the king of the north, where he shall put all under subjection; and he shall also carry captive into Egypt their gods, their princes, their gold, their silver, and all their precious spoils, and he shall continue several years when the king of the north can do nothing against him* (if he had not been called into Egypt by domestic reasons, he would have entirely stripped Seleucus, says Justin).

And so he shall return into his kingdom, but his sons (Seleucus Ceraunus, Antiochus the Great) *shall be stirred up, and shall assemble a multitude of great forces.*

And their army shall come and overthrow all; as a result, the king of the south (Ptolemy Philopator) *shall be irritated, and shall also form a great army and fight* (against Antiochus the Great) *and conquer* (at Raphia). *And his troops shall become insolent, and his heart shall be lifted up* (this Ptolemy desecrated the temple: Josephus). *He shall cast down many ten thousands, but he shall not be strengthened by it.*

For the king of the north (Antiochus the Great) *shall return with a greater multitude than before, and in those times also a great number of enemies shall stand up against the king of the south* (during the reign of the young Ptolemy Epiphanes); *also the apostates* (those who abandon their religion to please Evergetes, when he sent his troops to Scopas) *and robbers of your people shall exalt themselves to establish the vision; but they shall fall* (for Antiochus will again take Scopas, and conquer them).

And the king of the north shall destroy the ramparts and the most fortified cities, and all the arms of the south shall not withstand.

And everything shall yield to his will. He shall stand in the land of Israel, and it shall yield to him.

And thus he shall think to make himself master of all the empire of Egypt (despising the youth of Epiphanes, says Justin).

And for that he shall make alliance with him, and give his daughter (Cleopatra, in order that she may betray her husband. On which Appian says that, doubting his ability to make himself master of Egypt by force, because of the protection of the Romans, he wished to attempt it by cunning). *He shall wish to corrupt her, but she shall not stand on his side, nor be for him. Then he shall turn his face to other designs, and shall think to make himself master of some isles* (that is, seaports), *and shall take many* (as Appian says).

But a great prince shall oppose his conquests and shall cause the reproach offered by him to cease (Scipio Africanus, who stopped the progress of Antiochus Magnus, because the latter offended the Romans in the person of their allies). *He shall then return into his kingdom and there perish, and be no more.* (He was slain by his soldiers.)

And he who shall stand up in his estate (Seleucus Philopator or Soter, the son of Antiochus Magnus) *shall be a tyrant, a raiser of taxes in the glory of the kingdom* (which is the people). *But within a few days, he shall be destroyed, neither in anger nor in battle.*

And in his place shall stand up a vile person, unworthy of the honor of the kingdom, but he shall come in skillfully by flatteries.

All armies shall bend before him; he shall conquer them, and even the prince **with whom he has made** *a covenant. For having renewed the league with him, he shall work deceitfully and enter with a small people* into his province, peaceably and without fear. He shall take the fattest places, and shall do what his fathers had not done, and ravage on all sides. He shall forecast great devices during his time.

25.

[57] Prophecies [4]

Isaiah 1:21: *Change of good into evil and God's vengeance.*   S721/L486

———

Isaiah 10:1: *Woe unto them who decree unrighteous decrees.*[22]

Isaiah 26:20. *Come, my people, enter into your chambers and shut the doors about you: hide yourself as it were for a moment, until the indignation passes.*[23]

———

Isaiah 28:1. *Woe to the crown of pride.*[24]

———

Miracles. The earth mourns and languishes; Lebanon is ashamed and hewn down, etc. Isaiah 23:9.[25]

Now I will rise, said the Lord; now I will be exalted; now I will lift myself.[26]

———

All nations [. . .] are as nothing. Isaiah 40:17.[27]

Who has declared from the beginning, that we may know,   S722/L486 *and beforetime, that we may say: "He is righteous"? Isaiah 41:26.*[28]

———

I will work, and who shall let it? Isaiah 43:13.[29]

Do not prophesy in the name of the Lord, so that you do   S723/L486 *not die by our hand.*

---

[22] *Vae qui conditis leges iniquas.* Isaiah 10:1.

[23] *Vade, populus meus, intra in cubicula tua, claude ostia tua super te. Abscondere modicum ad momentum, donec pertranseat indignatio.* Isaiah 26:20.

[24] *Vae coronae superbiae.* Isaiah 28:1.

[25] *Luxit et elanguit terra, confusus est Libanus et obsorduit*, etc. In fact, this is Isaiah 33:9.

[26] *Nunc consurgam, dicit Dominus, nuc exaltabor, nunc sublevabor.* Isaiah 33:10.

[27] *Omnes gentes, quasi non sint.* Isaiah 40:7.

[28] *Quis annuntiavit ab exordio ut sciamus, et a principio ut dicamus: "Justus es"?* Isaiah 41:26.

[29] *Operabor, et quis avertet illud?* Isaiah 43:13.

Therefore thus said the Lord . . . [30] Jeremiah 11:21.

If they say to you: "Where shall we go forth?" Then you shall say to them: "Thus said the Lord: Such as are for death, to death; and such as are for the sword, to the sword; and such as are for the famine, to the famine; and such as are for captivity, to captivity." Jeremiah 15:2.[31]

The heart is deceitful above all things, and desperately wicked: who can know it?[32] That is to say, Who can know all its evil? For it is already known to be wicked.

I the Lord search the heart; I try the reins.[33] Jeremiah 17:9.

Come and let us devise devices against Jeremiah, for the law shall not perish from the priest, nor counsel from the wise, nor the word from the prophet.[34]

Be not a terror unto me; you are my hope in the day of evil. Jeremiah 17:7.[35]

Trust in external sacrifices.   Jeremiah 7:14.   S724/L486

I will do to this house, which is called by my name, in which you trust, and to the place I gave to you and to your fathers, as I have done to Shiloh.[36]

Therefore do not pray for this people.[37]

Outward sacrifice is not the essential point.   S725/L486

Jeremiah 7:22.

For I did not speak to your fathers, nor command them in the day that I brought them out of the land of Egypt, concerning burnt offerings and sacrifices.

But this thing I commanded them, saying: "Obey my voice, and I will be your God, and you shall be my people, and walk in all the ways that I have commanded you, that it may be well unto you."

---

[30] *Non prophetabis in nomine Domini et non morieris in manibus nostris. Propterea haec dicit Dominus . . .* Jeremiah 11:21.

[31] *Quod si dixerint ad te: "Quo egrediemur!" dices ad eos: "Heac dicit Dominus: Qui ad mortem, ad mortem; et qui ad gladium, ad gladium; et qui ad famen, ad famen; et qui ad captivitatem, ad captivitatem."* Jeremiah 15:2.

[32] *Pravum est cor omnium et incrustabile; quis cognoscet illud?* Jeremiah 17:9.

[33] *Ego dominus scrutans cor et probans renes.* Jeremiah 17:10.

[34] *Et dixerunt: "venite et cogitemus contra Jeremiam cogitationes. Non enim peribit lex a sacerdote neque sermo a propheta."* Jeremiah 18:18.

[35] *Non sis tu mihi formidini, tu spes mea in die afflictionum.* Jeremiah 17:17

[36] *Faciam domui huic in qua invocatum est nomen meum et in qua vos habetis fiduciam et loco quem dedi vobis et patribus vestris feci Silo.* Jeremiah 7:14.

[37] *Tu ergo noli orare pro populo hoc.* Jeremiah 7:16.

But they did not listen.[38]

A multitude of doctrines.   Jeremiah 11:13.

According to the number of your cities were your gods, O Judah; and according to the number of the streets of Jerusalem have you set up altars to that shameful thing.

Therefore, do not pray for this people.[39]

Neither can he say: "Is there not a lie in my right hand?"[40]   S726/L486
Isaiah 44:20.

Remember these, O Jacob and Israel, for you are my servant. I have formed you. You are my servant, O Israel; you shall not be forgotten of me.

I have blotted out your sins, as thick as a cloud. Return unto me, for I have redeemed you.[41] 44:21, etc.

Sing, O heavens, for the Lord has done it . . . for the Lord has redeemed Jacob and glorified himself in Israel. Thus says the Lord, your redeemer and he who formed you from the womb: "I am the Lord who makes all things; who stretches forth the heavens; who spreads abroad the earth by myself."[42] 44: 23–24.

In a little wrath, I hid my face from you for a moment, but   S727/L486
with everlasting kindness will I have mercy on you, said the Lord your redeemer.[43] Isaiah 54:8.

---

[38] *Quia non sum locutuscum patribus vestris et non praecepi eis, in die qua exudi eos de tera Egypti, de verbo holocautomatum et victimarum. Sed hoc verbus praecepi eis dicens: "Audite vocem meam, et ero vobis Deus, et vos eritis mihi populus, et ambulate in omni via quam mandavi vabis, ut bene sit vobis." —Et non audierunt.* Jeremiah 7:22–23, plus the first line of 24.

[39] *Secundum numerum enim civitatem tuarum erant dei tui, Juda, et secundum numerum viarum Jerusalem posuisti aram confusionis. Tu ergo noli orare pro populo hoc.* Jeremiah 11:13–14.

[40] *Neque dicet: "Forte mendacium est in dextera mea?"*

[41] *Memento horum, Jacob, et Israel, quoniam servus meus es tu. Formavi te, servus meus es tu, Israel, ne obliviscaris mei. Delevi ut nubem iniquitates tuas, et quasi nebulam peccata tua. Revertere ad me, quoniam redemi te.* Isaiah 44:21–22.

[42] *Laudate, caeli, quoniam miseridordiam fecit Dominus . . . quoniam redemit Dominus Jacob, et Israel gloriabitur. Haec dicit Dominus, redemptor tuus et formator tuus ex utero: "Ego sum Dominus, faciens omnia, extendens caelos solus, stabiliens terra, et nullus mecum."* Isaiah 44:23–24.

[43] *In momento indignationis abscondi faciem meam parumper a te, et in misericordia sempieterna misertus sum tui, dixit redemptor tuus Dominus.* Isaiah 54:8.

[Where is he] who led them by the right hand of Moses with   S728/L486
his glorious arm, dividing the water before them, to make him-
self an everlasting name?[44] Isaiah 63:12.

Thus you did lead your people, to make yourself an everlasting
name.[45] 14.

Doubtless you are our father, though Abraham is ignorant of us, and
Israel does not acknowledge us.[46] Isaiah 66:17

Why have you made us err from your ways and hardened our heart
from your fear?[47] Isaiah 63:17.

"They who sanctify themselves and purify themselves . . . shall be con-
sumed together," said the Lord.[48] Isaiah 66:17.

Yet you say: "Because I am innocent, surely his anger shall turn from
me."
Behold, I will plead with you, because you say: "I have not sinned."[49]
Jeremiah 2:35.

To do evil, they are wise, but to do good, they have no knowledge.[50]
Jeremiah 4:22.
I beheld the earth, and, lo, it was without form, and void;   S729/L486
and the heavens, and they had no light.
I beheld the mountains, and, lo, they trembled, and all the hills moved
lightly. I beheld, and, lo, there was no man, and all the birds of the heav-
ens fled. I beheld, and, lo, the fruitful place was a wilderness, and all the

------

[44] *Qui eduxit ad deteram Moysem bracchio majestis suae, qui scidit aquas anteeos ut faceret*
sibi nomen sempieternum. Isaiah 63:12.

[45] *Sic aduxisti populum tuum facere tibi nomen gloriae.* Isaiah 63:14.

[46] *Tu enim Pater noster, et Abraham nescivit nos, et Israel ignoravit nos.* Isaiah 63:16.

[47] *Quare indurasti cor nostrum ne timeremus te?* Isaiah 63:17.

[48] *"Qui sanctificabantur et mundus se putabant . . . simul consumentur," dicit Dominus.*
Isaiah 66:17.

[49] *Et dixisti: "Absque peccato et innocens ego sum. Et propterea averatur furor tuus a me."*
Ecce ego judicio contendam tecum, eo quod dixeris: "Non peccavi." Jeremiah 2:35.

[50] *Sapientes sunt ut faciant mala, bene autem facere nescierunt.* Jeremiah 4:22.

cities there were broken down at the presence of the Lord, and by his fierce anger.[51] Jeremiah 4:23, etc.

For thus has the Lord said: "The whole land shall be deso-   S730/L486
late; yet will I not make a full end."[52]

Jeremiah 5:4: *Therefore I said: "Surely these are poor; they are foolish, for they do not know the ways of the Lord nor the judgments of their God."*

I will get myself to the great men and speak to them, for they have known the ways of the Lord.

But these have altogether broken the yoke, and burst the bonds.

That is why a lion out of the forest shall slay them [. . .]; a leopard shall watch over their cities.[53]

Shall I not visit for these things, said the Lord; shall not my   S731/L486
soul be avenged on such a nation as this?[54] Jeremiah 5:29.

A wonderful and horrible thing is committed in the land.   S732/L486

The prophets prophesy falsely, and the priests bear rule by their means; and my people love to have it so: and what will you do in the end of this?[55] Jeremiah 5:30.

Thus said the Lord: "Stand in the ways, and see, and ask for the old paths, where is the good way, and walk in them, and you shall find rest for your souls." But they said, "We will not walk in them."

"Also I set watchmen over you, saying, hearken to the sound of the trumpet." But they said: "We will not hearken."

"Therefore hear, you nations [. . .] what is among them. Hear, o earth: behold, I will bring evil upon this people," etc.[56] Jeremiah 6:16.

---

[51] *Aspexi terram, et ecce vacua erat et nihili, et caelos, et non erat lux in eis. Vidi montes, et ecce movebantur, et omnes conturbati sunt. Intuitus sum, et non erat homo, et omne volatile ceali recessit. Aspexi, et ecce Carmelus desertus et omnes urbes ejus destructae sunt a facie Domini et a facie irae furoris ejus.* Jeremiah 4:23–26.

[52] *Haec enim dicit Dominus: "deserta erit omnis terra, sed tamen consummationem non faciam."* Jeremiah 4:27.

[53] *Ego autem dixi: "Forsitan pauperes sunt et stulti ignorantes viam Domini, judicium Dei sunt. Ibo ad optimates et loquar eis. Ipsi enim congnoverunt viam Domini. Et ecce magis hi simul confregerunt jugum, ruperunt vincula. Idcirco percussit eos leo de silva, pardus vigilans super civitates eorum."* Jeremiah 5:4–6.

[54] *Numquid super his non visitabo, dicit Dominus aut super gentem hujuscemodi no ulciscetur anima mea?"* Jeremiah 5:29.

[55] *Stupor et mirabilia facta sunt in Terra: Prophetae prophetabant mendacium, et sarcedotes appaudebant manibus, et populus meus dilexit talia. Quid igitur fiet in novissimo ejus?* Jeremiah 5:30–31.

[56] *Haec dicit Dominus: "Sate super vias, et videte, et interrogate de semitis antiquis quae sit vita bona, et ambulate in ea, et invenietis refrigerium animabus vestris." Et dixerunt: "non*

From the prophets of Jerusalem has profaneness gone forth   S733/L486
into all the land.[57] Jeremiah 23:15.

*They still say to those who despise me: "The Lord has said, you shall
have peace," and they say to everyone who walks in the corruption of his
own heart: "No evil shall come upon you.*[58] Jeremiah 23:17.

[58] Prophecies [5]

During the life of the Messiah   S734/L487

Speaks in a riddle:[59] Ezekiel 17.

His forerunner: Malachi 2.

He will be born a child: Isaiah 9.

He will be born in the town of Bethlehem: Micah 5. He will appear
mainly in Jerusalem and will be born of the family of Judah and of David.

He is to blind the learned and the wise: Isaiah 6; Isaiah 8; Isaiah 29;
and to preach the Gospel to the lowly and the poor, to open the eyes of
the blind: Isaiah 29; Isaiah 61; to give health to the sick and bring light
to those who languish in darkness: Isaiah 61.

He is to teach the perfect way and be the teacher of the gentiles:
Isaiah 55, 42:1–7.

The prophecies are to be unintelligible to the impious: Daniel 12;
but intelligible to those who are well instructed: Hosea, last chapter: 10.

The prophecies, which represent him as poor, represent him as
master of the nations: Isaiah 52:16, etc.; 53; Zechariah 9:9.

The prophecies that foretell the time only foretell him as master of the
gentiles and suffering, and not as in the clouds, nor as judge. And those
that represent him thus as judge and in glory, do not indicate the time.

He is to be the victim for the sins of the world: Isaiah 39:53, etc.

He is to be the precious cornerstone: Isaiah 28:16.

He is to be a stone of stumbling and offense: Isaiah 8.

Jerusalem is to dash against this stone.

The builders are to reject this stone: Psalms 117:22.

God is to make this stone the chief cornerstone.

---

*ambulabimus." "Et constitui speculatores: audite vocem tubae." Et dixerent: "Non au-
diemus." "Audite gentes, quanta ego faciam eis. Audi, terra: ecce ego adducam mala."* Jeremiah 6:16–19.

[57] *A prophetis enim Jerusalem egressa est pollutio super omnem terram.* Jeremiah 23:15.

[58] *Dicunt his qui blasphemant me: "Locutus est Dominus, pax erit vobis," et omni qui am-
bulat in pravitate cordi sui dixerunt: "Non veniet super vis malum."* Jeremiah 23:17.

[59] *Aenigmatis.* Ezekiel 17:2.

And this stone is to grow into a huge mountain and fill the whole earth: Daniel 2.

So, he is to be rejected, despised, betrayed: [Psalms] 108:8; sold: Zechariah 11:12; spit upon, buffeted, mocked, afflicted in innumerable ways; given gall to drink: Psalms 68:22; pierced: Zechariah 12:10; his feet and his hands pierced, [he is] slain, and lots cast for his raiment: Psalms [22].

He will rise again: Psalms 15; the third day: Hosea 6:3.

He will ascend to heaven to sit on the right hand: Psalms 110.

The kings will arm themselves against him: Psalms 2.

Being on the right hand of the Father, he will be victorious over his enemies.

The kings of the earth and all peoples will worship him: Isaiah 60.

The Jews will continue as a nation: Jeremiah.

They will wander, without kings, etc: Hosea 3.

Without prophets: Amos.

Looking for salvation and not finding it: Isaiah.

By slaying him in order not to receive him as the Mes- S734/L488
siah, the Jews have given him the final proof of being the Messiah.

And by continuing not to recognize him, they made themselves irreproachable witnesses.

Both by slaying him and by continuing to deny him, they have fulfilled the prophecies

Calling of the gentiles by Jesus Christ: Isaiah 52:15; Isaiah S734/L487
55:5; Isaiah 60.

Psalms 71.

Hosea 1:9: *You are not my people, and I will not be your God, when you are multiplied after the dispersion. In the places where it was said, "You are not my people," I will call them "my people."*

[59] Prophecies [6]

Perpetual captivity of the Jews 735/L489

Jeremiah 11:11: *I will bring evil upon Judah from which they shall not be able to escape.*

Figures

The Lord had a vineyard, from which he looked for grapes, and it brought forth only wild grapes. "I will therefore lay it waste, and destroy it; the earth shall only bring forth thorns, and I will forbid the clouds from [raining] upon it."

Isaiah 5:7: *The vineyard of the Lord is the house of Israel. And the men of Judah are his pleasant plant. I looked that they should do justice, and they bring forth only iniquities.*

Isaiah 8:

Sanctify the Lord with fear and trembling; let him be your only dread, and he shall be to you for a sanctuary. But he will be a stone of stumbling and a rock of offense to both the houses of Israel. He will be a gin and a snare to the inhabitants of Jerusalem. And many among them shall stumble against that stone, and fall, and be broken, and be snared, and perish there.

Hide my words, and cover my law for my disciples.

I will then wait in patience upon the Lord that hides and conceals himself from the house of Jacob.

Isaiah. 29: *Be amazed and wonder, people of Israel; stagger and stumble, and be drunken, but not with wine; stagger, but not with strong drink. For the Lord has poured out upon you the spirit of deep sleep. He will close your eyes; he will cover your princes and your prophets that have visions.*

Daniel 12: *The wicked shall not understand, but those well instructed shall understand.*

———

Hosea, last chapter, last verse, after many temporal blessings, says: *Who is wise, and he shall understand these things?* etc.

And the visions of all the prophets will become to you as a sealed book, which men deliver to one who is learned and who can read; and he says: "I cannot read it, for it is sealed." And when the book is delivered to them who are not learned, they say: "I am not learned."

And the Lord said to me: "Because this people do honor me with their lips, but have removed their heart far from me and their fear toward me is taught by the precept of man" (there is the reason and the cause of it, for if they adored God in their hearts, they would understand the prophecies).

Therefore, behold, I will proceed to do a marvelous work among this people, even a marvelous work and a wonder: for the wisdom of their wise men shall perish, and their understanding shall be [hidden].

Prophecies proofs of divinity

Isaiah 41:

If you are gods, come near and we will incline our heart to your words. Teach us the things that have been at the beginning, and declare for us the things to come.

By this we shall know that you are gods. Yea, do good or do evil, if you can. Let us then behold it and reason together.

Behold, you are of nothing, and only an abomination, etc. Who (among contemporary writers) *has declared from the beginning that we may know of the things done from the beginning and origin, so that we may say: "You are righteous." There is none who teaches us; yea, there is none who declares the future.*

———

Isaiah 42: *I am the Lord, and I will not give my glory to another. I have foretold the things that have come to pass, and things that are to come I do declare. Sing unto God a new song in all the earth.*

[Isaiah 43:]

Bring forth the blind people who have eyes and do not see, and the deaf who have ears and do not hear. Let all the nations be gathered together. Who among them can declare this, and show us former things and things to come? Let them bring forth their witnesses, that they may be justified! Or let them hear, and say, it is truth!

You are my witnesses, says the Lord, and my servant whom I have chosen, so that you may know and believe me, and understand that I am he.

I have declared and have saved, and I alone have done wonders before your eyes: you are my witnesses, said the Lord, that I am God.

For your sake, I have brought down the forces of the Babylonians. I am the Lord, your Holy One and Creator.

I have made a way in the sea, and a path in the mighty waters. I am he who drowned and destroyed forever the mighty enemies that resisted you.

Do not remember the former things, and do not consider the things of old.

Behold, I will do a new thing; now it shall spring forth; shall you not know it? I will even make a way in the wilderness, and rivers in the desert.

This people have I formed for myself; I have established them to show forth my praise, etc.

I, even I, am he who blots out your transgressions for my own sake, and will not remember your sins. Put in remembrance your ingratitude: see you, if you may be justified. Your first father has sinned, and your teachers have transgressed against me.

Isaiah 44:

I am the first, and I am the last, says the Lord. Who shall equal himself to me? Let him declare the order of things since I appointed the ancient people, and the things that are coming.

Do not fear: have I not told you all these things? You are my witnesses.

Prediction of Cyrus

For Jacob's sake, my elect, I have called you by your name.

Isaiah 45:21: *Come and let us reason together. Who has declared this from ancient time? Who has told it from that time? Have not I, the Lord?*

Isaiah 46: *Remember the former things of old, and know there is none like me, declaring the end from the beginning, and from ancient times the things that are not yet done; saying, my counsel shall stand, and I will do all my pleasure.*

Isaiah 42:9: *Behold, the former things have come to pass, and new things do I declare; before they spring forth, I tell you of them.*

Isaiah 48:3:

I have declared the former things from the beginning; I did them suddenly; and they came to pass. Because I know that you are obstinate, that your spirit is rebellious and your brow brass, I have even declared it to you before it came to pass: lest you should say that it was the work of your gods, and the effect of their commands.

You have seen all this; and will you not declare it? I have shown you new things from this time, even hidden things, and you did not know them. They are created now, and not from the beginning; I have kept them hidden from you, lest you should say, Behold, I knew them.

Yea, you did not know; yea, you did not hear; yea, from that time your ear was not opened. For I knew that you would deal very treacherously, and were called a transgressor from the womb.

Reprobation of the Jews and conversion of the gentiles.

Isaiah. 65:

I was sought by those who did not ask for me; I was found by those who did not seek for me; I said, "Behold me, behold me," to a nation that did not call upon my name.

I have spread out my hands all the day to an unbelieving people who walks in a way that was not good, after their own thoughts; a people who provokes me to anger continually by the sins they commit in my face; who sacrifices to idols, etc.

These shall be scattered like smoke in the day of my wrath, etc.

I will assemble together your iniquities, and the iniquities of your fathers, and will recompense you for all according to your works.

Thus says the Lord, "For my servants' sake, I will not destroy all Israel; but I will save some, as one does the new wine found in the cluster, of which one says, 'Do not destroy it, for a blessing is in it.'

Thus I will bring forth a seed out of Jacob and out of Judah, an inheritor of my mountains, and my elect and my servants shall inherit it and my fertile and abundant plains.

But I will destroy all others, because you have forgotten your God to serve strange gods. I called, and you did not answer; I spoke, and you did not hear; and you did choose the thing I forbade."

Therefore thus says the Lord, "Behold, my servants shall eat, but you shall be hungry; my servants shall rejoice, but you shall be ashamed; my servants shall sing for joy of heart, but you shall cry and howl for vexation of spirit.

And you shall leave your name for a curse unto my chosen. For the Lord shall slay you, and call his servants by another name, that he who blesses himself in the earth shall bless himself in God, etc.

Because the former troubles are forgotten.

For, behold, I create new heavens and a new earth; and the former things shall not be remembered, nor come into mind.

But be you glad and rejoice forever in that which I create. For, behold, I create Jerusalem for rejoicing, and her people for joy. And I will rejoice in Jerusalem and joy in my people; and the voice of weeping shall no more be heard in her, nor the voice of crying.

Before they call, I will answer; and while they are yet speaking, I will hear. The wolf and the lamb shall feed together, and the lion shall eat straw like the bullock; and dust shall be the serpent's meat. They shall not hurt nor destroy in all my holy mountain."

Isaiah 56:3:

<Thus says the Lord, "Keep your judgment, and do justice: for my salvation is near to come, and my righteousness to be revealed.

Blessed is the man who does this, who keeps the Sabbath, and keeps his hand from doing any evil.>

Neither let the strangers who have joined themselves to me say, 'God will separate me from his people.'"

For thus says the Lord: "Whoever will keep my Sabbath, and choose the things that please me, and take hold of my covenant; even unto them will I give in my house a place and a name better than that of sons and of daughters: I will give them an everlasting name that shall not be cut off."

[Isaiah 59:9–11:]

It is for our iniquities that justice is far from us. We wait for light, but behold obscurity. We hope for brightness, but walk in darkness.

We grope for the wall like the blind; we stumble at midday as in the night: we are in desolate places as dead men.

We roar all like bears, and mourn sore like doves. We look for judgment, but there is none. We hope for salvation, but it is far from us.

Isaiah 66:18:

But I know their works and their thoughts; it shall come that I will gather all nations and tongues, and they shall see my glory.

And I will set a sign among them, and I will send those that escape from them to the nations, to Africa, to Lydia, to Italy, to Greece, and to the people who have not heard my fame, neither have seen my glory. And they shall bring your brothers.

Jeremiah 7. Reprobation of the Temple.

Go to Shiloh, where I set my name at the first, and see what I did to it for the wickedness of my people (for I have rejected it, and made myself a temple elsewhere).

And now, because you have done all these works, says the Lord, I will do to this temple, in which my name is called, in which you trust, and to the place I gave to your fathers, as I have done to Shiloh.

And I will cast you out of my sight, as I have cast out all your brothers, even the seed of Ephraim (rejected forever).

Therefore do not pray for this people.

———

Jeremiah 7:22: *What use is it to add sacrifice to sacrifice? For I did not speak to your fathers, when I brought them out of the land of Egypt, concerning burnt offerings or sacrifices. But this thing I commanded them, saying, "Obey and be faithful to my commandments, and I will be your God, and you shall be my people."* (It was only after they had sacrificed to the golden calf that I commanded sacrifices to turn into good an evil custom.)

———

Jeremiah 7:4: *Do not trust in lying words, saying, "The temple of the Lord, the temple of the Lord, the temple of the Lord, are these."*

[60. Prophecies, Jews, Corruption]

Nature corrupted S736/L491

Man does not act by reason, which constitutes his being.

We have no king but Caesar. S736/L490

The Jews witnesses for God: Isaiah 43:9, 44:8. S736/L494

———

They are visibly a people expressly created to serve as a   S736/L495
witness to the Messiah:

Isaiah 43:9, 44:8: They keep the books, and love them, and do not understand them.

And all this was foretold: that God's judgments are entrusted to them, but as a sealed book.

Harden their heart. But how? By flattering their concupis-   S736/L496
cence and giving them the hope of satisfying it.

The sincerity of the Jews S736/L492

After they no longer had prophets: Maccabees.

Since Jesus Christ: Masorah.
This book will be a testimony for you.[60]
Defective final letters.

_____

Sincere against their honor, and dying for it, this has no example in the world, and no root in nature.

Prophecy   S736/L497

Your name shall be a curse to my chosen, and I will give them another name.[61]

Prophecies fulfilled.   S736/L493
[1] Kings 13:2.
[2] Kings 23:16.

_____

Joshua 6:26.
[1] Kings 16:34.

_____

Deuteronomy 33.

_____

Malachi 1:11. The sacrifice of the Jews rejected, and the sacrifice of the heathen (even outside Jerusalem), and in all places.

_____

Moses foretold the calling of the gentiles before dying: Deuteronomy 32:21, and the reprobation of the Jews.

_____

Moses foretold what would happen to each tribe.

Prophecy   S736/L498

Amos and Zechariah: they have sold the just one, and therefore will never be recalled.
Jesus Christ betrayed.
Egypt shall no longer be remembered: see Isaiah 43:16–17–18–19; Jeremiah 23:6–7.

Prophecy

The Jews shall be scattered abroad: Isaiah 27:6.
A new law: Jeremiah 31:32.

_____

[60] Isaiah 30:8.
[61] Isaiah 65:16.

The second temple glorious. Jesus Christ will come there: Haggai 2:7–8–9–10. Malachi. Grotius.

The calling of the gentiles: Joel 2:28; Hosea 2:24; Deuteronomy 32:21; Malachi 1:11.

What man ever had more renown?   S736/L499

The whole Jewish people foretell him before his coming.

The gentile people worship him after his coming.

The two peoples, gentile and Jewish, regard him as their center.

And yet, what man enjoys this renown less? Of thirty-three years, he lives thirty without showing himself. For three years he passes for an impostor; the priests and the chief people reject him; his friends and his nearest relatives despise him. Finally, he dies, betrayed by one of his own disciples, denied by another, and forsaken by all.

What part, then, has he in this renown? Never had man so much renown; never had man more ignominy. All that renown has served only for us, to render us capable of recognizing him; and he had none of it for himself.

[61] Figurative Law

Figures   S737/L501

To show that the Old Testament is—is only—figurative, and that the prophets understood by temporal blessings other blessings, is to show: 1. that this would be unworthy of God. 2. that their discourses express very clearly the promise of temporal blessings, and yet they say that their discourses are obscure and that their meaning will not be understood; as a result, it appears that this hidden meaning was not the one they openly expressed, and that consequently they meant to speak of other sacrifices, of another deliverer, etc. They say that they will be understood only in the fullness of time: Jeremiah 33, last verse.[62]

The second proof is that their discourses are contradictory, and cancel out one another. So that, if we suppose that they did not mean by the words "law" and "sacrifice" anything other than what Moses meant, there is a plain and gross contradiction. Therefore they meant something else, sometimes contradicting themselves in the same chapter.

---

[62] In fact, it is the last verse of chap. 30.

Now, to understand the meaning of an author . . .

It is fine to see the story of Herod, of Caesar, with the eyes   S737/L500
of faith.

Reason for figures   S738/L502

R. <They had to address a carnal people and to make
them the depositary of the spiritual covenant.>

To inspire faith in the Messiah, it was necessary there should have
been precedent prophecies, and that these should be conveyed by persons above suspicion, diligent, faithful, unusually zealous, and known to
all the world.

To accomplish all this, God chose this carnal people, to whom he
entrusted the prophecies that foretell the Messiah as a deliverer and dis-
penser of those carnal blessings this people loved.

And thus they have had an extraordinary passion for their prophets
and, in sight of the whole world, have had charge of these books that
foretell their Messiah, assuring all nations that he should come and in
the manner foretold in the books, which they held open to the whole
world. Yet this people, deceived by the poor and ignominious advent of
the Messiah, have been his most cruel enemies. So that they, the people
in the world least open to the suspicion of favoring us, the most strict
and most zealous there could be for their law and prophets, have kept
the books incorrupt.

Hence those who have rejected and crucified Jesus Christ, who has
been to them an offense, are those who have charge of the books that
testify of him and who state that he will be an offense and rejected. So,
they have shown it was he by rejecting him, and he has been proved alike
both by the righteous Jews who received him and by the unrighteous
ones who rejected him, both facts having been foretold.

For this reason, the prophecies have a hidden spiritual meaning to
which this people were hostile, under the carnal meaning they loved. If
the spiritual meaning had been revealed, they would not have been
capable of loving it, and, unable to bear it, they would not have been
zealous for the preservation of their books and their ceremonies. And if
they had loved these spiritual promises and had preserved them uncor-
rupted until the time of the Messiah, their testimony would have had no
force, because they would have been friends.

That is why it was good that the spiritual meaning was concealed.
But, on the other hand, if this meaning had been so hidden as not to appear at all, it could not have served as a proof of the Messiah. What then
was done? It was hidden under the temporal meaning in a multitude of
passages, and was so clearly revealed in some, in addition the time and
the state of the world being so clearly foretold that [the facts] were

brighter than the sun; and in some places this spiritual meaning is so clearly expressed that it would require blindness, like the one flesh imposes on mind when subdued by it, not to recognize this meaning.

This, then, was how God acted: this meaning is concealed under another in countless places, and revealed in some, though rarely; but in such a way that the places where it is concealed are equivocal and can suit both meanings, whereas the places where it is disclosed are unequivocal and can suit only the spiritual meaning.

So that this cannot lead into error and could only have been misunderstood by so carnal a people.

For when blessings are promised in abundance, what was to prevent them from understanding the true blessings, if not their cupidity, which limited the meaning to earthly blessings?

But those whose only blessing lay in God referred them to God alone.

For there are two principles that divide the wills of men: cupidity and charity. It is not that cupidity cannot exist along with faith in God, and charity with worldly riches; but cupidity uses God and enjoys the world, and charity does the opposite.

Now the ultimate end is what gives names to things.

Everything that prevents us from attaining it is called an enemy. Thus creatures, however good, are the enemies of the righteous, when they turn them away from God; and God himself is the enemy of those whose covetousness he confounds.

Thus, as the word enemy is dependent on the ultimate end, the righteous understood by it their passions, and the carnal the Babylonians. And thus these terms were obscure only for the unrighteous. And this is what Isaiah says: *Seal the law among my disciples.*[63] And that Jesus Christ shall be a *stone of stumbling*, but *Blessed are they who shall not be offended in him.*

Hosea, last verse, says it perfectly: *"Who is wise? And he shall understand these things. The righteous shall know them, for the ways of the Lord are right [. . .], but the transgressors shall fall therein."*

And yet this Covenant, made to blind some and enlighten   S738/L503
others, pointed, in those very persons it blinded, to the truth
that should be recognized by others. For the visible blessings they received from God were so great and so divine that he indeed appeared able to give them those that are invisible and a Messiah.

---

[63] *Signa legem in electis meis.* Isaiah 8:16.

For nature is an image of grace, and visible miracles are images of the invisible ones: *That you may know . . . I say to you: "Arise."*[64]

Isaiah, 51, says that Redemption will be like the crossing of the Red Sea.

God has therefore shown by the deliverance from Egypt and from the sea, by the defeat of kings, by the manna, by the whole genealogy of Abraham, that he was able to save, to send down bread from heaven, etc., so that the people hostile to him are the figure and representation of the very Messiah whom they do not know.

He has therefore taught us at last that all these things were only figures, and what is *true freedom, a true Israelite, true circumcision, true bread from heaven*, etc.

———

In these promises, each one finds what he has most at heart: temporal or spiritual blessings, God or creatures; but with this difference: that those who look for creatures there find them, but with many contradictions, with a prohibition against loving them, with the command to worship God alone, and to love only him, which is the same thing; and, finally, that the Messiah did not come for them. Whereas those who look for God there find him, and without any contradiction, with the command to love only him, and that the Messiah has come in the time foretold to give them the blessings for which they ask.

———

Thus the Jews had miracles, prophecies they saw fulfilled. And the teaching of their law was to worship and love one God alone; it was also perpetual. Thus it bore all the marks of the true religion; and so it was. But the teaching of the Jews must be distinguished from the teaching of the Jewish law. Now, the teaching of the Jews was not true, although it had miracles, prophecy, and perpetuity, because it lacked this other point of worshipping and loving God alone.

Kirkerus — Usserius.[65]

———

[64] *Ut sciatis . . . tibi dico: Surge*; Mark 2:10, 11.

[65] A reference to Conrad Kircher, author of *Concordantiae Veteris Testamenti Graecae* (1607), and James Usher, author of *Annales Veteris et Novi Testamenti* (1650).

[V. Fragments not Registered by Copy B]

[62. Unregistered Fragments][1]

Men often take their imagination for their heart, and they   S739/L975
believe they are converted as soon as they think of being
converted.

The last thing we discover in writing a book is what to put   S740/L976
in first.

For, although these events had taken place some 2,000 years   S741
before, so few generations had passed that they were as new to the
men of those times as events occurring some 300 years ago are to us
today. This is because the earliest men lived so long. So that Shem, who
saw Lamech, etc.

This proof is sufficient to convince reasonable people of the truth of
the Flood and the Creation. And it shows God's Providence, for, seeing
that the Creation was beginning to recede into the past, he provided a
historian who can be called contemporary and entrusted a whole people to the care of his book.

And what is still more remarkable is that this book was accepted
unanimously and without contradiction, not only by the whole Jewish
people, but also by all the kings and peoples of the earth, who received
it with an altogether particular respect and veneration.

[The Memorial][2]   S742/L913

The year of grace 1654

Monday, November 23, feast of Saint Clement, Pope and martyr,
and of others in the {Roman} Martyrology.

Eve of Saint Chrysogonus, martyr, and others.

From about half past ten in the evening until about half past mid-
night.

---

[1] Fragments S739–40 come from the 1678 edition of the *Pensées*; S741 was attached to
the first copy; S742 is an autograph fragment sewn in the lining of Pascal's jacket, found
after his death; S744–70 come from the Manuscript Périer; S771 was attached to the second copy; fragments S772–85 come from the Manuscript Joly de Fleury, S786 from the
Portefeuilles Vallant, S787–803 from the Recueil Original, and S804–12 from the Manuscripts Guerrier; S813 was an annotation discovered in 1952.

[2] The main variants from Louis Périer's copy of the autograph are indicated by curly
brackets { }.

Fire

God of Abraham, God of Isaac, God of Jacob.[3]

    not of philosophers and scholars.

Certainty, {joy,} certainty, feelings, joy, peace.

God of Jesus Christ.

My God and your God.[4]

Your God shall be my God.[5] {Ruth}

Forgetfulness of the world and of everything, except God.

He can only be found by the ways taught in the Gospels.

Greatness of the human soul

Righteous Father, the world had not known you, but I have known you.[6] {John}

Joy, joy, joy, tears of joy

I have cut myself off from him. ────────────

They have forsaken me, the fountain of living waters.[7]

My God, will you forsake me?[8] ────────────

Let me not be cut off from him forever!

And this is life eternal, that they might know you, the only true God, and Jesus Christ whom you have sent.[9]

    Jesus Christ. ────────────

    Jesus Christ. ────────────

I have cut myself off from him. I have fled from him, denied him, crucified him. ────────────

    Let me never be cut off from him.

    He can only be kept by the ways taught in the Gospel.

Sweet and total renunciation

{Total submission to Jesus Christ and to my director.

Eternally in joy for one day's effort on earth.

I will not forget your word.[10] Amen.}

---

[3] Exodus 3:6.

[4] *Deum meum et Deum vestrum.* John 20:17.

[5] Ruth 1:16.

[6] John 17:25.

[7] *Dereliquerùnt me fontem aquae vivae.* Jeremiah 2:13

[8] Cf. Matthew 27:46.

[9] John 17:3.

[10] *Non obliviscar sermones tuos.* Psalms 119:16.

The nature of self-love and of this human self is to love   S743/L978
only self and to consider only self. But what will it do? It cannot prevent this object it loves from being full of faults and wretchedness. It wants to be great, and sees itself small; it wants to be happy, and
sees itself wretched; it wants to be perfect, and sees itself full of imperfections; it wants to be the object of men's love and esteem, and it sees
that its defects deserve only their dislike and contempt. This embarrassment in which it finds itself produces in it the most unrighteous and
criminal passion imaginable, for it conceives a mortal hatred against
this truth admonishing it and convincing it of its faults. It wants to annihilate this truth, but, unable to destroy it in its essence, it destroys it as
far as possible in its own knowledge and in that of others; that is to say, it
devotes every care to hiding its faults both from others and from itself,
and it cannot endure that others should point them out or notice them.

No doubt it is an evil to be full of faults; but it is a still greater evil to
be full of them and to be unwilling to recognize them, since this adds
the further evil of a deliberate illusion. We do not want others to deceive
us, and we do not think it fair that they should be held in higher esteem
by us than they deserve; it is not, then, fair that we should deceive them
and should want them to esteem us more highly than we deserve.

Thus, when they discover only the imperfections and vices we really
have, it is clear they do us no wrong, since it is not they who cause them;
they rather do us good, since they help us free ourselves from an evil:
namely, the ignorance of these imperfections. We must not be angry at
their knowing our faults and despising us: it is but right that they should
know us for what we are and despise us, if we are despicable.

Such are the feelings that would arise in a heart full of equity and
justice. What, then, must we say of ours, when we see it in an altogether
different disposition? For is it not true that we hate the truth and those
who tell it us, and we like them to be deceived in our favor, and prefer
to be esteemed by them as being other than what we are in fact?

Here is a proof of it that horrifies me. The Catholic religion does not
require us to reveal our sins indiscriminately to everyone. It allows them
to remain hidden from all other men; but it makes a single exception, to
whom we are ordered to reveal the innermost recesses of our heart and
show ourselves as we are. There is only this one man in the world whom
it orders us to undeceive, and it binds him to an inviolable secrecy,
which makes this knowledge exist in him as if it did not exist. Can anything more charitable and pleasant be imagined? And yet the corruption of man is such that he finds even this law harsh; and it is one of the
principal reasons why a great part of Europe has rebelled against the
Church.

How unjust and unreasonable is the heart of man, which finds it bad to be required to do with respect to one man what it would be right to do, in some measure, with all men! For is it right that we should deceive them?

There are different degrees in this aversion for the truth; but it may be said that it exists in everyone in some degree, because it is inseparable from self-love. It is this false delicacy that requires those who are under the necessity of rebuking others to choose so many roundabout ways and qualifications to avoid giving offense. They must minimize our faults, appear to excuse them, intersperse praise and evidence of love and esteem. Even then, this medicine does not cease to be bitter to self-love. It takes as little as possible, always with disgust, and often with a secret resentment against those administering it.

Hence it happens that those who have an interest in being loved by us avoid rendering us a service they know to be disagreeable. They treat us as we want to be treated: we hate the truth, and they hide it from us; we desire flattery, and they flatter us; we like to be deceived, and they deceive us.

So, each degree of good fortune elevating us in the world removes us further from the truth, because we are most afraid of wounding those whose affection is most useful and dislike most dangerous. A prince can be the laughingstock of all Europe, and he alone will know nothing of it. I am not surprised: to tell the truth is useful to those to whom it is spoken, but disadvantageous to those who tell it, because they become so disliked. Now, those who live with princes love their own interest more than that of the prince they serve; and so they take care not to provide him a benefit that would be harmful to themselves.

This misfortune is no doubt greater and more common among the wealthiest; but those less wealthy are not exempt from it, since there is always some advantage in getting people to love us. Human life is thus only a perpetual illusion; we do nothing but deceive and flatter each other. No one speaks about us in our presence as he would in our absence. The union among men is founded on mutual deceit; few friendships would endure if everyone knew what his friend said about him when he was not there, even though he was then speaking sincerely and dispassionately.

Man is, therefore, only disguise, falsehood, and hypocrisy, both in himself and with regard to others. He does not want to be told the truth. He avoids telling it to others. And all these dispositions, so far removed from justice and reason, have a natural root in his heart.

Every time the Jesuits take the Pope unawares, all of   S744/L914
Christendom becomes guilty of perjury.

The Pope is very easily taken unawares, because he has so much to do and places so much credence in the Jesuits. And the Jesuits are very capable of taking him unawares by means of calumny.

Hearing the rumor about the Feuillants, I went off to see   S745/L915
him, said my old friend. Talking of piety, he thought that I
had some feeling for it and that I might easily be a Feuillant.

And that I might profitably write something against innovators, especially these days.

We have recently gone against our general chapter, whose position is that we should sign the Bull.

That he wished God might inspire me.

Father, must one sign?

                                  3   S746/L916

If they do not give up probability, their good maxims are
no more holy than the bad ones, for they are based on human authority.
And thus, if they are more just, they will be more reasonable, but not
more holy: they take after the wild stem on which they are grafted.

If what I say does not help enlighten you, it will help the people.

If these are silent, the stones will speak.

Silence is the greatest persecution. The saints were never silent. It is true that a vocation is needed; but it is not from the Council's decrees that we must learn whether we are called, it is from the necessity to speak. Now, after Rome has spoken, and we think it has condemned the truth, and they have written it down, and the books saying the contrary have been censured, the more unjustly we are censured and the more violently they want to stifle speech, the louder we must cry out, until there comes a Pope who listens to both parties and consults antiquity to do justice.

As a result, the good Popes will find the Church still in an uproar.

The hope that Christians have of possessing an infinite   S746/L917
blessing is mingled with actual enjoyment as well as with
fear. For unlike those who would hope for a kingdom of which they
would have no part, being subjects, Christians hope for holiness and
freedom from injustice; and some part of this is theirs already.

The Inquisition and the Society: the two scourges of the   S746/L916
truth.

Why do you not accuse them of Arianism? For, if they said that Jesus
Christ is God, perhaps they did not understand by it that he is so by
nature, but as it is said: *You are gods.*[11]

If my *Letters* are condemned at Rome, what I condemn in them is
condemned in heaven.

To your tribunal, Lord Jesus, I call.[12]

You yourselves are corruptible.

I feared that I had written badly, seeing myself condemned, but the
example of so many pious writings makes me believe the contrary. It is
no longer permitted to write well.

So corrupt or ignorant is the Inquisition!

It is better to obey God than men.[13]

I fear nothing; I hope for nothing. The bishops are not like that. Port-
Royal is afraid, and it is bad policy to separate them, for they will no
longer be afraid and will cause greater fear.

I do not even fear your censures, mere straws unless they are founded
on those of tradition. .

Do you censure everything? What! Even my respect? No. Therefore,
tell me what, or you will do nothing, unless you point out the wrong
and why it is wrong. And this is what they will have great difficulty in
doing.

---

[11] *Dii estis.* Psalms 81:6.

[12] *Ad tuum, Domine Jesu, tribunal appello.*

[13] Acts 5:29.

Probability

They have amusingly explained safety. For, after having established that all their paths are safe, they no longer call safe the one that leads to heaven, with no danger of failing to arrive there by it, but the one that leads there with no danger of straying from it.

My Reverend Father   S747

If I have given you some displeasure with my other *Letters* by making obvious the innocence of those whom you insisted on sullying, I will give you joy with this one, by showing you the pain with which you have filled them. Console yourself, my Father; those you hate are distressed. And if the Bishops in their dioceses execute the counsel you give them to require us to swear and sign that we believe as fact something we do not believe and are not required to believe, you will reduce your adversaries to the ultimate sadness of seeing the Church in that state. I have seen them, my Father, and I admit that I have been extremely satisfied. I have seen them not in a philosophic generosity or in that disrespectful firmness that makes one arrogantly follow what he believes to be his duty; nor in that soft and timid cowardice that prevents one from seeing the truth or following it; but in a sweet and solid piety, full of self-defiance, of respect for the power of the Church, love for peace, and tenderness and zeal for the truth, desire to know it and defend it, fear for their infirmities, regret for having been put to these trials, and yet hope that God will deign to uphold them by his light and strength, and that Jesus Christ's grace, which they uphold and for which they suffer, will itself be their light and their strength. And in the end I saw in them the character of Christian piety that causes strength to emerge . . .

I have found them surrounded by people they know who also came upon this subject to lead them to what they believed to be best in the present state of things. I have heard the counsels given to them; I have noticed the manner in which they received them and the replies they made to them. In truth, my father, if you had been present, I believe that you yourself would admit that there is nothing in their proceedings not infinitely removed from the air of revolt and heresy, as the whole world could understand by the temperance they brought to the matter, which you will see here, to preserve all together these two things infinitely dear to them: the peace and the truth.

For after they have been presented in general with the penalties they will receive by their refusal, and the scandal that could arise in the Church as a result, if this New Constitution were presented for them to sign, they remarked . . .

If the Jesuits were corrupt and it were true that we were alone, this would be even more reason for us to remain firm.

The Day of Judgment   S747/L979

What war has established, let not a feigned peace remove.[14]

As an angel of the Lord [. . .] moved neither by blessing nor by cursing.[15]

They are attacking the greatest of Christian virtues: namely, love of truth.

If the signature means this, allow us to explain, so that there is no room for equivocation: for we must agree that many think that signing signifies consent.

So this, Father, is what you call the meaning of Jansenius! So this is what you cause the Pope and bishops to understand!

If the proper official did not sign, the decree would be invalid. If the Bull were not signed, it would be valid. Therefore it is not . . .

We are not guilty of not believing, and we will be guilty for swearing without believing . . .

Fine questions. He . . .

"But might you be mistaken?" I swear that I believe I might be mistaken. But I do not swear that I believe I am mistaken.

I am sorry to be telling you everything; I am only giving an account.

With Escobar, this puts them on top. But they do not take it like that, and showing how much they dislike seeing themselves between God and the Pope . . .

The rivers of Babylon flow, and fall, and carry away.   S748/L918

———

O holy Zion, where everything is firm and nothing falls!

———

We must sit atop these waters, not under or in them, but above, and not standing but seated, so as to be humble remaining seated and in safety remaining above. But we shall stand in the porches of Jerusalem.

———

Let us see if this pleasure is stable or flowing! If it passes away, it is a river of Babylon.

The Mystery of Jesus   S749/L919

Jesus suffers in his Passion the torments men inflict upon him. But in his agony he suffers the torments he inflicts on himself. *And*

---

[14] *Quod bellum firmavit, pax ficta non auferat.*

[15] *Neque benedictione, neque maledictione movetur, sicut angelus Domini.* 2 Samuel 14:17.

he was troubled.[16] This torture is inflicted by no human, but by an almighty hand. And he must be almighty to bear it.

———

Jesus seeks some comfort at least from his three dearest friends, and they are asleep. He prays them to bear with him a while, and they leave him with complete indifference, having so little compassion that it could not prevent their sleeping even for a moment. And so Jesus was abandoned alone to the wrath of God.

———

Jesus is alone on the earth, not only without anyone to feel and share his suffering, but without anyone even to know of it. Heaven and he were alone in this knowledge.

———

Jesus is in a garden, not of delight, like the first Adam, who was lost there with all of mankind; but of agony, where he saved himself and all of mankind.

———

He suffers this anguish and this abandonment in the horror of the night.

———

I believe that Jesus never complained but on this single occasion. But then he complained as though he could no longer bear his extreme suffering: *My soul is sorrowful, even unto death.*[17]

———

Jesus seeks companionship and comfort from men. This is the single occasion in all his life, it seems to me. But he receives none, for his disciples are asleep.

———

Jesus will be in agony until the end of the world. We must not sleep during that time.

———

Jesus, in the midst of this universal desertion, with his friends chosen to watch with him, finding them asleep, is vexed because of the danger to which they expose, not him, but themselves; cautions them for their

---

[16] *Turbare semetipsum.* John 11: 33.

[17] Matthew 26:38; Mark 14:34.

own salvation and their own good, with a sincere tenderness for them during their ingratitude, and warns them that *the spirit is willing and the flesh weak*.[18]

―――

Jesus, finding them still asleep, without their being restrained by any consideration either for themselves or for him, has the kindness not to awaken them, and leaves them to their rest.

―――

Jesus prays in the uncertainty of the Father's will, and fears death. But, once he knows it, he goes forward and offers himself to death: *Let us be going*.[19] *He went forth* (John).[20]

―――

Jesus prayed to men and was not heard.

―――

Jesus, while his disciples slept, brought about their salvation.

―――

He brought it about for each of the righteous while they slept, both in the nothingness before their birth, and in the sins after their birth.

―――

He prays only once that the cup might pass away, and then with submission; and twice that it should come if it must.

―――

Jesus is soul weary (*ennui*).

―――

Jesus, seeing all his friends asleep and all his enemies vigilant, commits himself wholly to his Father.

―――

Jesus does not see in Judas his enmity, but God's order, which he loves, and he perceives it so little that he calls him friend.

―――

Jesus tears himself away from his disciples to enter into his agony. We must tear ourselves away from our nearest and dearest to imitate him.

―――

---

[18] Matthew 26:41; Mark 14:38.

[19] *Eamus.* Matthew 26:46; Mark 14:42.

[20] *Processit.* John 18:4.

While Jesus remains in agony and in the greatest pain, let us pray longer.

We ourselves[21] could not have received any general   S750/L920
maxims. If you look at our *Constitutions*, you will hardly recognize us: they make us out to be beggars, kept out of courts, and yet, etc. But this is not infringing them, for God's glory is everywhere.

There are different ways of achieving it. Saint Ignatius chose certain ones, and now we choose others. It was better at the beginning to propose poverty and retreat. Later on it was better to choose the rest. For it would have caused alarm to begin at the top. This goes against nature.

It is not that the general rule fails to insist on adherence to the *Institutions*, for there would be abuses. You would find few like us, who know how to elevate ourselves without vanity.

Unam sanctam.[22]

The Jansenists will pay the penalty.

Father Saint-Jure. —Escobar.

So important a man.[23]

Acquaviva, December 14, 1621. —Tanner q. 2, dub. 5, n. 86.[24]

Clement and Paul V. God visibly protects us.

Against hasty judgments and scruples.

Saint Teresa 474.

Roman, Rose.

By a false crime.[25]

Subtlety for its own sake.

———

All the truth on one side. We extend it to both.

Two obstacles: the Gospel; the laws of the state. *From the greater to the lesser. More recent.*[26]

To speak of personal vices.

Fine letter of Acquaviva, June 18, 1611, against probable opinions.

---

[21] That is, the Jesuits. See fragment S789.

[22] A reference to the 1302 Bull *Unam sanctam* of Pope Boniface VIII, according to which the Pope would be master not only of spiritual, but also of temporal powers.

[23] *Tanto viro*: allusion to a scandalous question of the Jesuit Lamy; see *Sixième écrit des curés de Paris.*

[24] A. Tanner (1578–1632), author of *Universa theologia* (1626–1627). Claudio Acquaviva was general of the Jesuits, 1581–1615.

[25] *Falso crimine*: Allusion to a thesis of a Louvain Jesuit. See Pascal's *Fifteenth Provincial Letter.*

[26] A *majori ad minus. Junior.*

Saint Augustine 282.

And for Saint Thomas, in the places where he specifically dealt with these matters.

Clemens Placentinus, 277.[27]

And novelties.

And it is no excuse for superiors not to have known, because they ought to have known. 279–194, 192.

———

For morality: 283, 288.

The Society is important to the Church: 236; for good or ill: 156.

Acquaviva: the confessions of women: 360.[28]

We implore God's mercy, not that he may leave us at   S751/L919 peace in our vices, but that he may deliver us from them.

———

If God gave us masters by his own hand, oh, how necessary will it be for us to obey them with a good heart! Necessity and events are infallibly so.

———

Console yourself; you would not seek me if you had not found me.

———

I thought of you in my agony, I have shed such drops of blood for you.

———

It is tempting me rather than testing yourself, to think whether you would do well in the absence of this or that thing. I will act in you if it happens.

———

Let yourself be guided by my rules. See how well I have led the Virgin and the saints, who have let me act in them.

———

The Father loves everything I do.

———

---

[27] Clemens Placentius was the pseudonym of Giulio Scoti, an ex-Jesuit who published the anti-Jesuit treatise *De potestate pontificia* (1646).

[28] The page references in this and similar fragments intended for the *Provincial Letters* are to the *Historia Jesuitica* of R. Hospinianus, and the letters are from editions of the correspondence of Jesuit Generals. The scraps of Latin include references to these works, to various Jesuit polemics, and to papal Bulls.

Do you want it always to cost me the blood of my humanity, without your shedding tears?

———

Your conversion is my affair. Do not fear, and pray with confidence as though for me.

———

I am present with you through my word in Scripture, through my spirit in the Church and through inspiration, through my power in priests, through my prayer in the faithful.

———

Physicians will not heal you, for you will die in the end; but it is I who heal you and make the body immortal.

———

Suffer bodily chains and servitude; I deliver you only from spiritual servitude at present.

———

I am more a friend to you than this or that one, for I have done for you more then they; and they would not suffer what I have suffered from you, and they would not die for you at the time you were unfaithful and cruel, as I have done and am ready to do, and do, among my chosen and in the Holy Sacrament.

———

If you knew your sins, you would lose heart. —I shall lose it then, Lord, for I believe their malice on your assurance. —No, for I, by whom you learn, can heal you of them, and what I tell you is a sign that I will heal you. In proportion to your expiation of them, you will know them, and it will be said to you: "Behold your sins are forgiven you."

Repent, then, for your hidden sins and for the secret malice of those you know.

———

Lord, I give you all.

———

I love you more ardently than you have loved your filth, *like those sullied [. . .] for the mire.*[29]

———

---

[29] *ut immundus [. . .] pro luto.* Isaiah 64:6–8

May mine be the glory, not yours, worm and clay.

———

Testify to your director that my own words are an occasion for you of evil and vanity or curiosity.

———

I see my abyss of pride, curiosity, concupiscence. There is no relation between me and God or Jesus Christ the Righteous. But he has been made sin for me: all your scourges have fallen upon him. He is more abominable than I. And, far from abhorring me, he feels honored that I go to him and comfort him. But he has healed himself and will heal me all the more surely.

I must add my wounds to his, and join myself to him, and he will save me in saving himself.

But this must not be appended to the future.

———

You shall be as gods, knowing good and evil.[30] Everybody acts as a god in judging: "This is good or bad," and in being too distressed or delighted by events.

———

Do small things as though they were great, because of the majesty of Jesus Christ, who does them in us and lives our life; and great things as though they were small and easy, because of his omnipotence.

Pilate's false justice serves only to makes Jesus Christ suffer, for he has him scourged by his false justice and then put to death. It would have been better to put him to death at once. Thus are the falsely honorable. They do good works and bad ones to please the world and to show that they are not wholly of Jesus Christ, for they are ashamed to be; and finally, when it comes to great temptations and opportunities, they put him to death.

We understand the prophecies only when we see the   S751/L936 events happen. Thus the proofs of retreat and direction, silence, etc., are proofs only to those who know and believe them.

———

Saint Joseph so internal in a law wholly external.

———

Outward penances dispose inward, as humiliations to humility. Thus the . . .

———

[30] *Eritis sicut dii scientes bonum et malum.* Genesis 3:5.

People of every condition and even the martyrs have   S752/L921
reason to fear, according to Scripture.

The greatest pain of purgatory is the uncertainty of the judgment.

———

A hidden God.[31]

It is true that entering into piety produces pain. But this   S753/L924
pain does not arise from the piety that begins to make its way
in us, but from the impiety still there. If our senses were not opposed to
penitence and our corruption were not opposed to God's purity, there
would be nothing painful to us in this. We suffer only to the extent that
the natural vice in us resists supernatural grace: our heart feels torn between these contrary efforts. But it would be very unfair to impute this
violence to God, who is drawing us in, instead of attributing it to the
world, which is holding us back. It is like a child whom a mother tears
from the arms of robbers: in the pain it suffers, [it] should love the loving and legitimate violence of one who gives it its freedom, and hate
only the imperious and tyrannical violence of those who detain it unjustly. The cruelest war that God can wage with men in this life is to
leave them without that war he came to bring. *I came to bring war,* he
says, and to teach them of this war. *I came to bring fire and the sword.*[32]
Before him the world lived in this false peace.

On the miracle   S753/L922

As God has made no family happier, let him also make it
be that he finds none more thankful.

———

On confessions and absolutions without signs of regret.   S753/L923

God considers only what is internal; the Church judges
only by what is external. God absolves as soon as he sees repentance in
the heart, the Church when it sees it in works. God will make a Church
pure inside, to confound, by its internal and altogether spiritual holiness,
the internal impiety of the proud and of the Pharisees. And the Church
will be an assembly of men whose external customs are so pure as to
confound the customs of the heathens. If there are hypocrites among
them so well disguised that it does not recognize their venom, it will tol-
erate them. For, although they are not accepted by God, whom they
cannot deceive, they are accepted by men, whom they do deceive. And

———

[31] *Deus absconditus.* Isaiah 45:15.
[32] Matthew 10:34; Luke 12:49.

thus the Church is not dishonored by their conduct, which appears holy . . .

The law has not destroyed nature, but instructed it. Grace   S754/L925 has not destroyed the law, but put it into effect.

———

Faith received at baptism is the source of the whole life of Christians and converts.

We make an idol of truth itself, for truth apart from charity   S755/L926 is not God, but his image and an idol that we must neither love nor worship. Still less must we love or worship its opposite, which is falsehood.

———

I may well love total darkness, but if God commits me to a state of semidarkness, I am displeased by such darkness as is there; and, because I do not see in it the merits of total darkness, it does not please me. This is a fault and a sign that I am making an idol of darkness, separated from God's order. Now, we should worship only in his order.

What use would it do me?   S756/L927
Abominable.
Singlin.[33]

What use would it do me to remember something, if it   S756/L928 can equally hurt and help me, and if everything depends on God's blessing, which he gives only to things done for him, according to his rules and in his ways, the manner being thus as important as the thing, and perhaps more so, since God can bring good out of evil, and without God we bring evil out of good?

———

Do not compare yourself to others, but to me. If you do   S756/L929 not find me in those to whom you compare yourself, you are comparing yourself to someone abominable.

If you find me in them, compare yourself to them.

But whom will you be comparing? Yourself, or me in you? If it is you, it is someone abominable; if it is I, you compare me to myself.

Now I am God in all.

———

---

[33] Antoine Singlin (1607–1664) was associated with Port Royal and was one of Pascal's spiritual directors.

I speak to you and often counsel you, because your guide cannot speak to you. For I do not want you to lack a guide.

———

And perhaps I do so in response to his prayers, and thus he leads you without your seeing it.

———

You would not seek me if you did not possess me.
Do not therefore be troubled.

———

Anything can be fatal to us, even the things made for our   S756/L927
use, as in nature walls can kill us, and stairs can kill us, if we
do not proceed carefully.

———

The least movement affects all of nature: the whole sea changes be-cause of a rock. Thus, in grace, the least action affects everything by its consequences; therefore everything is important.

———

In every action, we must look beyond the action to our present, past, and future state, and to whatever is affected by it, and see the connec-tions among all these things. And then we shall be very restrained.

External works   S756/L928

There is nothing so dangerous as what pleases God and man, for states that please God and men have some element pleasing to God, and some other element pleasing to men, like the greatness of Saint Teresa: what is pleasing to God is her deep humility in her revela-tions; what is pleasing to men is her illuminations. And so we kill our-selves to imitate her discourses, thinking to imitate her state, and thus to love what God loves and put ourselves in the state God loves.

———

It is better not to fast, and be humbled by it, than to fast and be self-satisfied.

Pharisee, publican.[34]

Why has God established prayer?   S757/L930

1. To communicate to his creatures the dignity of causality.
   But to conserve his preeminence, he grants prayer to whom he pleases.

---

[34] Cf. Luke 18:9–14.

2. To teach us from whom we derive virtue.

3. To make us deserve other virtues through our work.

Objection: but we may believe that prayer derives from ourselves.

This is absurd. For even when we have faith, we may not have virtues, so how should we have faith? Is there not a greater distance from lack of faith to faith than from faith to virtue?

_____

Worthy: this word is ambiguous.

_____

Which made us worthy of such a Redeemer.[35]

_____

Which made it worthy to touch God's hallowed limbs.[36]

_____

Worthy to touch God's hallowed limbs.[37]

_____

I am not worthy.[38] *Who eats unworthily.*[39]

_____

You are worthy to receive.[40]

_____

Find me worthy.[41]

_____

God bestows only according to his promises.

He has promised to grant justice to prayers.

He has never promised prayer except to the children of the promise.

_____

Saint Augustine formally stated that strength would be taken from the righteous.

But he said it by chance. For the occasion to say it might not have presented itself. But his principles make it clear that, the occasion being present, it was impossible for him not to say it, or say anything to the

---

[35] *Meruit habere Redemptorem.* Office for Holy Saturday.

[36] *Meruit tam sacra membra tangere.* Office for Good Friday.

[37] *Digno tam sacra membra tangere.* Hymn *Vexilla regis.*

[38] *Non sum dignus.* Luke 7:6

[39] *Qui manducat indignus.* I Corinthians 11:29.

[40] *Dignus est accipere.* Revelation 4:11.

[41] *Dignare me.* Office of the Holy Virgin.

contrary. It is then rather that he was forced to say it, the occasion being present, than that he said it, the occasion for it having been present. The one is of necessity, the other of chance. But the two are all that we can ask.

And will this one scoff at the other?   S758/L932

Who should scoff? And yet this one does not scoff at the other, but pities him.

I love poverty because he loved it. I love riches because   S759/L931
they afford me the means of helping the wretched. I keep
faith with everyone. I do not render evil to those who wrong me, but I wish them a condition like mine, in which one receives neither evil nor good on the part of men. I try to be just, true, sincere, and faithful to all men. And I have a tender heart for those whom God has more closely united to me. And whether I am alone or in the sight of men, all my actions are done in the sight of God, who must judge them, and to whom I have consecrated them all.

These are my feelings.

And every day of my life I bless my Redeemer, who implanted these in me, and who made a man full of weakness, wretchedness, concupiscence, pride, and ambition into a man free from all these evils, by the power of his grace, to which all the glory for this is due, since I derive from myself only wretchedness and error.

They say that the Church says what it does not say, and   S760/L980
does not say what it does say.

Concupiscence of the flesh, concupiscence of the eyes,   S761/L933
pride, etc.

There are three orders of things: flesh, mind, and will.

The carnal are rich men, kings: they have as object the body.

The curious and scholarly: they have as object the mind.

The wise: they have as object righteousness.

God must reign over everything, and everything should be related to him.

In things of the flesh, concupiscence reigns properly.

In things of the mind, curiosity properly.

In wisdom, pride properly.

It is not that we cannot glory in wealth or knowledge, but that it is not the place for pride. For while granting a man that he is learned, you can still convince him that he is wrong to be conceited.

The proper place for conceit is in wisdom. For you cannot grant a man that he has become wise but that he is wrong to glory in it. For it is right that he should.

Now, God alone gives wisdom. And that is why *he who glories, let him glory in the Lord.*[42]

Nature has perfections, to show that it is the image of   S762/L934
God, and faults, to show that it is only his image.

———

Since men are not accustomed to fashion merit, but only   S762/L935
to reward it when they find it fashioned, they judge God by
themselves.

20 V. Sick bodies are the figures in the Gospel for the   S763/L938
state of the sick soul. But, because one body cannot be sick
enough to express it well, several were needed. Thus there are the deaf,
the dumb, the blind, the paralytic, the dead Lazarus, the possessed: all
these together are in the sick soul.

When our passion leads us to do something, we forget our   S763/L937
duty: this is similar to our liking a book and reading it, when
we ought to be doing something else. Now, to remember our duty, we
must decide to do something we dislike, and then make the excuse that
we have something else to do, and in this way remember our duty.

The servant does not know what his lord does,[43] for the   S764/L939
master tells him only what to do and not its purpose. And this
is why he often obeys slavishly and sins against the purpose. But Jesus
Christ has told us the purpose.

And you defeat that purpose.

Jesus did not want to be killed without the forms of   S765/L940
justice, for it is far more ignominious to die by justice than by
an unjust sedition.

We do not get bored with eating and sleeping every day,   S766/L941
for hunger returns, as does slumber. Without that we would
get bored with them.

So, without the hunger for spiritual things, we would get bored with
them: *Hunger after righteousness* (Eighth Beatitude).[44]

Conclusion   S766/L942

Are we safe? Is this principle safe? Let us examine it.
Our evidence null and void. Saint Thomas.

———

[42] *Qui gloriatur, in Domino glorietur.* Corinthians 1:31; 2 Corinthians 10:17.
[43] John 15:15.
[44] Matthew 5:6, 10.

It seems to me that Jesus Christ allowed only his wounds   S767/L943
to be touched after his resurrection.
Touch me not.[45]
We must unite ourselves only to his sufferings.

———

He gave himself in communion as a mortal in the Last Supper, as
risen from the dead to the disciples at Emmaus, as ascended into
heaven to the whole Church.

———

The external must be joined to the internal to obtain   S767/L944
anything from God; that is, we must go down on our knees,
pray with our lips, etc., so that the proud man who would not submit to
God may now submit to his creature. To expect help from these externals is superstition. Not to want to be joined to the internal is conceit.

———

Of all the mysteries, repentance alone was clearly   S767/L945
declared to the Jews, and by Saint Jehan [John] the forerunner;[46] and then the other mysteries [were declared], to indicate that this
order must be observed in every man, as in the entire world.

25 Bb. — 2. To consider Jesus Christ in every person and   S768/L946
in ourselves: Jesus Christ as a father in his Father, Jesus
Christ as a brother in his brothers, Jesus Christ as a poor man in the
poor, Jesus Christ as a rich man in the rich. Jesus Christ as doctor and
priest in priests. Jesus Christ as sovereign in princes, etc. For by his glory
he is everything that is great, being God, and by his mortal life he is
everything that is puny and abject. That is why he took on this unhappy
condition, so that he could be in every person and the model of every
condition.

The just man acts by faith[47] in the least things: when he   S768/L947
reproves his servants, he wishes their correction by the spirit
of God, and prays God to correct them, expecting as much from God as
from his own reproofs, and prays God to bless his corrections. And so in
all his other actions.

We distance ourselves only by distancing ourselves from   S769/L948
charity.

---

[45] *Noli me tangere.* John 20:17.

[46] Matthew 3:1–2; Mark 1:4.

[47] Romans 1:17.

_____

Our prayers and virtues are abominable before God if they are not the prayers and virtues of Jesus Christ. And our sins will never be the object of mercy, but of God's justice, if they are not the sins of Jesus Christ.

_____

He adopted our sins, and [accepted] us into his covenant. For virtues are proper to him, and sins foreign. Virtues are foreign to us, and our sins are proper to us.

_____

Let us change the rule we have thus far adopted for judging what is good. We had as rule our own will; let us now take God's will: anything he wills is good and right for us; anything he does not will is bad and wrong.

Anything God does not will is forbidden. Sins are forbidden by God's general statement that he did not will them. Other things left without a general prohibition, which we call permitted for that reason, are nevertheless not always permitted; for, when God removes some particular from us, and when, through the event, which is a manifestation of God's will, it becomes apparent that God does not will that we should have the thing, it is then forbidden to us as sin, since God's will is that we should not have one any more than the other. The sole difference between these two things is that it is certain that God will never will the sin, while it is not certain that he will never will the other thing. But as long as God does not will it, we must regard it as sin—as long as the absence of God's will, which alone is all goodness and all justice, renders it unjust and wrong.

What would the Jesuits be without probability, and proba-   S770/L981
bility without the Jesuits?

Take away probability, and you can no longer please the world. Bring in probability, you can no longer displease it. It used to be difficult to avoid sins, and difficult to atone for them. Now it easy to avoid them by any number of tricks, and easy to atone for them.

_____

We have made uniformity out of diversity, for we are all   S770/L982
uniform, in that we have all become uniform.

Just as the only object of peace within states is to assure   S771/L974
the preservation of people's property, so the only object of
peace within the Church is to assure the preservation of the truth,
which is its property and the treasure in which its heart lies. And, just as
it would be contrary to the purpose of peace to allow foreigners into a
state to pillage it without resistance, for fear of disturbing the peace

(because, as peace is only just and useful for safeguarding property, it becomes unjust and pernicious when it allows this to be lost, so war, which can defend it, becomes both just and necessary), likewise, in the Church, when truth is injured by enemies of the faith, when attempts are made to uproot it from the hearts of the faithful and to make error reign, would remaining at peace be serving or betraying the Church? And is it not clear that, just as it is a crime to disturb the peace when truth reigns, it is also a crime to remain at peace when the truth is being destroyed? There is therefore a time when peace is just and a time when it is unjust. It is written that *there is a time for war and a time for peace*,[48] and it is the interest of the truth that distinguishes between them. But there is not a time for truth and a time for error, and it is written, on the contrary, that *the truth of the Lord endures forever*;[49] and that is why Jesus Christ, who said that he had come to bring peace, said also that he had come to bring war;[50] but he did not say that he had come to bring both truth and falsehood.

Truth is therefore the first rule and ultimate purpose of things.

It is good to induce people inwardly renewed by grace to   S772
perform works of piety and penance proportionate to their ability,
because both of these are preserved by the proportion between the goodness of the works and the spirit in which they are performed. When someone not yet inwardly renewed is constrained to perform extraordinary works of piety and penance, both of these are spoiled: the man corrupting the works through his wickedness, and the works proving too much for the weakness of the man, who is unable to bear them. It is a bad sign when someone is seen producing beyond himself from the moment of his conversion. The order of charity is to drive roots into one's heart before producing good works beyond.

I feel in myself a malice that prevents me from agreeing with   S773
what Montaigne says, that vivacity and firmness weaken in us
with age.[51] I would not wish that to be so. I am envious of myself. This self at twenty is no longer me.

---

[48] Ecclesiastes 3:8.

[49] Psalms 116:2.

[50] John 14:27; Matthew 10:34.

[51] Cf. Montaigne, *Essays* I, chap. 57: "It is possible that for those who use their time well, knowledge and experience grow with living; but vivacity, quickness, firmness, and other qualities much more our own, more important and essential, fade and languish" (Frame trans., p. 238; Screech trans., p. 368).

Sleep, you say, is the image of death; as for me, I say that it is   s774
rather the image of life.

Aristotle, who wrote a treatise *On the Soul*, only talks, accord-   s775
ing to Montaigne, about the effects of the soul,[52] which nobody
fails to know, and says nothing about its essence, origin, or nature,
which is what people want to know.

People withdraw and hide for eight months in the countryside   s776
so that they can shine for four at Court.

No pleasure has any taste for me, says Montaigne, *without com-*   s777
munication:[53] a sign of man's esteem for man.

Scripture sends man to the ants:[54] a clear sign of the cor-   s778
ruption of his nature. How fine it is to see the master of the world
sent off to the animals as though to the masters of wisdom!

Someone realizing he has said or done a foolish thing always   s779
thinks this will be the last time. Far from concluding that he will
do many more foolish things, he concludes that this one will prevent
him from doing so.[55]

Philosophers in the schools talk of virtue and rhetoricians of   s780
eloquence without knowing these things. Present the former with
a truly virtuous man, but without luster, and the latter with a discourse
full of elegant words, but without witticisms; they will make nothing of
them.

Sudden death alone is feared, and that is why confessors   s781/L984
live with the great.

He plays the disciple without ignorance and the teacher   s782/L992
without presumption. Annat.

I find nothing easier than to treat all of that as fiction. But I   s783
find nothing harder than to answer it.

---

[52] See Montaigne, *Essays* II, chap. 12: "Let us not forget Aristotle: [. . .] for he speaks
neither of the essence, nor of the origin, nor of the nature of the soul, but only of the effect. Lactantius, Seneca, and most of the dogmatists have admitted that this was something they did not understand. And after all that enumeration of opinions: '*Which one is
true among these pronouncements, some god will see,*' says Cicero" (Ariew and Grene
trans., p. 104).

[53] Montaigne, *Essays* III, chap. 9 (p. 986 in the 1652 ed.).

[54] Proverbs 6:6–8.

[55] Cf. Montaigne, *Essays* III, chap. 13: "To learn we have said or done a foolish thing, that
is nothing. We must learn that we are nothing but fools. It is a far broader and more important lesson" (Frame trans., p. 822; Screech trans., p. 1219).

Why does God not show himself? Are you worthy of it?—Yes.   S784
—You are quite presumptuous, and thus unworthy.—No.—
Then you are unworthy of it.

God is hidden. But he lets himself be found by those who seek   S785
him.

There have always been visible signs of him throughout the ages.
Ours are the prophecies. Other ages had other signs.

These proofs all support one another. If one is true, so is the other.
Thus every age, having proofs proper to itself, has known the others
through them.

Those who saw the Flood believed in the Creation, and believed in
the Messiah who was to come. Those who saw Moses believed in the
Flood and the fulfillment of the prophecies.

And we who see the prophecies fulfilled should believe in the Flood
and Creation.

The most unreasonable things in the world become most   S786/L977
reasonable, because of the unruliness of men. What is less
reasonable than to choose the eldest son of a queen to rule a state? We
do not choose as captain of a ship the passenger who comes from the
best home. Such a law would be ridiculous and unjust; but because men
are and will always be unruly, it becomes reasonable and just, for who
could be chosen? The most virtuous and most able? That immediately
has us coming to blows, everyone claiming to be this most virtuous and
able person. Let us then attach this qualification to something undeni-
able. He is the king's eldest son: that is clear, there is no argument about
it. Reason can do no better, because civil war is the greatest of evils.

That we have treated them as humanely as possible in   S787/L949
order to keep a middle course between the love of truth and
the duty of charity.

That piety does not consist in never rising up against our brothers. It
would be very easy, etc.

It is false piety to preserve the peace to the detriment of truth.

It is also false zeal to preserve the truth at the expense of charity.

———

Thus they did not complain about it.

———

There is a time and a place for their maxims.

———

Their vanity actually arises from their errors.
Resembling the Fathers through their faults,

And the martyrs through their punishment.

———

Yet they will not deny any of them.

———

They had only to take the *Extract* and deny it.

———

They even prepare war against him.[56]

———

Mr. Bourzeis: at least they cannot deny that he opposed the condemnation.[57]

Paul IV, in his Bull *Cum ex apostolatus officio*, published in 1558: S788/L950

We ordain, lay down, decree, and define that each and every one of those who have been led astray or have fallen into heresy or schism, of whatever rank and condition they may be, laymen, ecclesiastics, priests, bishops, archbishops, patriarchs, primates, cardinals, counts, marquis, dukes, kings, and emperors, in addition to the aforementioned sentence and penalties, shall for that alone, without any ministry by right or by fact, be deprived wholly, completely, and perpetually of their orders, bishoprics, benefices, offices, kingdom, or empire, and never be allowed to occupy them again. Let us leave their punishment to the discretion of the secular power, granting no indulgence to those who may in true repentance return from the error of their ways, except that, through the benevolence and clemency of the Holy See, they may be deemed worthy to be confined in a monastery, there to do perpetual penance on bread and water. But remaining always deprived of every dignity, order, prelacy, county, dukedom, or kingdom. And those who shelter and protect them shall, for that alone, be judged to be excommunicated and disgraced, deprived of every kingdom, dukedom, good, and property, which shall fall by right and ownership to whoever first takes possession of them.

If they have slain any excommunicated person, we do not consider them guilty of homicide, on the grounds that, burning with zeal for their Catholic mother against the excommunicated, they happened to kill any of them.[58]

---

[56] *Sanctificant proelium.* Micah 3:5.

[57] The Abbe de Bourzeis was an Augustinian theologian who stopped writing on questions of grace after the Papal Bull of 1653 and even signed the Formulary of 1661.

[58] *Si hominem excommunicatum interfecerunt, non eos homicidas reputamus, quod adversus excommunicatos zelo catholicae matris ardentes aliquem eorum trucidasse contigerit.*

23 q. 5 of Urban II.

121. The Pope forbids the king to marry his children S788/L951
without his permission. 1294.

———

We wish you to know.[59] 124. 1302.
Childish.
Have you the right idea about our Society?   S789/L952

———

The Church has survived for so long without these questions.

———

Others ask them, but it is not the same.

———

What comparison is there, do you think, between 20,000 separated
and 200 million united, who will die for one another? An immortal
body.

———

We support one another to the death. Lamy.[60]

———

We push our enemies. Mr. Puys.[61]

———

Everything depends on probability.

———

The world has a natural need for a religion, but a gentle one.

———

I want to show this to you by making an unusual assumption. So, I
will say: "Even if God did not support us by a particular act of providence, for the good of the Church I want to show you that, even humanly speaking, we cannot perish."
Grant me this principle and I will prove everything. The fact is that
the same fortunes run in both Society and Church.
Without these principles, nothing can be proved.

---

[59] *Scire te volumus.*

[60] Lamy was a Jesuit (Amico) who claimed that a priest could justly kill those who would
risk the reputation of his community; other Jesuits who would not have agreed with him
still felt that they needed to defend his opinion as probable. See fragment S750.

[61] Mr. Puys was a theologian from Lyon who was slandered by the Jesuit d'Alby; see fragment S796.

People do not live for long in overt impiety, or naturally in great austerity.

An accommodating religion is fit to last.

We seek them out through libertinage.

About individuals who do not want to dominate by strength of arms, I do not know whether they could do any better.

Kings, Pope.

Third request; 246.

---

6. Right and sincere faith toward devotion.

6. 452. Kings as nursing fathers.

4. Hated because of their merits.

Apology of the University. 159. Decree of the Sorbonne.

<Kill> the Kings. 241, 228.

Jesuits hanged. 112.

Religion. And society.

A Jesuit is all kinds of men.[62]

Colleges, parents, friends, children to choose.

Constitutions

253. Poverty, ambition.

257. Mainly the princes, great nobles who may do harm and serve.

12. Useless, rejected.

Looking well.

Wealth, nobility, etc. What! Were you afraid that they might have failed to be accepted sooner?

27.

47. Give one's property to the Society for the glory of God. Declarations.

51, 52. Unanimity of opinions. **Declarations.** Submit to the Society and thus preserve uniformity. Now, today, uniformity lies in diversity, for Society wants this.

117. **Constitutions:** Gospel and Saint Thomas. **Declarations:** Any accommodating theology.

---

[62] *Jesuita omnis homo.*

65. Rare, pious scholars. Our former members changed their minds.

23. 74. Begging.

19. Do not give to relatives, and rely on the advisers assigned by the superior.

1. Do not practice self-examination. **Declarations**.

2. Total poverty. For performing masses, for sermons, or in compensatory alms.

4. Declarations, the same authority as the *Constitutions*. End, read the *Constitutions* every month.

149. The *Declarations* ruin everything.

154. Do not provoke the giving of perpetual alms, nor ask for them as rightful, nor alms-box.

Declarations: not as alms (but rather as compensation).[63]

200. 4. Advise us of everything.

190. **Constitutions**: do not want troop. **Declarations**: troop, interpreted.

A universal and immortal body.

———

Great and unscrupulous affection for the community: **dangerous**.

Without our *Constitutions*, we would all be rich because of religion. Thus we are poor.

———

With and without the true religion, we are strong.

Clemens Placentinus

Our generals feared the discredit resulting from external occupations: 208, 152, 150; from the court: 209, 203, 216, 218; from not following the most certain and authoritative views, Saint Thomas, etc.: 215, 218.

Payments against the *Constitutions*:[64] 218.

Women: 225, 228.

Princes and politics: 227, 168, 177. Politics: 181.

Probability, novelty: 279, 156. Novelty, truth.

To pass the time and be entertained, rather than to help souls: 158.

Lax opinions: 160. Mortal into venial sin.

Contrition: 162.

Politics: 162.

Courtliness:[65] <164> or 162.

---

[63] *Non tanquam eleemosyna (sed tanquam compensatio).*

[64] Stipendium contra *Constitutiones*

[65] *Aulicismus*

Amenities of life increase for the Jesuits: 166.

Father Le Moine, 10,000 crowns, outside his province.

Apparent and false goods that deceive them: 192ff.

See how weak is man's foresight! All the things our first generals feared would lead to the loss of the Society are just those by which it has flourished: by the great, by our *Constitutions* being thwarted, by the multitude of religious people, the variety and novelty of opinions, etc.: 182, 157.

The original spirit of the Society extinct: 170, 171–4, 183–7. *It is not the same any more.*[66] Vittelescus. 183.

Complaints of the generals. None from Saint Ignatius, none from Laynez, a few from Borgia and Acquaviva, innumerable from Mutius, etc.[67]

[The first column, most likely in Arnauld's handwriting,   S790/L955
refers to passages from *Epistolae praepositorum generalium
ad Patres et Fratres Societatis Jesu* (Antwerp, 1635) and the second, in
Pascal's handwriting, has his comments in French.]

Ep. 16 Acquavivae.
De formandis concionatoribus.
p. 373. *Longe falluntur qui ad . . .
irrigaturae.*

Read the Fathers in order to have them conform to your imagination, instead of forming your thought on that of the Fathers.

Ep. 1 Mutii Vittelesci.
p. 389. *Quamvis enim probe
norim . . . et absolutum.*
p. 390. *Dolet ac queritur . . . esse
modestiam.*

modesty.

p. 392. *Lex ne dimidiata . . .
reprehendit.*
408. *Ita feram illam . . . etiam
irrumpat.*
409. *Ad extremum pervelim . . .
circumferatur.*

Mass. I do not know what he says. Politics.
Because of the bad luck or rather the singular good luck of the Society, this fact is attributed to all. Obey the bishops exactly; let it not appear as if we pretend to

---

[66] *Non e piu quella.*

[67] Ignatius of Loyola, Diego Laynez, Francisco Borgia, Claudio Acquaviva, and Mutius Vittellesci were all generals of the Jesuits.

410. *Querimoniae . . . deprehendetis.* p. 412.

412. *Ad haec si a litibus . . . aviditatis.*
413. *Patris Borgiae . . . videbitur illam futuram.*
415. *Ita res domesticas . . . Nunc dimittis*, etc.
Ep. 2 Mutii Vittelesci.
432. *Quarto nonnullorum . . . quam ardentissime possum urgere.*
433. *Quoniam vero de loquendi licentia . . . aut raro plectarur.*
Ep 3 Vittelesci.
p. 437. *Nec sane dubium . . . nihil jam detrimenti acceperit.*
p. 440. *Ardentissime Deum exoremus . . . operati non est gravatus, et tu fili hominis*, etc. *Ezechiel* 37.
p. 441. *secundum caput . . . tanti facinus.*
p. 442. *Haec profero una si deficiet . . . qui haec molitur*, etc.
p. 443. *Ex hoc namque vitio . . . importunum praebeas.*

p. 443. *Spectabit tertium caput . . . mutatus est color optimus.* 445. *De paupetate . . . non adversentur veritati.* 445. *Nobilis quidam Roma . . . collocabit.*
p. 446. *Faxit Deus . . . atque si praetermitterentur.*

measure ourselves against them, following the example of Saint Xavier.
Testaments. Suits.
They amplify; they even invent false stories.

Probability: *Tueri pius potest, probabilis est. Auctore non caret.*
Failure to punish the slanderous.

Lest the society be spoiled.

Lack of obedience in order to seek after their reputation.
Lack of obedience, seeking the support of the great.
They do indecent things, outside the state of the Society, and say that the great lords harass them on account of them. But it is they who harass them. So that either we must have them as enemies, if we refuse them, or lose the Society, by agreeing with it.
Chastity.
Poverty, the attenuation of opinions contrary to the truth.

Grapevines, etc.

Examine the motive for the censure by considering the S791/L954 phenomena. Produce a hypothesis suitable for all of them.

———

The habit makes the doctrine.

———

I distrust this doctrine, because it is too gentle for me, considering the wickedness that is said to be in me.

———

In the year 1647, grace for all; in 1650, it was more rare, etc.

———

At the slightest inconvenience caused by grace, they create other kinds (of graces), for they dispose of it as if it were their work.

———

In the end, Mr. Chamillard[68] is so close to it that, if there are degrees leading down to nothingness, this sufficient grace is now the closest it can be.

———

Everyone was taken by surprise, for such a thing had never been seen in Scripture or in the Fathers, etc.

———

How long, Father, has this been an article of faith? It is at the most only since the words *proximate power* came in. And I believe it created this heresy by being born, and was born solely for this end.

———

I distrust their union, considering their particular disagreements. I will wait for them to agree before taking sides: for the sake of one friend, I would make too many enemies. I am not learned enough to reply to them.

———

As if there had never been similar occasions within the Church, but I believe what my priest says about it.

———

Luther: everything outside the truth.

———

Only one tells the truth.

---

[68] Michael Chamillard, professor at the Sorbonne who ultimately judged Arnauld as extremely orthodox.

Heretical member.

Unam sanctam.

The *Enluminures* did us harm.

The same proposition is good in one author and evil in another.
Yes, but there are therefore other bad propositions.

Some people defer to censure, others to reasons; but all defer to reasons. I am surprised, then, that you did not take the general path instead of the particular one, or at least that you did not make contact with it.

Plurality of graces.
Jansenist translators.

<Saint Augustine has the most of it because his enemies are so divided.> Another thing to be considered is an uninterrupted tradition of twelve [hundred years]: popes, councils, etc.

Mr. Arnauld must have some really bad opinions, given that they infect those he embraces.

The advantage to them of the censure is that when they are censured, they will fight, saying they are imitating the Jansenists.

I am so relieved! No Frenchman is a good Catholic!

Litanies. Clement VIII. Paul V. Censure. God visibly protects us.

Man is quite mad.
He cannot create a mite.[69]

---

[69] See Montaigne, *Essays* II, chap. 12: "Man is quite mad. He does not know how to produce a mite, and produces gods by the dozens" (Ariew and Grene trans., p. 91).

Instead of gods, the grace to go there.

Everyone declares that they are so.[70] Mr. Arnauld (as well   S792/L955
as his friends) protests that he condemns them in themselves,
wherever they may be found; that if they are in Jansenius, he condemns
them there; that even if they are not there, if the heretical meaning of
these propositions condemned by the Pope can be found in Jansenius,
he condemns Jansenius.

But you are not satisfied with these protestations. You want him to assert that these propositions occur word for word in Jansenius. He has
replied that he cannot assert this, because he does not know whether it
is the case; that he has looked for them there, as well as countless others,
without ever finding them there. They have begged you and all your associates to say in which pages they occur. No one has ever done so. And
yet you want to cut him off from the Church for this refusal, although
he condemns everything it condemns, for the sole reason that he will
not assert that certain words, or a certain meaning, occur in a book in
which he has never found them, and in which no one will point them
out to him. In truth, Father, this pretext is so empty that the Church has
perhaps never known so strange, unjust, and tyrannical a procedure.

There is no need to be a theologian to see that their only heresy consists in their opposition to you. I have felt this in myself, and we see the
general hardship it causes in all those who have attacked you.

The clergy of Rouen, Jansenists.

Vow of Caen.

You believe your intentions to be so honorable that you make them
the subject of a vow.

Two years ago, their heresy was the Bull. Last year it was *inward*. Six
months ago, it was *word for word*.[71] Now it is the meaning.

Do I not clearly see that all you want is to make them heretics? Holy
Sacrament.

I have quarreled with you on behalf of the others.

You are quite ridiculous to make so much noise over the propositions. This is nothing; it must be heard.

---

[70] That is, everyone recognizes the five propositions as heretical.

[71] *Totidem.*

<The Doctors of the Sorbonne> Without authors' names. But since your intentions were known, there were seventy against it.—Date the decree.

———

So that the person you had not been able to convict of heresy from his own words, etc.

———

For everything becomes known.

———

He either knows it or he doesn't, or he is doubtful, or a sinner, or a heretic.

———

Preface.
Villeloin.[72]
Jansenius, Aurelius,[73] Arnauld, *Provincial Letters.*
What reasons do you have for it? You say I am a Jansenist, that Port Royal maintains the five propositions, and that thus I maintain them: three lies.
By considering only the heathen.
This same light that reveals supernatural truths reveals them without error, whereas the light that, etc.
How could the meaning of Jansenius occur in propositions that are not by him?
And I beg you not to come and tell me that it is not you who is doing all this.
Spare me that answer.

———

Either it is in Jansenius or not. If it is there, he is thus condemned for it. If not, why do you want to have him condemned?
If just one of your Father Escobar's propositions were condemned, I would bring Escobar in one hand and the censure in the other, and make of this a formal argument.
The Pope has not condemned two things. He only condemned the meaning of the propositions.

---

[72] Michel de Marolles, the abbé de Villeloin, wrote *Discours sur la cause janséniste*, favorable to Port-Royal, as a preface to his translation of the New Testament.
[73] Pseudonym of Saint Cyran.

Will you say he did not condemn it? But the meaning of Jansenius is contained in it, said the Pope. I see very well that the Pope thought so because of your *word for word*,[74] but he did not say so on pain of excommunication.

———

Why should he, and the bishops of France, not have believed it? You said *word for word*[75] and they did not know that you are capable of saying it, even though it was not so. Impostors! My fifteenth *Letter* had not been seen.

Diana[76]

S793/L956

This is what Diana does.

11. **It is permitted not to give benefices without responsibility for souls to the most worthy.** The Council of Trent seems to say the opposite, but here is how he proves it: **For if that were so, all prelates would be in a state of damnation, for all of them do this.**

11. **King and Pope are not obliged to choose the most worthy. If that were so, the Pope and kings would bear a terrible responsibility.**

21. And elsewhere: **If this opinion were not correct, penitents and confessors would have much to do. And that is why I think it should be followed in practice.**

22. And in another place, where he sets out the conditions necessary for making a sin mortal, he puts in so many circumstances that it becomes barely possible to commit mortal sin; and when he has established his point, he exclaims: **How gentle and light is the yoke of the Lord!**[77]

11. And elsewhere: **We are not obliged to give away our surplus as alms for the ordinary needs of the poor. If the contrary were true, most of the rich and their confessors would have to be condemned.**

I was getting impatient with these arguments, when I said to the good Father: "But who prevents us from saying that they are so?" — "It is what he anticipated as well in this passage," he replied, "where after saying: 22. **If that were true, the richest would be damned**, he adds: **To this Arragonius replies that they are so; and Bauny, a Jesuit, adds, moreover, that their confessors are, too. But I reply with Valentia, another Jesuit, and other authors, that there are several reasons for excusing the rich and their confessors.**"

———

[74] *Totidem.*

[75] *Totidem.*

[76] Diana is a Theatine casuist from Palermo (1585–1663). See Pascal's *Fifth* and *Sixth Provincial Letters.*

[77] Matthew 11:30: "For my yoke is easy and my burden is light."

I was delighted with this argument, when he finished off with this one:

"If this opinion about restitution were true, oh, how many restitutions would have to be made!"

"Oh, my Father," I said, "what a good reason!"—"Oh," said the Father, "what an accommodating man!"—"Oh, my Father," I replied, "but for your casuists, how many people would be damned! Oh, my Father, how broad you make the path that leads to heaven! Oh, what a lot of people find it! Here is . . . "

It is, in its idiom, wholly the body of Jesus Christ, but it cannot be said to be the whole body of Jesus Christ.[78]   S794/L957

———

The union of two things without change does not enable us to say that one becomes the other.

In this way, the soul is united to the body,

and the fire to the wood, without change.

But change is needed to make the form of the one become the form of the other.

Thus the union of the Word to mankind.

———

Because my body without my soul would not constitute the body of a man, then my soul united to any matter whatsoever will constitute my body.

This does not distinguish the necessary condition from the sufficient condition. The union is necessary, but not sufficient.

The left arm is not the right.

———

Impenetrability is a property of matter.

———

Numerical[79] identity, with respect to the same time, requires the identity of matter.

———

---

[78] This seems to be a commentary on Descartes' letter to Denis Mesland of February 9, 1645, concerning the Eucharist. Pascal must have had a copy of the original, since the letter was published only in 1811 and not in Claude Clerselier's volumes of Descartes' correspondence.

[79] *De numero.*

Thus, if God united my soul to a body in China, the same body *numerically the same*[80] would be in China.

———

The same river that runs there is *numerically the same*[81] as the one running at the same time in China.

Part I, 1, 2, c. 1, section 4.[82]   S795/L958

What is more absurd than to say that inanimate bodies have passions, fears, dreads? That insensible bodies, lifeless, and even incapable of life, have passions that presuppose at least a sensitive soul to receive them? Moreover, that the object of their dread is the void? What is there in the void that could make them afraid? Is there nothing more lowly and ridiculous?

This is not all. [We claim] that they have in themselves a principle of movement to shun the void. Do they have arms, legs, muscles, nerves?

If does not signify indifference.   S795/L959
Malachi.
Isaiah.
Isaiah, *If you wanted*, etc.[83]
The day when.[84]

You threaten me.   S796/L960

I am no heretic; I have not maintained the five propositions. You say it and do not prove it. I say that you have said this, and I do prove it.

———

I say you are impostors; I prove it to you; and that, impudently, you do not hide it: d'Alby, Brisacier, Meynier;[85] and that you authorize it: **Cancel**.[86]

Since you have only touched upon this, it is to approve all the rest.

By virtue of senatorial decrees and plebiscites:[87] to ask for similar passages.

---

[80] *Idem numero.*

[81] *Idem numero.*

[82] *Treatise on the Vacuum.*

[83] *Si volueritis.* Isaiah 1:19.

[84] *In quacumque die.*

[85] All of these are Jesuits accused of slander.

[86] **Elidere.**

[87] *Ex senatus-consultis et plebiscitis.* See Fragment S94.

When you believed Mr. Puys an enemy of the Society, he was an un-worthy pastor of his church, ignorant, heretical, of bad faith and morals. Now he is a worthy pastor, of good faith and morals.

––––––

To slander: *it is a great blindness of the heart.*[88] Not to see it as evil: *it is a greater blindness.*[89] To defend it instead of confessing it as a sin: *then the depth of wickedness encompasses man,*[90] etc. 230, Prosper. ***Cancel.***[91] Caramuel.[92]

––––––

The great lords are divided in civil wars.
And so are you in the civil war between men.

––––––

I am very glad you publish the same thing I do.
Given to contention.[93] Saint Paul.
He has given me cause.[94]

––––––

The saints indulge in subtleties to make themselves out to be crimi-nals, and impeach their better actions, and these indulge in subtleties in order to excuse the most wicked ones.

––––––

Do not pretend that this is what happens in a debate.
We will have your whole works printed, and in French: we will have the whole world as judge.

––––––

A building of equal beauty outside, but on a bad foundation, built by the heathen sages. And the devil deceives men by an apparent resem-blance, based on the most different foundation.

––––––

Never had man so good a cause as mine, and never have others fur-nished so fine a target as you.

––

[88] *Haec est magna caecitas cordis.*

[89] *Haec est major caecitas cordis.*

[90] *Tunc homines concludit profunditas iniquitatis.*

[91] *Elidere.*

[92] Juan Caramuel (1606–1682), a Spanish Cistercian whose moral opinions gained for him the title of Prince of the Laxists.

[93] *Ex contentione.* Romans 2:8.

[94] *Me causam fecit.*

The people of the world do not believe they are on good paths.

The more they indicate weakness in my person, the more they authorize my cause.

You say I am a heretic. Is that allowed? And if you do not fear that men render justice, do you not fear that God will render it to me?

You will feel the force of the truth, and you will yield to it.

I pray people to do me the justice of no longer taking them at their word.
We will need to require the world to believe you on pain of mortal sin. —*Cancel*.[95]

It is a sin to believe slander rashly.

He did not easily trust a slanderer.[96] Saint Augustine.

And by falling on all sides, he made me fall,[97] in accordance with the maxim of the slanderers.

There is something supernatural in such blindness. *Destiny they deserved*.[98]

I am alone against 30,000. Not at all. You keep the court, the deception; I the truth. It is my whole strength. If I lose it, I am lost. I shall not lack accusers and persecutors. But I possess the truth, and we shall see who will prevail.
I do not deserve to defend religion, but you do not deserve to defend error. And I hope that God, in his mercy, having no regard to the evil in

---

[95] *Elidere.*

[96] *Non credebat temere calumniatori.*

[97] *Fecitque cadendo undique me cadere.*

[98] *Digna necessitas.* Wisdom of Solomon 19:4.

me, and having regard to the good in you, will grant us all the grace that
truth will not fail in my hands, and that falsehood will not . . .

———

Most impudent Liars.[99]

———

230. —The extreme sin is to defend it. **Cancel**.[100]

———

340, 23. The fortune of the wicked.

———

A man shall be commended according to his wisdom.[101]

———

66. *Work in order to lie.*[102]
80. Alms.
False piety, double sin.
B. You are ignorant of the prophecies, if you do not know   S797/L961
that all this must happen: princes, prophets, Pope, and even
the priests; and yet the Church must subsist.

By the grace of God, we have not reached that point. Woe to these
priests! But we hope that God will grant us the mercy that we shall not
be among them.

2 Saint Peter, chap. 2: false prophets in the past, images of future
ones.

It must indeed be, says the Feuillant, that this is not so   S798/L962
certain, for controversy indicates uncertainty.

Saint Athanasius, Saint Chrysostom.

Morals. Unbelievers.

———

The Jesuits have not made the truth uncertain, but they have made
their own impiety certain.

Contradiction has always been around in order to blind the wicked.
For everything offensive to truth or charity is bad. This is the true
principle.

---

[99] *Mentiris impudentissime.* See Provincial Letter xvi.

[100] *Elidere.*

[101] *Doctrina sua noscetur vir.* Proverbs 12:8.

[102] *Labor mendaci.*

It is indifferent to the human heart whether to believe   S799/L963
there are three or four persons in the Trinity, but not, etc. As
a result, they chafe to support the one but not the other.

It is good to do the one, but we must not set aside the other. The
same God who told us, etc.

And thus whoever believes the one but not the other does not believe
it because God said so, but because his inclination does not deny it and
it is easy to consent to it and thus to have, without bother, a testimony of
his conscience that it . . .

But it is false testimony.

Letter on how Jesuits established themselves violently   S799/L964
everywhere.

———

Supernatural blindness.

———

This morality that has as its head a crucified God.

———

Here are the ones who vow to obey *as if with Christ!*[103]

———

The decadence of the Jesuits.

———

Our religion, which is wholly divine.

———

A casuist, mirror!
If you find it good, it is a good sign.

———

It is a strange thing that there is no way of giving them the idea of
religion.

———

A crucified God.

———

By taking up this punishable matter of the schism, they will be
punished.

———

[103] *Tanquam Christo.*

But what a reversal! By embracing it, children love the corruptors. The enemies abhor them.

———

We are the witnesses.

———

For the crowd of casuists, it is so far from being a subject of accusation against the Church that it is, on the contrary, a subject of lamentation by the Church.

———

And so that we are not suspect.

Like the Jews who bring forward their Books, which for the gentiles are not suspect, they bring to us their *Constitutions*.

So that if it is true, on the one hand, that some lax   S800/L965 religious persons and some corrupt casuists, who are not members of the hierarchy, are steeped in these corruptions, it is certain, on the other hand, that the true pastors of the Church, who are the true guardians of the Divine Word, have preserved it unchangeably against the efforts of those who have tried to destroy it.

And thus the faithful have no pretext to follow that laxity, offered to them only by the foreign hands of these casuists, instead of the sound doctrine presented to them by the paternal hands of their own pastors. And the impious and heretics have no ground for giving these abuses as evidence of the defect in God's providence over his Church. For, as the Church consists properly in the body of the hierarchy, we are so far from being able to conclude from the present state of matters that God has abandoned it to corruption, that it has never been more apparent than at the present time that God visibly protects it from corruption.

For if some of these men, who by an extraordinary vocation have made profession of withdrawing from the world and adopting the religious habit in order to live in a more perfect state than ordinary Christians, have fallen into aberrations that horrify ordinary Christians, and have become to us what the false prophets were among the Jews, this is a private and personal misfortune, which must indeed be deplored, but from which nothing can be inferred against the care God takes of his Church, since all these things are so clearly foretold, and it has been so long since announced that these temptations would arise on the part of this kind of people; so that when we are well instructed, we see in this evidence of God's care, rather than of his forgetfulness in regard to us.

We must hear both sides; this is what I have been careful   S801/L966 to do.

When we have heard only one side, we are always biased in its favor. But the opposite side makes us change our mind. Instead, in this case, the Jesuit confirms it.

———

Not what they do, but what they say.[104]

———

The outcry is directed only against me. I want it that way. I know to whom I am accountable.

———

Jesus was a stone of stumbling.[105]

———

Open to condemnation, condemned.

———

   Politics.
We have found two obstacles to our plan of making things easier for men: one, the internal laws of the Gospel; the other, the external laws of religion and the state.
   We are masters of the first, and here is how we have dealt with the others: *amplify, restrict, from the greater to the less.*[106]
   More recent.[107]
   Probable.
   They reason like those who prove that it is night at noon.
   If reasons as bad as these are probable, anything may be.
   First reason: *Master of conjugal acts.*[108] Molina.
   Second reason: *He cannot be compensated.*[109] Lessius.
   Oppose not saintly, but abominable maxims.
   Bauny, burner of barns.[110]
   Mascarenhas, Council of Trent, on priests in state of mortal sin, *as soon as possible.*[111]

---

[104] Matthew 23:3.

[105] Isaiah 8:14; see fragment S269.

[106] *Amplianda, restringenda, a majori ad minus.*

[107] *Junior.*

[108] *Dominus actuum conjugalium.*

[109] *Non potest compensari.* See fragment S603.

[110] The Jesuit Bauny maintained that if someone had asked a soldier to burn a neighbor's barn, he would not be held responsible for reparations, since he had not burned the barn himself.

[111] *Quam primum.*

Difference between dinner and supper.   S802/L968

———

In God, the word does not differ from the intention, for he is true; nor the word from the effect, for he is powerful; nor the means from the effect, for he is wise. Saint Bernard, *Ultimus sermo in Missus*.[112]

———

Saint Augustine, *City of God*, v. 10. This rule is general: God can do everything, except those things due to which, if he could do them, he would not be omnipotent, such as dying, **being deceived, etc., lying**, etc.

———

Several evangelists for the confirmation of the truth. Their discrepancy useful.

———

The Eucharist after the Lord's Supper: truth after the figure.

———

The ruin of Jerusalem, a figure of the ruin of the world.
Forty years after the death of Jesus.

———

Jesus does not know either as a man or as emissary. Matthew 24:36.

———

Jesus condemned by the Jews and Gentiles.

———

The Jews and Gentiles prefigured by the two sons.

———

Saint Augustine, *City of God*, xx. 29.
Work out your own salvation with fear.[113]   S803/L969

———

Those poor in grace
Ask and it shall be given you.[114] Therefore is it in our power to ask? On the contrary, it is not, because obtaining is, and prayer is not. For since salvation is not in our power and obtaining is, prayer is not in our power.

———

---

[112] *Last Sermon on the Missus*; cf. Luke 1:26.

[113] Phillipians 2:12.

[114] *Petenti dabitur*. Matthew 7:7.

The righteous man should then no longer hope in God, for he should no longer hope but try to obtain that for which he asks.

Let us conclude, then, that since man is now incapable of using this proximate power and God is unwilling to let this become a means whereby he should be estranged from him, it is only by an efficacious power that he is not estranged.

Therefore, those who are estranged from God do not have this power without which there is no estrangement from God, and those who are not estranged from God do have this power.

Therefore, those who cease to pray, having persevered for some time in prayer by this efficacious power, lack that efficacious power.

And thus God abandons them first in this sense.

Mr. de Roannez said:[115] "Reasons come to me afterward,   S804/L983
but at first a thing pleases or shocks me without my knowing
the reason, and yet it shocks me for that reason which I discover only afterward."—But I believe, not that it shocks for the reasons we discover afterward, but that we discover these reasons only because it does shock.

Now, probability is necessary for the other maxims, like   S805/L985
that of Lamy and of the slanderer.

By their fruits.[116] Judge their faith by their morals.

Probability does not mean much without corrupt means, and the means are nothing without probability.

There is pleasure in being confident in our ability to do well and in our knowing how to do well. The grace: *"To know and be able."*[117] Probability brings such pleasure, for we can give an account to God by relying on their authors.

Heretics, who take advantage of the doctrine of the   S806/L986
Jesuits, must be made to know that it is not that of the
Church, and that our divisions do not separate us from the altar.

If in differing we condemned, you would be right. Uni-   S807/L987
formity without diversity is useless to others; diversity without uniformity is ruinous for us.[118] The one is harmful outside; the other inside.

---

[115] De Roannez was the governor of Poitou and a close friend of Pascal.

[116] *A fructibus eorum.* Matthew 7:20.

[117] *Scire et posse.*

[118] Sellier has *vous*, but it must be a slip for *nous*.

. . . But it is impossible that God should ever be the end,   S808/L988
if he is not the beginning (*principe*). We direct our sight up-
ward, but rest upon the sand. And the earth will dissolve, and we shall
fall while looking at the heavens.

The Jesuits have tried to combine God and the world, and   S809/L989
have only earned the contempt of God and the world. For, as
regards conscience, this is evident; and, as regards the world, they are
not good cabbalists. They have power, as I have often said, but it is with
respect to other religious persons. They enjoy enough credit to get a
chapel built or preach a jubilee, but not to secure appointments to
bishoprics or governorships. On their own admission, they hold that
monks have a very silly position in the world (Father Brisacier, Bene-
dictines). Yet you give way beneath those more powerful than yourselves, and use what small credit you enjoy oppressing those who
intrigue less than you in the world.

The Jesuits   S810/L990

In corrupting the bishops and the Sorbonne, they have
not succeeded in making their judgment just, but they have succeeded
in making their judges unjust. And thus, when they are condemned for
it in the future, they will say *ad hominem* that the judges are unjust, and
so will refute their judgment. But that is useless. For, as they cannot now
conclude that the Jansenists have been properly condemned solely because they have been condemned, similarly they will then be unable to
conclude that they are wrongly condemned themselves because they are
condemned by judges open to corruption. For their condemnation will
be just because it is delivered, not by judges who are always just, but by
judges who are just in this respect; and this will be shown by other proofs.

As the two chief interests of the Church are preserving the   S811/L991
piety of the faithful and converting heretics, we are overcome with grief when we see the factions formed today to introduce
those errors most liable to exclude heretics from ever entering into
communion with us, and fatally to corrupt the pious Catholics remaining to us. These undertakings so openly directed today against the truths
of religion, and those most important for salvation, do not merely fill us
with distaste, but with fear and dread; because, apart from what every
Christian ought to feel about such disorders, we have the additional
obligation of providing the remedy and using the authority given us by
God in order to see that the people he has committed to our charge, etc.

Their whole society of casuists cannot give assurance to a   S812/L993
conscience in error, and that is why it is important to choose
good guides.

Thus they will be doubly culpable, both for having followed the ways they should not have followed, and for having listened to teachers to whom they should not have listened.

Thus the Jesuits cause people either to embrace errors or to   S813
swear they have embraced them, and have them fall into error or into perjury, and rot either the mind or the heart.

CONCORDANCE

L	S	L	S	L	S
L1	S37	L36	S70	L70	S104
L2	S38	L37	S71	L71	S105
L3	S38	L38	S72	L72	S106
L4	S38	L39	S73	L73	S107
L5	S39	L40	S74	L74	S108
L6	S40	L41	S75	L74	S109
L7	S41	L42	S76	L75	S110
L8	S42	L43	S77	L76	S111
L9	S43	L44	S78	L77	S112
L10	S44	L45	S78	L78	S113
L11	S45	L46	S79	L79	S114
L12	S46	L47	S80	L80	S115
L13	S47	L48	S81	L81	S116
L14	S48	L49	S82	L82	S116
L15	S49	L50	S83	L83	S117
L16	S50	L51	S84	L84	S118
L17	S51	L52	S85	L85	S119
L18	S52	L53	S86	L86	S120
L19	S53	L54	S87	L87	S121
L20	S54	L55	S88	L88	S122
L21	S55	L56	S89	L89	S123
L22	S56	L57	S90	L90	S124
L23	S57	L58	S91	L91	S125
L24	S58	L58	S92	L92	S126
L25	S59	L59	S93	L93	S127
L26	S60	L60	S94	L94	S128
L27	S61	L61	S95	L95	S129
L28	S62	L62	S96	L96	S130
L29	S63	L63	S97	L97	S131
L30	S64	L64	S98	L98	S132
L31	S65	L65	S99	L99	S132
L32	S66	L66	S100	L100	S133
L33	S67	L67	S101	L101	S134
L34	S68	L68	S102	L102	
L35	S69	L69	S103	L103	S135

L	S	L	S	L	S
L104	S136	L143	S176	L182	S213
L105	S137	L144	S177	L183	S214
L106	S138	L145	S178	L184	S215
L107	S139	L146	S179	L184	S216
L108	S140	L147	S180	L185	S217
L109	S141	L148	S181	L186	S218
L110	S142	L149	S182	L187	S219
L111	S143	L149	S274	L188	S220
L112	S144	L150	S183	L189	S221
L113	S145	L151	S184	L190	S222
L114	S146	L152	S185	L190	S223
L115	S147	L153	S186	L191	S224
L116	S148	L154	S187	L192	S225
L117	S149	L155	S187	L193	S226
L118	S150	L156	S188	L194	S227
L119	S151	L157	S189	L195	S228
L120	S152	L158	S190	L198	S229
L121	S153	L159	S191	L199	S230
L121	S154	L160	S192	L200	S231
L122	S155	L161	S193	L200	S232
L123	S156	L162	S194	L201	S233
L124	S157	L163	S195	L202	S234
L125	S158	L164	S196	L203	S235
L126	S159	L165	S197	L204	S236
L127	S160	L166	S198	L205	S237
L128	S161	L167		L206	S238
L129	S162	L168	S199	L207	S239
L130	S163	L169	S200	L208	S240
L131	S164	L170	S201	L209	S241
L132	S165	L171	S202	L209	S242
L133	S166	L172	S203	L210	S243
L133	S167	L173	S204	L211	S244
L134	S168	L174	S205	L212	S245
L137	S169	L175	S206	L213	S246
L138	S170	L176	S207	L214	S247
L139	S171	L177	S208	L215	S248
L140	S172	L178	S209	L216	S249
L140	S173	L179	S210	L217	S250
L141	S174	L180	S211	L218	S251
L142	S175	L181	S212	L219	S252

L	S	L	S	L	S
L220	S253	L260	S291	L299	S330
L221	S254	L261	S292	L300	S331
L222	S255	L262	S293	L301	S332
L223	S256	L263	S294	L302	S333
L224	S257	L264	S295	L303	S334
L225	S258	L265	S296	L304	S335
L226	S258	L266	S297	L305	S336
L227	S259	L267	S298	L306	S337
L228	S260	L268	S299	L307	S338
L229	S261	L269	S300	L308	S339
L230	S262	L270	S301	L309	S340
L231	S263	L271	S302	L310	S341
L232	S264	L272	S303	L311	S342
L233	S265	L273	S304	L312	S343
L234	S266	L274	S305	L313	S344
L235	S267	L275	S306	L314	S345
L236	S268	L276	S307	L315	S346
L237	S269	L277	S308	L316	S347
L238	S270	L278	S309	L317	S348
L239	S271	L278	S310	L318	S349
L240	S272	L279	S311	L319	S350
L241	S273	L280	S312	L320	S351
L242	S275	L281	S313	L321	S352
L243	S276	L282	S314	L322	S353
L244	S277	L283	S315	L323	S354
L245		L284	S316	L324	S355
L246	S278	L285	S317	L324	S357
L247	S279	L286	S318	L325	S356
L248	S280	L287	S319	L326	S358
L249	S281	L288	S320	L327	S359
L250	S282	L289	S321	L328	S360
L251	S283	L290	S322	L329	S361
L252	S284	L291	S323	L330	S362
L253	S285	L292	S324	L331	S363
L254	S286	L293	S324	L332	S364
L255	S287	L294	S325	L333	S365
L256	S288	L295	S326	L334	S366
L257	S289	L296	S327	L335	S368
L258	S290	L297	S328	L336	S367
L259	S290	L298	S329	L337	S369

L	S	L	S	L	S
L338	S370	L377	S409	L417	S36
L339	S371	L378	S410	L418	S680
L340	S372	L379	S411	L419	S680
L341	S373	L380	S412	L420	S680
L342	S374	L381	S413	L421	S680
L343	S375	L382	S414	L422	S680
L344	S376	L383	S2	L423	S680
L345	S377	L384	S3	L424	S680
L346	S378	L385	S4	L425	S680
L347	S379	L386	S5	L426	S680
L348	S380	L387	S6	L427	S681
L349	S381	L388	S7	L428	S682
L350	S382	L389	S8	L429	S682
L351	S383	L390	S9	L430	S683
L352	S384	L391	S10	L431	S683
L353	S385	L392	S11	L432	S684
L354	S386	L393	S12	L433	S685
L355	S387	L394	S13	L434	S686
L356	S388	L395	S14	L435	S687
L357	S389	L396	S15	L436	S688
L358	S390	L397	S16	L437	S689
L359	S391	L398	S17	L438	S690
L360	S392	L399	S18	L439	S690
L361	S393	L400	S19	L440	S690
L362	S394	L401	S20	L441	S690
L363	S395	L402	S21	L442	S690
L364	S396	L403	S22	L443	S690
L365	S397	L404	S23	L444	S690
L366	S398	L405	S24	L445	S690
L366	S399	L406	S25	L446	S690
L367	S400	L407	S26	L447	S690
L368	S401	L408	S27	L448	S690
L369	S401	L409	S28	L449	S690
L370	S402	L410	S29	L450	S690
L371	S403	L411	S30	L451	S691
L372	S404	L412	S31	L452	S692
L373	S405	L413	S32	L453	S693
L374	S406	L414	S33	L454	S694
L375	S407	L415	S34	L455	S695
L376	S408	L416	S35	L456	S696

L	S	L	S	L	S
L457	S696	L486	S732	L520	S453
L458	S697	L486	S733	L521	S453
L459	S697	L487	S734	L522	S453
L460	S699	L487	S734	L523	S453
L461	S700	L488	S734	L524	S453
L462	S701	L489	S735	L525	S454
L463	S702	L490	S736	L526	S454
L464	S703	L491	S736	L527	S454
L465	S703	L492	S736	L528	S454
L466	S703	L493	S736	L529	S454
L467	S704	L494	S736	L530	S455
L468	S705	L495	S736	L531	S456
L469	S706	L496	S736	L532	S457
L470	S707	L497	S736	L533	S457
L471	S708	L498	S736	L534	S457
L472	S709	L499	S736	L535	S457
L473	S710	L500	S737	L536	S458
L474	S711	L501	S737	L537	S458
L475	S711	L502	S738	L538	S458
L476	S711	L503	S738	L539	S458
L477	S712	L504	S672	L540	S458
L478	S713	L505	S672	L541	S459
L479	S714	L506	S673	L542	S459
L480	S715	L506	S674	L543	
L481	S716	L507	S675	L544	S460
L482	S717	L508	S676	L545	S460
L483	S718	L508	S677	L546	S460
L484	S719	L508	S678	L547	S460
L485	S720	L508	S679	L548	S460
L486	S721	L509	S669	L549	S460
L486	S722	L510	S669	L550	S461
L486	S723	L511	S669	L551	S461
L486	S724	L512	S670	L552	S461
L486	S725	L513	S671	L553	S462
L486	S726	L514	S671	L554	S463
L486	S727	L515	S452	L555	S464
L486	S728	L516	S452	L557	S465
L486	S729	L517	S452	L558	S465
L486	S730	L518	S452	L559	S466
L486	S731	L519	S453	L560	S467

L	S	L	S	L	S
L561	S468	L601	S498	L641	S529
L562	S469	L602	S500	L642	S529
L563	S470	L603	S500	L643	S529
L564	S471	L604	S501	L644	S529
L565	S471	L605	S502	L645	S530
L566	S472	L606	S502	L646	S531
L567	S473	L607	S504	L647	S532
L568	S473	L608	S504	L648	S533
L569	S473	L609	S504	L649	S534
L570	S474	L610	S503	L650	S535
L571	S474	L611	S503	L651	S536
L572	S475	L612	S505	L652	S536
L573	S476	L613	S506	L653	S537
L574	S477	L614	S507	L654	S538
L575	S478	L615	S508	L655	S539
L576	S479	L616	S509	L656	S540
L577	S480	L617	S510	L657	S541
L578	S481	L618	S511	L658	S542
L579	S482	L619	S512	L659	S543
L580	S482	L620	S513	L660	S544
L581	S483	L621	S514	L661	S544
L582	S484	L622	S515	L662	S544
L583	S485	L623	S516	L663	S544
L584	S485	L624	S517	L664	S545
L585	S486	L625	S518	L665	S546
L586	S486	L626	S519	L666	S547
L587	S486	L627	S520	L667	S547
L588	S487	L628	S521	L668	S547
L589	S488	L629	S522	L669	S548
L590	S489	L630	S523	L670	S549
L591	S490	L631	S524	L671	S550
L592	S492	L632	S525	L672	S551
L593	S493	L633	S526	L673	S552
L594	S491	L634	S527	L674	S553
L595	S491	L635	S528	L675	S554
L596	S493	L636	S528	L676	S555
L597	S494	L637	S529	L677	S556
L598	S495	L638	S529	L678	S557
L599	S496	L639	S529	L679	S558
L600	S497	L640	S529	L680	S559

L	S	L	S	L	S
L681	S560	L721	S598	L757	S626
L682	S561	L722	S600	L758	S627
L683	S562	L722	S602	L759	S628
L684	S563	L722	S603	L760	S629
L685	S564	L723	S601	L761	S629
L686	S565	L723	S604	L762	S629
L687	S566	L724	S605	L763	S629
L688	S567	L725	S606	L764	S630
L689	S568	L726	S607	L765	S631
L690	S569	L727	S608	L766	S631
L691	S570	L728	S609	L767	S632
L692	S571	L728	S610	L768	S633
L693	S572	L729	S611	L769	S634
L694	S573	L730	S612	L770	S635
L695	S574	L731	S613	L771	S636
L696	S575	L732	S613	L772	S636
L697	S576	L733	S614	L773	S637
L698	S577	L734	S615	L774	S638
L699	S577	L735	S616	L775	S639
L700	S578	L736	S617	L775	S640
L701	S579	L737	S617	L776	S641
L702	S580	L738	S617	L777	S642
L703	S581	L739	S617	L778	S643
L704	S582	L740	S617	L779	S643
L705	S583	L741	S617	L780	S644
L706	S584	L742	S617	L781	S644
L707	S585	L743	S617	L782	S645
L708	S586	L744	S618	L783	S645
L709	S587	L745	S618	L784	S645
L710	S588	L746	S619	L785	S645
L711	S589	L747	S620	L786	S645
L712	S590	L748	S621	L787	S645
L713	S591	L749	S622	L788	S645
L714	S592	L750	S622	L789	S645
L715	S593	L751	S622	L790	S645
L716	S594	L752	S622	L791	S645
L717	S595	L753	S623	L792	S646
L718	S596	L754	S624	L793	S646
L719	S597	L755	S625	L794	S647
L720	S598	L756	S625	L795	S648

L	S	L	S	L	S
L796	S649	L836	S423	L875	S440
L797	S650	L837	S424	L876	S440
L798	S650	L838	S424	L877	S441
L799	S651	L839	S424	L878	S442
L800	S652	L840	S425	L879	S442
L801	S653	L840	S428	L880	
L802	S653	L841	S426	L881	S443
L803	S653	L842	S427	L882	S444
L804	S653	L843	S427	L883	S444
L805	S653	L844	S427	L884	S444
L806	S653	L845	S427	L885	S445
L807	S654	L846	S429	L886	S445
L808	S655	L847	S430	L887	S445
L809	S656	L848	S430	L888	S445
L810	S657	L849	S430	L889	S445
L811	S658	L850	S431	L890	S445
L812	S658	L851	S432	L891	S445
L813	S658	L852	S433	L892	S446
L814	S658	L853	S433	L893	S447
L815	S659	L854	S434	L894	S448
L816	S659	L855	S435	L895	S448
L817	S659	L856	S436	L896	S448
L818	S660	L857	S437	L897	S448
L819	S660	L858	S437	L898	S448
L820	S661	L859	S438	L899	S448
L821	S661	L860	S439	L900	S448
L822	S663	L861	S439	L901	S449
L823	S664	L862	S439	L902	S449
L824	S665	L863	S439	L903	S450
L825	S666	L864	S439	L904	S450
L826	S667	L865	S439	L905	S450
L827	S667	L866	S440	L906	S451
L828	S668	L867	S440	L907	S451
L829	S668	L868	S440	L908	S451
L830	S419	L869	S440	L909	S451
L831	S420	L870	S440	L909	S451
L832	S421	L871	S440	L910	S451
L833	S421	L872	S440	L911	S451
L834	S422	L873	S440	L912	S451
L835	S423	L874	S440	L913	S742

L	S	L	S	L	S
L914	S744	L941	S766	L968	S802
L915	S745	L942	S766	L969	S803
L916	S746	L943	S767	L970	S417
L917	S746	L944	S767	L971	S415
L918	S748	L945	S767	L972	S416
L919	S749	L946	S768	L973	S698
L919	S750	L947	S768	L974	S771
L920	S751	L948	S769	L975	S739
L921	S752	L949	S787	L976	S740
L922	S753	L950	S788	L977	S786
L923	S753	L951	S788	L978	S743
L924	S753	L952	S789	L979	S747
L925	S754	L953		L980	S760
L926	S755	L954	S791	L981	S770
L927	S756	L955	S790	L982	S770
L928	S756	L955	S792	L983	S804
L929	S756	L956	S793	L984	S781
L930	S757	L957	S794	L985	S805
L931	S759	L958	S795	L986	S806
L932	S758	L959	S795	L987	S807
L933	S761	L960	S796	L988	S808
L934	S762	L961	S797	L989	S809
L935	S762	L962	S798	L990	S810
L936	S751	L963	S799	L991	S811
L937	S763	L964	S799	L992	S782
L938	S763	L965	S800	L993	S812
L939	S764	L966	S801		
L940	S765	L967	S599		

INDEX

By reference to fragments numbered according
to Sellier's edition of copy B

322